International Intervention, Identity and Conflict Transformation

I0131136

This book addresses the challenges of international intervention in violent conflicts and its impact on groups in conflict.

When the international community intervenes in a violent internal conflict, the intervening powers may harden divisions, constructing walls between groups, or they may foster transformation, soften barriers and build bridges between conflicting groups. This book examines the different types of external processes and their respective contributions to softening or hardening divisions between conflicting groups. It also analyzes the types of conflict resolution strategies, including integration, accommodation and partitioning, and investigates the conditions under which the international community decides to pursue a particular strategy, and how the different strategies contribute to solidification or transformation of group identities. The author uses three case studies, Bosnia and Herzegovina (BiH), Northern Ireland and Israel-Palestine, to reveal how different types of external interventions impact on the identities of conflicting groups. The volume seeks to address how states and international organizations ought to intervene in order to stimulate the building of bridges rather than walls between conflicting groups. In doing so, the book sheds light on some of the pitfalls in international interventions and highlights the importance of united external process and inclusive identity strategies that promote transformation and bridge differences between conflicting groups.

This book will be of much interest to students of intervention, peace and conflict studies, ethnic conflict, security studies and IR.

Timea Spitka is Sophie Davis Postdoctoral Fellow in Gender, Conflict Resolution and Peace at the Hebrew University, Israel, and has a PhD in International Relations.

Routledge Studies in Peace and Conflict Resolution
Series Editors: Tom Woodhouse and Oliver Ramsbotham
University of Bradford

Reconciliation after Terrorism
Strategy, possibility or absurdity?
Judith Renner and Alexander Spencer

Post-War Security Transitions
Participatory peacebuilding after
asymmetric conflicts
*Edited by Veronique Dudouet,
Hans Giessman and Katrin Planta*

Rethinking Peacebuilding
The quest for just peace in the Middle
East and the Western Balkans
*Edited by Karin Aggestam and
Annika Björkdahl*

Violent Conflict and Peacebuilding
The continuing crisis in Darfur
Johan Brosché and Daniel Rothbart

Peacebuilding and NGOs
State–civil society interactions
Ryerson Christie

Peace Negotiations and Time
Deadline diplomacy in territorial disputes
Marco Pinfari

**History Education and Post-Conflict
Reconciliation**
Reconsidering joint textbook projects
*Edited by Karina V. Korostelina and
Simone Lässig*

Conflict Resolution and Human Needs
Linking Theory and Practice
*Edited by Kevin Avruch and
Christopher Mitchell*

**Human Rights Education and
Peacebuilding**
A comparative study
Tracey Holland and J. Paul Martin

Post-Conflict Studies
An Interdisciplinary Approach
*Edited by Chip Gagnon and
Keith Brown*

**Arab Approaches to Conflict
Resolution**
Mediation, negotiation and settlement
of political disputes
*Nahla Hamdan and
Frederic S. Pearson*

**UN Peace Operations and
International Policing**
Negotiating complexity, assessing
impact and learning to learn
Charles T. Hunt

**Civil Resistance and Conflict
Transformation**
Transitions from armed to nonviolent
struggle
Edited by Véronique Dudouet

Communication and Peace
Mapping an emerging field
*Edited by Julia Hoffmann and
Virgil Hawkins*

**Migration and Security in the
Global Age**
Diaspora communities and conflict
Feargal Cochrane

Gender, Peace and Security
Implementing UN Security Council
Resolution 1325
*Edited by Theodora-Ismene Gizelis
and Louise Olsson*

**Conflict Transformation and
Reconciliation**
Multi-level challenges in deeply
divided societies
Sarah Maddison

**International Intervention, Identity
and Conflict Transformation**
Bridges and walls between groups
Timea Spitka

International Intervention, Identity and Conflict Transformation

Bridges and walls between groups

Timea Spitka

Routledge
Taylor & Francis Group

LONDON AND NEW YORK

First published 2016
by Routledge
2 Park Square, Milton Park, Abingdon, Oxon OX14 4RN

and by Routledge
711 Third Avenue, New York, NY 10017

First issued in paperback 2017

Routledge is an imprint of the Taylor & Francis Group, an informa business

British Library Cataloguing-in-Publication Data
A catalogue record for this book is available from the British Library

Library of Congress Cataloging-in-Publication Data
Names: Spitka, Timea, author.
Title: International intervention, identity and conflict transformation : bridges and walls between groups / Timea Spitka.
Description: New York, NY : Routledge, 2016. | Series: Routledge studies in peace and conflict resolution | Includes bibliographical references and index.
Identifiers: LCCN 2015025485| ISBN 9781138823815 (hardback) | ISBN 9781315741864 (ebook)
Subjects: LCSH: Conflict management–International cooperation. | Intervention (International law) | International relations.
Classification: LCC JZ6368 .S65 2016 | DDC 327.1/17–dc23
LC record available at http://lccn.loc.gov/2015025485

ISBN 13: 978-0-8153-6518-1 (pbk)
ISBN 13: 978-1-138-82381-5 (hbk)

Typeset in Times New Roman
by Wearset Ltd, Boldon, Tyne and Wear

For Amir, Ariella, Yannay and Yasmin, I hope this book contributes to the shifting of the tide, so that one day soon you can be proud of where you were born.

Contents

Acknowledgments

I would like to thank the Leonard Davis Institute at Hebrew University and editors at Routledge Publications for making this book not only possible but a pleasure to write. This book began as a PhD thesis and therefore I would like to give special thanks to my PhD advisors Becky Kook and Joel Peters for allowing me to pursue a topic that continues to be close to my heart. Second, I would like to thank the PhD committee, namely Oren Yiftachel and Arie Kacovic, who approved my proposal while under some duress huddled outside under blankets in a café on a cold night in Tel Aviv. Sadly, Dan Bar On, who was also on the committee and whom I would like to thank, could not be there. I wish to also sincerely thank those who took the time to read through various sections of this manuscript and provided me with greatly needed feedback, including Dan Miodownik, Arie Kacovic, Guy Ben Porat, Amal Jamal, Doron Shultziner, Eduard Iricinsci as well as the anonymous readers. Finally, a special thank you to my supportive partner Shlomi Segall and my kids: Amir, Ariella, Yasmin and Yannay. This book is for them.

Introduction

Conflict transformation goes beyond suppressing or ending the conflict into the realm of permanently transforming relations between conflicting groups. Conflicts may be suppressed only to ignite at a later stage or ended unjustly with individuals unable to meet basic human needs and attain fundamental human rights. Conflict transformation also entails a fundamental transformation in the relationship between groups that ensures every individual is able to meet at minimum his or her basic human needs. The term "conflict transformation" emphasizes the need to alter attitudes at grass-roots level for meaningful peace to occur. Ongoing disputes such as the Israeli-Palestinian conflict continue not only because conflicting groups are unable to agree on a settlement but international intervention has contributed to building walls rather than bridges between the groups.

Underlying assumptions about group identity frame the manner in which international actors understand conflicts and their roots causes, and construct the tools and goals for intervention. For a successful prognosis of a conflict, one needs a proper diagnosis. Since group identities underlie the way conflicts are diagnosed, in order to have a successful third-party intervention, it is essential that they are accurately understood. How do the representatives of intervening states and organizations interpret group identities in conflict? What are the consequences of their interpretations on the type of intervention process and strategies? This book argues that, regardless of intention, international intervention process and conflict resolution strategies impact on the identity of groups in conflicts. The fundamental question is: under what conditions do external processes and strategies include elements that promote a transformation in hostile group identities, and under what conditions do international intervention process and strategies harden divisions between groups? In other words, is the international community contributing to building walls or bridges between conflicting groups?

With ever-increasing interaction between countries, more effective international political and judicial bodies and softer barriers against international intervention within domestic conflicts, intervention today in violent domestic conflicts has become more common and rapid, but not necessarily more effective. Well-intended interventions have heightened conflicts or frozen hostile relations between groups. Interveners have proposed or, at times, imposed unworkable institutional frameworks, which have built barriers, and have drawn the interveners perpetually into the very conflicts they sought to alleviate. A serious challenge for the intervener, one that is not adequately addressed in the literature, is how to approach group identities in a violent conflict. The interpretation of the identity of the groups in conflict is determined by numerous factors, including cultures, perceptions, international norms, interests and common practices. Perceptions of group identity frame the conflict and thus influence the type of intervention. The type of international intervention consequently impacts on the identity of the groups in conflict.

Interpretations of group identities form the road map for understanding of conflicts and largely guide international intervention process and strategies. The identity of groups in conflict, based on ethnicity, religion, class, ideology, or instrumental factors, is our basis for interpreting violent conflicts. Perceptions on the nature of group identities, whether salient or fluid, form a significant component of the reasoning behind differing external approaches. The interpretation by policy makers regarding the nature of group identities in a violent conflict has serious implications. Determining group identity to be constant or malleable to change has dramatic implications on policy and type of strategies. If it is malleable to change, as argued in this book, what role is the international community playing in the transformation of group identities when intervening in the conflict? The type of process and type of strategies taken are based on the perceptions of the nature of identity of groups in conflict and have an impact on the potential for the long-term transformation of a conflict. How do external interveners interpret and address internal group identities in a conflict situation? What are the common international practices concerning conflicting groups within a state?

In this book, I argue that there are two fundamental aspects of international intervention which impact on identity of conflicting groups: external *process*; and external *strategies*. External process mirrors how the main external interveners intercede in a particular conflict. International intervention process can be united or divided. In other words, the external parties can intervene jointly, supporting the same side, or support opposite sides in the conflict. Second, intervention process can take place in a neutral or a partisan manner. In a partisan intervention process, one group is deliberately supported at the expense of the other. The intervention can also take place on behalf of neither group, utilizing a neutral approach. The process is the first part of a dual typology examining how external intervention takes place, which I argue has a significant impact on groups in conflict.

External conflict resolution *strategies* are the second vital variable analyzing the type of approaches proposed and at times imposed by the interveners to resolve a conflict. International interveners can advocate strategies ranging from integration, accommodation to partitioning as an approach to resolving differences between conflicting groups. This may include strategies found within the terms of a peace agreement, separation agreements, design of institutions and the type of power sharing arrangements and integration. Analogous to the external process, the chosen strategy advocated or imposed by an outside actor has potentially a long-term impact on groups in conflict. The critical question asked in this book is: under what conditions do international process and external strategies contribute to the transformation or the reification of conflicting group identities?

The book argues that the type of intervention process – united, divided, neutral or partisan – stimulates a shift in salience of conflicting group identities. The fundamental question is: under what conditions do external processes include elements that promote a positive shift between group identities and under what conditions do international intervention process harden group identities? My working assumption is that united intervention, where key stakeholders intervene in the same manner, can contribute to a positive transformation of groups in conflict. My second assumption is that divided international intervention, where external interveners support opposing groups, not only weakens the intention of the intervention, it also likely affirms or hardens the identities of the groups in conflict. Supported by opposing sides, conflicting parties feel no need to transform their goals, positions or narratives.

As will be discussed in Chapter 2, the effect of neutral versus partisan intervention is more complex since it is far more dependent on the already existing power dynamics between the groups. A united–neutral intervention may contribute to a transformation unless the dominant group is behaving in an aggressive manner. A neutral intervention against an uncooperative and aggressive group may have little impact on the behavior of aggressive leadership of the group. However, a united partisan intervention may have a transformative impact on an uncooperative and aggressive group. Based on the above argument, external process would contribute towards positive group identity transformation under the condition of a united and neutral intervention and might contribute towards transformation under the condition of united partisan intervention. However, it should be noted that a partisan intervention against a group might also increase the salience of the said group, since the group will feel under threat. Thus, a partisan intervention may not necessarily have the desired identity transformation.

International conflict resolution strategies also impact on the identity of groups in conflict. External strategies proposed in conflicts may harden or soften differences between the conflicting groups. Institutions suggested or imposed on conflicting groups may build bridges or walls that can have long-term impact. It is useful to discern under what conditions external interveners promote inclusive versus exclusive notions of group identity. Inclusive strategies are those that promote common bonds and ensure that all groups are included in a national strategy. On the other hand, exclusive identity strategies are those that would exclude particular groups on a national level, such as in cases of ethno-democracy. As will be discussed, integration and accommodation can all be based on either inclusive or exclusive principles. On the other hand, partitioning territory along ethnic/religious lines is built along exclusive principles, excluding groups not linked to the territory.

Adopted international strategies have a powerful impact on the conflicting groups. Power-sharing arrangements, including accommodation and integration, can potentially be inclusive or exclusive. Both may also be transformative, in that they may address issues of misbalance and can soften divisions between groups. However, this depends on the type of accommodation and integration as well as the nature of the balance of power relations between the groups. Partitioning along group lines or assimilative arrangements are more likely to harden identities and widen divisions between hostile groups. Partitioning options that link group identity with territory may also heighten conflict and even spur ethnic cleansing as groups vie for control of specific geographical areas. On the other hand, arrangements that ignore identity issues and institutionally exclude groups are likely to induce fear of assimilation and may also harden identities and serve to heighten the conflict.

Based on the above discussion, I examine the impact of the external conflict resolution strategies that will be analyzed in the theoretical section and the three case studies. The main strategies discussed include integration, accommodation and partitioning; however, since full integration was not proposed by external interveners in any of the case studies, and is seldom proposed and adopted during or subsequent to a violent conflict, the research will focus on a hybrid of integration and accommodation, accommodation and partitioning. As referred to above, the fundamental question is: under what conditions do external strategies include elements that promote a positive shift in group identities and under what conditions do intervention strategies harden or solidify group identities. My working assumption is that inclusion fosters identity transformation while exclusion advances reification of conflicting group identities.

International interventionists may or may not be deliberately using a particular process or a strategy to impact on group identities. However, whether intended or not, external process and strategies have an impact. The type of process culminating in mediated or imposed agreements and institutions contributes to hardening or transforming group identities. Elaborating on external interventions in Northern Ireland, Israel-Palestine, and Bosnia and Herzegovina, this book will analyze external process and strategies managing antagonizing groups within each conflict and their impact on the identity of the groups in conflict. In all three conflicts, external versus internal intervention are blurred, in that none are entirely domestic disputes since groups have various ties to neighboring countries. The book will primarily focus on diplomatic intervention on the part of the key players namely: the United States (US), European Union (EU) and United Nations (UN) and the significant regional actors. When relevant, it will also examine how military and/or economic interventions affected diplomatic efforts.

External intervention in violent domestic disputes can contribute to freezing or transforming group identities. Official international interventions in violent conflicts have on many occasions tended to affirm rather than transform identities, supporting dominant forms of political and institutional partitioning between the hostile groups. Using lenses influenced by domestic and international perceptions, potential external interveners formulate their interpretations of the reality of groups in conflict and propose strategies and types of intervention. Whether intended or not, international interventions can result in the shifting, distorting or transforming of the identity of the conflicting groups. For example, in order to lure an advantageous type of intervention, leaders of conflicting groups can put forth their case in the most favorable light, hoping that international interveners will help their cause or, at the very least, refrain from obtrusive meddling. Thus, groups may highlight or transform their outward casings to lure potential supporters.

The type of conflict resolution intervention strategy has a pivotal impact on the identity of groups in conflict. The intervention may serve to strengthen, weaken or transform a conflicting group, shifting its position politically, institutionally or instrumentally. By being recognized externally, particular domestic leaders may be strengthened or weakened. Certain groups can become more central within the establishment of new institutions, shifting power relations within a country. Groups may strive for and receive greater status, for example, that of a national minority. Through recognition or peace agreements, groups can be granted a route towards the creation of an independent state. Interesting to note are the external normative qualifications determining which groups are deemed to deserve a state, which groups are suitable to be institutionally accommodated within the state and which groups are externally pressured to be integrated within the already existing state institutions. In other words, under what conditions do international interveners approach a conflict using a group strategy of partitioning, accommodation or integration? What is the impact of the type of intervention on the identities of the parties?

The particular strategy can stem from a number of reasons, including international norms, the interpretation of the conflict, the relationship between the intervener and the conflicting party or state, and the status of the state in conflict within the international arena. Due to internal or international strategic interest, the intervener may favor a particular group or the state over another group. External strategic preference can include disintegration or preservation of the state. In general, partitioning and accommodation arrangements tend to favor the conflicting group over the state. On the other hand, integrative arrangements are more favorable towards the state. However this is dependent on the type of arrangement and on the extent of inclusion and exclusion of individuals and groups. The successes of any of the strategies are also very much dependent on how group identities are approached and the degree of inclusion and exclusion.

Although group identity issues are at the core of violent conflicts, official international intervention has tended to ignore them or focus on ways of institutionalizing group differences into territorial divisions or static institutional arrangements. Demarcated correlation between a specific group identity and territory is the source of many conflicts, since it is built on strategies of exclusion. One can distinguish, however, between two types of approaches of groups belonging to the land. The first approach can be summed up as "this land belongs to us;" the second as "we belong to the land" (Bashir Bashir, from discussions with the author in Jerusalem in 2011). The former is a more Western, exclusive, concept that implies a denial of access to the land to others. "We belong to this land," on the other hand, is not necessarily exclusive. The condition of mutual belonging could be that everyone recognizes the land as important to the well-being of the groups living on the land and does not threaten exclusivity over land. The exclusive/inclusive distinction goes beyond territory to include the political and economic sphere.

This book uses an in-depth comparison of external intervention in three prom-inent case studies. There are many other cases that might have been used, includ-ing South Africa, Afghanistan, Sudan, Somalia, Iraq or Syria. Each conflict has its own regional and domestic complexities, as well as a type of intervention, which have to be taken into account when conducting a comparison. Every con-flict necessitates an in-depth examination of the dynamics of international inter-vention and provides ample material on the effects of intervention process and strategies within the conflict. As has been recommended by qualitative method-ologists, the cases were not selected on the bases of the dependent variable, or the impact of the external process on the conflict (Tansey 2014). Rather, they were selected because of the independent variable, third party intervention process and strategies. External intervention was abundant in all three cases, with potentially measurable indicators of the impact. The three case studies were also chosen based on the hypothesis that Northern Ireland was an example of a united–neutral external process and inclusive group strategies, Bosnia and Herzegovina an example of mixture of united–partisan process and exclusive group identity strategy, and Israel-Palestine a case of divided external process and exclusive group external strategies.

Measuring the impact of external intervention is challenging, since one needs to differentiate between legacies of domestic factors versus international inter-vention. As noted by scholars engaged in methodological debates, international and domestic variables interact in often-complex ways, which are difficult to untangle (Downs 2002; Tansey 2014). Establishing a clear chain of causal responsibility can be a challenge. This research addresses this methodological challenge by monitoring the effects of very different types of external processes: united, divided, neutral and partisan. In each of the case studies, I examine whether there is a correlation between the change in the type of process and the impact on groups in conflict.

The methodology in the research uses process tracing and counterfactual ana-lysis to examine causal relationship between external intervention and impact on group identities. Methodologically this creates some challenges, due to the neces-sity of establishing a direct correlation between external intervention and groups within a state. Domestic factors, which are generally the focus of the investigation when examining group identities within a state, can play a far more crucial role in shaping group identities. However, these are examined at length in other sources. An externally led peace process and external intervention in a violent conflict pro-vides a unique window of opportunity for international mediators to impact on group identities and their potential for transformation. International mediation attempts to transform relationships between groups may thus strengthen or weaken a group, and may encourage or impose a particular type of institutional framework, resulting in long-term consequences. Intervening states may also recognize new states, intervene on behalf of particular groups or back a type of leadership.

The research will analyze each case in depth to note under what conditions external processes and strategies included elements that promoted a positive shift in group identities and under what conditions international interventions contributed to hardening group identities. The three case studies selected in this research shed light on how different interpretations of group identities resulted in diverse intervention processes and strategies, and their impact on the conflict and identity of the conflicting parties. There are many similarities and differences in the cases, which was the justification for their selection for comparison. First, all three case studies have been abundantly and well researched, providing rich secondary material. Second, interventions in the case studies took place around the same time and were impacted by significant global events, such as the end of the Cold War and the rise of the EU. The period under investigation will focus on the same time period, from the 1990s until the present time. Third, the US took a vital role in all of the cases, while the EU has become an increasingly significant player. Finally, all three conflicts have been argued to be intractable ethnic or religious conflicts that are difficult or impossible to resolve. At the same time, the cases are examples of different types of external processes and strategies. I would argue that the Northern Ireland case is an example of a relatively positive intervention process and strategies that to a large extent contributed to resolving the conflict, while Israel-Palestine is an example of a negative intervention process and strategies which has for the most part not contributed to a resolution. Finally, Bosnia and Herzegovina consisted of a positive process but negative intervention strategies that ended the violence, but with divisive strategies that froze the conflicting relations between the groups.

Official international interventions in violent conflicts have on many occasions tended to affirm rather than transform identities, supporting dominant forms of political and institutional partitioning between the hostile groups. This book addresses the differences between the integrative, accommodative and partitioning options in Northern Ireland, Bosnia and Herzegovina and Israel-Palestine. Although affirmative approaches have been used and may be necessary to address different grievances, the recent experiences in conflicts such as in Israel-Palestine and in Bosnia and Herzegovina, have pointed to the dangers of relying on affirmative and partitioning strategies. I argue that conflict resolution should not only constitute attempts to negotiate agreements between existing groups but be a conscious effort to transform the identities of the conflicting groups, including the changing of group perceptions, attitudes and goals; an endeavor to promote a civic versus ethnic/religious identity, as well as attempts at the formation of new common and multi-layered identities.

The structure of this book unfolds as follows: Chapter 1 defines identity and examines the dynamic nature of group identity in conflict and conflict resolution. It outlines the manner in which group identity becomes distorted during a violent conflict. Due to this distortion, I argue that group identity strategies should be designed to transform a conflict, or, through the creation of an open and flexible institutional framework, be given the opportunity and the time to transform.

Chapter 2 develops a framework to examine international processes, representing four types of external interventions: united, divided, neutral and partisan. The process utilized by the external parties runs along a dual axis of intervention, shifting between united and divided, on the one hand, and neutral and partisan, on the other. The type of external process has an impact on the conflict and on the identities of the parties. A united intervention, where countries intercede in unison, is the ideal type of external intervention but challenging to achieve. By empowering opposite sides, a divided intervention tends to put fuel on the fire and thus a shift from a united towards a divided partisan intervention is likely to deepen a conflict, hardening the groups' positions. The impact of a neutral versus a partisan intervention depends on many factors, beginning with the power balance between the conflicting groups. A neutral intervention against an uncooperative and aggressive group may have little impact, while a united partisan intervention may have a transformative impact on an uncooperative and aggressive group.

Chapter 3 examines international interventionist strategies, including integration, accommodation, and partitioning, noting opportunities, challenges and potential consequences stemming from a choice of a particular strategy. The theoretical literature outlines two main strategies regarding the provisions of groups' rights within peace agreements and existing or new institutions. These are accommodating the group within a power sharing arrangement and integrating the group within the state's political and institutional framework. Although external interveners may not publicly advocate subsequent strategies, in practice the choice may be widened to include: partitioning of the state, assimilation, exclusion, and annihilating a conflicting group. International norms on minority group rights, as outlined by the UN Charter of Rights, favor integration. Accommodation, in line with international principles, is an international approach advocated only for groups recognized as natives or aboriginals (Kymlicka 1996). However, practice often differs from principles, and this is particularly the case in violent conflicts where external interveners commonly promote accommodation or partitioning over integration of the group within a state.

The next section of the book examines international intervention process and strategies within the case studies. Chapter 4 explores international intervention in Bosnia and Herzegovina (BiH) where, in an effort to end the conflict, the international community promoted numerous partitioning solutions that heightened the conflict and deepened divisions between the conflicting groups. The case of Bosnia is an example of a process that eventually ended a conflict but did so with detrimental identity strategies. In the end, the US mediated and imposed a peace agreement that froze the conflicting relationship between the groups and created an unworkable state. From the initial external intervention, European efforts focused on partitioning the country along ethno-religious lines. Despite the significant number of mixed marriages, groups were externally perceived as divided, primordial and unchanging. European attempts at partitioning along ethnic lines hardened differences and furthered ethnic cleansing. The Dayton Agreement, mediated by the US, was based on the principle of achieving a balance of power between the groups divided along ethno-religious lines. The agreement effectively froze the conflict, institutionalizing ethno-national group identities into a static consociational framework. Despite the billions of dollars invested in resolving the conflict, the international community has achieved little to positively transform the relations between the Bosniaks, Croats and Serbs. Also, in institutionalizing the political power relations along ethno-national lines, the peace agreement has effectively hindered identity transformation.

Chapter 5 examines international intervention in the Northern Ireland conflict. Northern Ireland, for the most part, highlights positive external process and strategies. The chapter notes that, through a transformative and inclusive mediation process and a flexible institutional framework, the Good Friday Agreement promoted multi-layered identity and transformation of the groups in the conflict. The past 15 years of an increasingly united external intervention process has served to deescalate the conflict. The shift from a divided partisan to a more neutral external intervention softened the differences between the conflicting groups, fostering transformation. United intervention was made possible with the termination of the partisan support of the respective patrons of the Unionists and the Nationalists, and a move towards a more neutral stance. The Good Friday Agreement took a flexible, inclusive approach on group identity. In the agreement, for the most part, group identities were not perceived as primordial, solid and unchanging but with the potential for change. Although partitioning has not been removed from the menu, the focus has not been on exclusive group control over territory but rather a move towards cooperation and collaboration. The increased united external intervention based on non-exclusive identity principles shifted the impact from escalating towards resolving the conflict.

Chapter 6 looks at the numerous attempts to broker a peace agreement in Israel-Palestine, examining the largely unhelpful external process and strategies. The prolonged divided external intervention in the Israeli–Palestinian conflict has been one source of escalation, deepening the divide between the conflicting groups. It is argued here that Palestinians and Jewish Israelis have grown further apart, not only because of events that took place but as a consequence of the continued divided material and idealistic support from their respective patrons. Although in principle much of the international community has shifted towards a united partisan position against Israel, in practice, powerful countries, most notably the US, have continued to support Israel. In addition, violent Palestinian factions have continued to receive moral and material support from neighboring states and groups, perpetuating a divided external intervention.

The emphasis of partitioning of land along ethno-religious lines as the only possible official solution to the conflict has also deepened divisions between the conflicting groups. Israeli and Palestinian group identities have externally been perceived as primordial, solid and impossible to change. The partition option along ethno-religious lines has encouraged further segregation, land grabs and exclusivity. The chapter observes that, although the two-state solution may presently be the only common acceptable international solution, a united and transformative approach is needed to build bridges between the hostile groups. Thus, despite numerous continuing international efforts to end the conflict, and regardless of intention, ongoing external intervention in Israel-Palestine has for the most part served to escalate rather than transform the conflict.

Chapter 7 conducts an overview of the success and failures of international intervention with a focus on the three conflicts, analyzing the impact on identity of the groups in conflict. The final chapter points to the dangers of linkage between group identity and territory during the height of the conflict. It stipulates that united external interventions have been the most likely to have transformative impact on group identities. It notes that official peace-making strategies have tended to be affirmative, heightening and institutionalizing the differences between the groups. It also construes that the trouble with institutional frameworks negotiated at the height of a conflict within groups is that they may freeze the relationship and group identity when it is at its most hostile and adversarial. The agreements in the long term may thus prevent a transformation and be a hindrance to resolution. The chapter concludes with lessons learned and recommendations for external interveners in violent conflict.

Examining the three case studies, this analysis sheds light on interpretation of group identities and the consequential international intervention process and strategies. Whether intended or not, differing processes and strategies have an impact on group identities in violent conflicts. The subsequent chapters will examine the criteria that the international community, in particular the US, UN and the EU, uses for its preference of a specific type of process and type of strategies and the impact of the choice on the groups' identity in conflict.

Although academics and practitioners are familiar with distortions of group identities as a result of violent conflict, they know far less about peace makers' attempts to promote positive shifts in group identities or to broker new common identities. Despite the vast body of literature on conflict resolution, few authors have focused on how external parties approach group identities in conflict. Dominant studies have ignored identity issues or have emphasized primordial and one-dimensional aspects of identity, ignoring its complicity and its potential for transformation. Identity groups have been studied significantly within the domestic arenas, but studies of external impact on groups have been minimal. There is also a significant gap between common macro international relations studies of intervention and micro social–psychological studies of group identity. Thus the subsequent chapters will attempt to take a step towards bridging the gap between studies of external intervention and complex studies of group identity.

References

Downs, George and Stephen John Stedman. 2002. "Evaluation Issues in Peace Implementation." In *Ending Civil Wars: The Implementation of Peace Agreements*, ed. Stephen John Stedman, Donald Rothchild and Elizabeth M. Cousens. Boulder CO: Lynne Rienner.

Kymlicka, Will. 1996. *Multicultural Citizenship*. Oxford: Oxford University Press.
Lederach, John Paul. 2005. *The Moral Imagination: The Art and Soul of Building Peace*. Oxford: Oxford University Press.
Lijphart, Arend. 2007. *Thinking about Democracy: Power Sharing and Majority Rule in Theory and Practice*. London: Routledge.
Tansey, Oisin. 2014. Evaluating the Legacies of State-Building: Success, Failure and the Role of Responsibility. *International Studies Quarterly* 58: 174–186.

1   The dynamics of group identity in conflict and conflict resolution

In 1996 war-torn Sarajevo, just a year after the signing of the Dayton Agreement that ended the bloodiest war in Europe since World War II, Serbian singer Dorde Balasevic gave a sold-out concert to enthusiastic Sarajevans. As the audience sang along to the folksy old ballads, there were few dry eyes in the crowded hall. How was it that a Serbian singer was so well received by a large, mostly Bosniac (Muslim) audience? Where was the ancient hatred that was reportedly suppressed by Tito's policies and responsible for the violence in Bosnia? The Sarajevo concert, one of the few successful events organized just after the war by the United Nations High Commissioner for Refugees (UNHCR), opens a gateway into some of the complexities of group identity. Prior to the war, Sarajevo was a mosaic of cultures and mixed marriages constituted during centuries of coexistence, leaving few families without at least one member from some other ethnic or religious group. As Bosnia became engulfed in the Yugoslavian conflict, individuals and families were perplexed about which side they were on. From one day to the next, millions of Bosniac Muslims, most of whom had for centuries led a European secular life but defined themselves as Muslims culturally, found themselves categorized by Serbian extremists as Turkish Muslims and as such publicly labeled by national extremists as "foreign invaders" and a target for removal or extermination. People's group identities, how they categorized themselves and, more significantly, how others categorized them, rapidly became a matter of life and death.

How we depict ourselves and how others define us is an essential trait of our existence. It defines who we are as individuals, as part of a group, and it guides our daily lives and interactions with others and the society around us. Identity is multi-layered but can be divided into two general but interrelated aspects. First, *personal identity*, consisting of segments of self that are based on individual characteristics such as profession, interests, personality traits, color, marital status, nationality, age, gender and religion. Second, *group identity*, consisting of those aspects of the self that are based on group membership, which include similar traits such as race, language, color, tribe, nationality, ethnicity, and religion but as they pertain to membership in a group (Tajfel 1978). Although both individual and group identities have similar characteristics, group identity is more than the sum of individual identities, moving beyond individual control and subject to a dynamic with a life of its own. Group identity may change, based on relations between groups and external and internal manipulations. Depending on circumstances such as violence, group identity can strengthen, weaken or be transformed. This research focuses on group aspects of identity, its dynamics within a violent conflict and its potential for transformation.

In this book, I argue that transformation of conflicting group identities is a fundamental element in conflict transformation. Group identity is fluid and dynamic, becoming distorted during a violent conflict, and hence needs to be transformed as part of conflict resolution. Without transformation or the potential for long-term transformation, groups cannot reach reconciliation and the conflict between groups may freeze or just shift into a different sphere. Although group identity change is one of the primary aspects in conflict resolution, those who adhere to primordial or instrumental definitions of group identity generally bypass it. External interveners frequently overlook the salience of group identity, leaving issues related to group identity to national leadership. Much of international mediation is focused on how to draw lines or divide territory between conflicting groups without questioning the salience of group identity and the nexus between a group and the territory. However, regardless of intention, international intervention in violent conflicts, namely international intervention process and strategies, impact on group identities. With or without intention, external intervention process and strategies may soften or harden barriers between conflicting groups. In order to examine the impact of the types of intervention one has to first understand the complexity of the dynamics of groups in a violent conflict.

The trouble with defining group identity is that it is multi-layered, complex, dynamic and open to multiple internal and external interpretations. None of us belongs to only one group; rather, there are a number of overlapping group identities that define who we are and where we belong in any given place and time. Ethnic, racial or religious identities have been traditionally regarded as the least permeable to change, but, in our increasingly mixed world, whether in Canada, Bosnia, India, Israel, Palestine or Iraq, these are far more complex, multi-layered and dynamic than are generally represented. There are, however, times in one's life, year, day or situation when a particular group membership may become the primary focal point above all others. The salience of the affiliation with the specific group may be related to the intensity of the situation. For instance, an act of direct discrimination on the basis of belonging to a particular group may heighten one's identification with the group targeted, strengthening the connection with the others in the group, and increasing the salience.

Many of us become more conscious of our own group identities when meeting a new curious person or attempting to pass through airport security, where complex answers as to which group one belongs to can be a subject either for an interesting discussion or for an unpleasant interrogation. For example, when entering Israel, being categorized as part of a particular group such as a Palestinian, a peace activist, or a human rights lawyer can lead to intense interrogation or refusal of entry. In the case of a violent intergroup conflict, the focus on a particular group membership may remain the focal point for some time. Significant differences between groups may not necessarily be related to the level of hostility. During the violence in Bosnia, a different spelling of a name on an identity card was the key determinant of belonging to a group and was commonly used by militias to determine the ultimate fate of the person, be that ethnic cleansing, incarceration or death. Defining the nature of group identity is vital since it reflects the underlying and core issues in any conflict and determines our understanding of a conflict. In turn, the interpretation of the conflict between the groups determines the type of resolution interveners may seek or prescribe.

Although there is overlap, most group identity theorists can be categorized into three different schools: primordial, instrumental, and constructivists (Tailor and Orkin 2001). The social–psychological approach, based on small group experiments, can be seen as the fourth approach, influencing instrumentalist and constructivist research. Each defines group identity in a different way and offers distinct explanations for outbreak of violence. The primordial approach emphasizes the ancient and deep-rooted side of collective identity (Birch 1989; Huntington 1998; Smith 2009). Most primordialists view collective identity as an organic progress, going through the stages of birth, development and maturity. Their focus is on the cultural, religious and ethnic differences that are perceived as impermeable to significant change. Many primordialists believe ethnic or religious conflict to be inevitable and rooted in human nature and/or in the cultural or religious characteristics of a particular group. A recent example of a primordialist approach is Samuel P. Huntington's influential work, *The Clash of Civilizations and the Remaking of the World Order*. In his analysis, cultural and religious differences are presumed to be solid, unchanging and directly linked to cooperation, coexistence or violence (Huntington 1998).

A fundamental weakness of the primordial approach is that it fails to account for salience of group identities. Based on ontological assumptions, primordial understanding of group identity approaches fails to explain upsurges in nationalism or conflict. In addition, the approach cannot account for why culturally similar or identical groups fight, while culturally different groups cooperate. On the whole, the primordial approach is considered the "old" theoretical approach to the study of group identity and has been, for the most part, abandoned by scholars in favor of other approaches that perceive identities in a less fixed and more dynamic manner. However, some academics, and many practitioners and top policy makers have retained a primordial understanding of group identity, influencing the type of intervention in conflicts.

Unlike the primordial theorists, instrumental theorists view group identities as goal-oriented and changing when there are comparative advantages to be gained (Brass 1991; Gellner 1983; Gurr 1996; Kreidie and Monroe 2002). The emphasis of most instrumental theorists is on relative deprivation or grievance, and bad leadership, which tend to incite nationalism, extremism and violence for personal or group gain. According to the pivotal instrumental theorist Ernest Gellner "Nationalism is primarily a political principle, which holds that the political and the national unit should be congruent." Therefore "if the rulers of the political unit belong to a nation other than that of the majority ruled, this, for the nationalists, constitutes a quite understandably intolerable breech of political propriety" (Gellner 1983, 1). Instrumentalists perceive it natural for leadership to rally their group in pursuit of a particular common goal. Some instrumental theorists utilize a rational choice approach that "suggests that there are tangible costs and benefits to be gained from conflict and that participants act with a rational calculus" (Kreidie and Monroe 2002, 9). Although there are tangible benefits to be gained in conflict, the use of a rational approach in violent conflicts can be hindering, since actors engaged in a conflict do not necessarily act rationally or at times even in their best self-interest or the interest of the group. The instrumental approach, however, is helpful in explaining the rise of nationalistic leadership, which commonly plays a key role in inciting conflicts.

Social psychology is the study of individual behavior in a social context and can be combined with either the instrumentalist or constructivist approaches. The emphasis is on the examination of perceptions, motivations, feelings and overt actions of individuals, which are utilized to identify how they influence, and are affected by, relations between groups (Taylor and Moghaddam 1987). The analysis has been particularly insightful in understanding perceptions and how relations between groups affect them. For example, Morton Deutsch maintains that parties respond to one another in terms of their respective expectations, and that their behavior in conflict is influenced by their negative expectations of each other (Deutsch 1973). Tajfel and Turner explain intergroup behavior through referring to psychological process, including social comparison and psychological distinctiveness. The central assumption in the Social Identity Theory (SIT), developed by Tajfel and Turner, is that individuals are motivated to achieve and maintain a positive self-identity (Tajfel and Turner 1979). Thus, individuals wish to alter their intergroup situation, so that their social identity can be comparatively improved. SIT conclusions are the result of small intergroup experiments in which individuals, divided into arbitrary group categorizations, indicate immediate preferences for their own group and demonstrate discriminative biases against members in the other group.

Reacting against primordialists, and drawing on research conducted by instrumentalists and Social Identity Theorists, constructivists focus on perceptions and less permanent aspects of group identities. According to constructivists, even ethnic or religious identities have been shown to be constructed, maintained and manipulated to impact on a conflict (Cornell and Hartmann 1998; Kriesberg 1998; Taras and Tanguly 2002). Although some traits such as language, religion, skin color, and origin are not easily modifiable, group identities are thought to be based not on ascribed traits but on shared values, beliefs, perceptions and concerns that are varyingly open to acquisition or transformation by choice (Kriesberg 2003). According to Brubaker, "groups that are definitively bounded, internally homogeneous and clearly differentiated don't actually exist. It is the shared sense or image of groupness that is real..." (Brubaker 2000). In *Ethnicity without Groups*, Brubaker stressed that "[e]thnicity, race, and nationhood are fundamentally ways of perceiving, interpreting, and representing the social world. They are not things *in* the world, but perspectives *on* the world" (Brubaker 2002, 17). Although many scholars have adopted a constructivist approach, this view is less common in the world of policy making. Policy strategies are often reflected from conventional scholarly literature or a populist and media view of violent conflicts that at times make simplistic primordial distinction between groups and mark their nature as static and unchanging.

The presumption of much of the conventional literature on violent conflicts has been that ethnic or religious diversity within a state has been the primary cause of violent conflicts. Samuel Huntington was not alone in arguing that the mere presence of ethnic diversity can cause conflict, due to differences in values of different cultures (Huntington 1998). Primordial scholars have presented ethnic identity as unchanging and impart it as a key explanatory variable triggering violent conflict (Smith 2009; Taras and Tanguly 2002). Recent findings in empirical literature have disputed this analysis, noting that ethnic diversity is not linked to higher levels of violence, but may rather reduce the risk of conflict. According to Collier, instead of diversity, it is rather ethnic dominance that can increase the risk of war (Collier 2000).

Violent conflict is not inherent to group identity but is commonly caused by lack of basic human needs, dysfunctional institutions and bad leadership. Fearon argues that "large scale ethnic violence is provoked by elites seeking to gain, maintain, or increase their hold on political power" (Fearon and Latin 2000). Recent literature has also shifted the debate on the causes of conflicts focusing on grievance, to noting the importance of greed (Aspinall 2007). In other words some elite leadership may be motivated less by the dire situation of the particular group they represent than by attempts to gain control over particular resources for their own benefit. This shift has deepened our understanding of conflict and allowed the identity of groups to be understood in a more profound way. Although grievance remains a key variable, salience of group identity may also be related to greed. However, the shift in salience of group identity has only recently been noted to be an important variable in intensity of conflict.

The importance of salience of group identity has been a focus of much constructivist literature. Most constructivists, however, admit some constant or long-term aspects of group identities and do not view group identities as completely fluid. As noted by prominent constructivist scholar Brubaker,

> If it [identity] is fluid, how can we understand the ways in which self-understandings may harden, congeal, and crystallize? If it is constructed, how can we understand the sometimes coercive force of external identifications? If it is multiple, how do we understand the terrible singularity that is often striven for – and sometimes realized – by politicians seeking to transform mere categories into unitary and exclusive groups?
>
> (Brubaker 2000, 1)

Still, group identity, including religious or ethnic, is not primordial, solid and unchanging. As noted by Kanchan Chandra

> [I]t is common to assume that because the attributes defining them [identities] are fixed in the short term, ethnic identity categories are also fixed in the short term. Individuals can change between identity *categories*, often quite rapidly, by combining and recombining elements from their set of attributes differently.
>
> (Chandra 2006, 18)

Membership in groups and the meaning of the membership is also not constant. Todd noted that multiple identities are not something one chooses and discards but are overlapping identities that fall within collective categories. Collective identities are reproduced based on "contact with others whom we recognize are like ourselves and on a related sense of belonging with those who share our categories and who recognize and respond positively to our immediate intuitive distinctions" (Todd 2008, 434). For instance, a particular group identity, such as a parent's heritage, may become more prominent when one visits the location of one's birth and finds a sense of shared belonging. Fearon and Latin note that social categories are distinguished by two main features:

> rules of membership that decide who is and who is not a member of the category; and content, that is sets of characteristics (such as beliefs, desires, moral commitments, and physical attributes) thought typical of members of the category, or behaviors expected or obliged of members in certain situations (roles).
>
> (Fearon and Latin 2000, 848)

Both the rules of membership and the content of the characteristics can become dynamic in the midst of a violent conflict and may determine one's affiliation and security.

This book pursues a constructivist approach that defines group identity as socially constructed, based on various traits, experiences and perceptions that people have. I contend that group identity is complex, multi-layered and dynamic, defining the group in relations to others and to the world in any given place and time. Groups are continuously creating and shifting rules of membership and notions of themselves and others, based on their perceived immediate present, past, and potentially also future reality. Although there are some traits that cannot be easily modified, the meaning or the perception of the meanings do change, as do their significance, membership rules and perception of characteristics. A person may emphasize different aspect of his or her group identity such as their skin color, gender, religion or ethnicity. For groups, this change goes beyond the shifting of narratives, and can determine the inclusive and exclusive nature of group identity and strategies of cooperation or conflict. Even when group membership remains solid over time, perceptions of the meaning of the group, its inclusive and exclusive nature and its relationship with other groups do change.

Who is part of "us" and who is one of "them" can become a matter of life and death in conflict and needs to be an integral part of conflict transformation. The common emphasis among constructivists is a dynamic, shared, imagined community that has a great capacity for change. As noted by Kriesberg, "people who share the same identity think of themselves of having common interest and a common fate" (Kriesberg 1998). The common shared sense of belonging and fate may fade or be heightened in midst of a violent conflict. Research that places a much higher emphasis on dynamic elements of identity in conflict is a step forward from research based on primordial understanding that determined conflicting groups as impermeable to significant change. Defining groups as solid and unchanging is not only false but creates hurdles in attempts at formulating transformative process and strategies.

Group identity and violent conflict

Every individual holds layers of group identity that define who they are; these layers can change according to events, perception of events, in relation to others and can also be subject to manipulation by leadership or a state. For individuals, group membership is rarely equal in strength, as membership in some groups is, at times, more vital than membership in others, depending on changing circumstances and realities. A group identity may also lay dormant until it is threatened, discriminated against, revived or incited by political, military or cultural leadership utilizing a particular group identity to attain power. Vamik Volkan maintains that

> individuals are not usually preoccupied with their large-group identity until it is threatened. When a group is in continuing conflict or a war with a neighbor group, members become acutely aware of their large group identity to the point where it may far outweigh any concern for individual needs, even survival.
>
> (Volkan 1997, 25)

In a conflict situation, it is the threatened group identity that generally becomes the dominant identity and overshadows others. For example, if members of a group experience discrimination or persecution on the basis of their religion, language or gender, than that particular group identity is likely to become the focal point above others (See Figure 1.1). The threatened identity may remain the dominant group identity until the relevant threat, such as discrimination or persecution of members of group, is removed. The process is far more dynamic than reflected in the literature. Volkan notes that "at the root of many group conflicts are bloodlines that establish a kind of border in times of crisis that cannot be crossed" (Volkan 1997, 20). However, even during a state of war, or at times because of the violent conflict itself, group identities and their

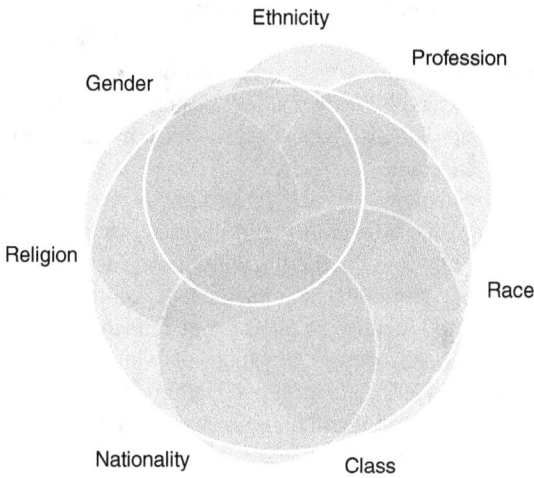

Figure 1.1 Mixed identities.

meaning can and do change. As noted by Kriesberg, when and how identities contribute to intractable conflict depends on the content of the group identities held. This includes numerous factors such as views of the other, nationalism, or the degree of inclusion and self-perception as victims (Kriesberg 2003).

For example, the Israeli–Palestinian conflict is one of the long-standing, antagonistic conflicts where the main presumption is that the only divisive lines are between Palestinians and Israelis. Although this is the deepest divide in the current state of unrest, when one examines the conflict in a more thorough light, one notes many other conflicting lines within the groups, such as those between moderates and extremists, seculars and religious, or those between political groups such as Hamas and Fatah, which have all, at certain times, reached levels of violence. There are also many other group identities including Druze, Christians, immigrants, Haredi, Americans, Russians, peace activists, settlers, to name a few, that create a far more complex environment.

One can also note some ongoing connections such as between proponents of the peace process, environmental groups, women's groups, members of the medical field and other minority groups such as Israeli and Palestinian homosexuals. For example, it is interesting to note that the lack of gay rights and persecution of homosexuals in Palestine has resulted in the immigration of some gay Palestinians into Israel. This does not mean that Palestinian and Israeli gays do not experience the gravity of the Israeli–Palestinian conflict, only that the lack of sexual freedom for many Palestinians gays represents a fundamental aspect of their group identity that is presently also under threat. However, some Palestinian gays who fled to Israel hoping for more freedom have been subject to racism and ended up in Israeli prisons or deported (Ritchie 2010). Membership of vulnerable groups has also been exploited for political gain. In 2014, members of an elite Israeli secret service unit made a public objection to the exploitation of individuals who are part of vulnerable groups. Forty-three members of the prestigious 8200 unit said that they would no longer serve the occupation by providing espionage to manipulate, recruit and exploit vulnerable Palestinians (Cohen 2014). Membership of vulnerable groups can also be subject to attack by extremists and manipulation by nationalistic leadership.

How it is that group identity can be fluid and yet differences between groups can be used as grounds for violence or even genocide? The dynamic and multi-layered nature of group identity does not make it insignificant. Identity is also a basic human need. Researching common basic human needs, conflict resolution theorist Johan Galtung ascertained identity as one of four fundamental internationally acknowledged basic human needs, the others of which are survival, freedom and well-being (Galtung 1996). According to Galtung, these four fundamental human needs are equally essential and non-negotiable. In other words, at minimum, humans strive to meet all of the above needs. The advantageous element of basic human needs is that they are not mutually exclusive. Thus, the attainment of basic needs for a particular group does not threaten the needs of another group. Still, when one of these basic human needs is under threat, people are willing to sacrifice the others to retrieve it. In the case of identity, when people feel that the fundamental aspect of their identity is under threat, they may be willing to sacrifice their freedom, well-being and even survival to get it back. Galtung's analysis is helpful in understanding the power of identity as well as the creation of conditions under which all humans can attain basic human needs. Creating conditions for meeting all basic human needs is one of the theoretical foundations in conflict transformation.

The power of group identity has been prevalent in academic literature. Troublesome, intractable conflicts involving a clash of group identities have often been categorized as "identity conflicts." Jay Rothman differentiates between resource and identity-based conflict. He defines identity conflicts as "deeply rooted in the underlying individual human needs and values that together constitute people's social identities, particularly in the context of group affiliation, loyalties, and solidarity" (Rothman 1997). Thus, rather than being just disputes over tangible resources, "identity conflicts" are rooted in the people's collective needs such as dignity, recognition, safety, control, purpose and efficacy (Rothman 1997, 9).

This is not to say that conventional issues, such as territorial disputes, do not play a role in the conflicts, it is rather to stress that group identity issues often lie at the core of the problem. Group identity is what defines the interpretations of the conflict and conflicts often become described as direct threats against a particular group. Even when the group's existence is not necessarily threatened, a perception of a threat to their essential identities makes a compromise difficult. When dealing with violent intergroup conflicts, however, all are identity conflicts or become so as soon as violence erupts. Therefore, although the research adds to the understanding of conflict between groups, the term "identity conflict" in a violent group conflict seems superfluous. In addition, while Rothman uses the distinction between identity and non identity conflicts to examine ways to tackle identity conflict, many theorists and practitioners have used the term "identity conflicts" to justify an avoidance of intervention.

The manipulation of group identity is commonly cited as one of the contributors to a violent conflict (Fearon and Latin 2000). One does not have to look far for evidence that "ethnic engineers" manufacture oppositional elements of identity and manipulate group identities. The manipulation of group identities can indeed be a key contributor to the escalation of conflict. Most cases of genocide can be attributed to high levels of dehumanization usually created and manufactured by extremist leadership (Adelman 2005). Individuals and groups tend to dehumanize their enemies; the level of their dehumanization generally correlates to the level or the intensity of the violence. In cases of genocide, the threatened groups have often been categorized using expressions characteristic to forms of low life, such as cockroaches or vermin.

Dehumanization takes place, first, by ignoring positive attributes of the other and, second, by attributing negative characteristics to groups that the perpetrators consider their enemy. Dehumanization makes people unable to see similarities between themselves and a perceived enemy (Schirch 2000). Eventually, as individuals and groups chip away at complexities of the identities of others, conflicting group identities become one-dimensional. Opposing group identities become narrow, exclusive, single-dimensional, and hostile to internal differentiations. As noted by Schirch, "As humans strip the humanity of the 'other' in conflict, they negate the identities they may share with their enemy, leaving a one-dimensional understanding of both their own and their enemy's identity" (Schirch 2000, 150). Although there have been numerous excellent studies of dehumanization, few authors have examined the opposite phenomenon or a re-humanization process. Transformation of group identity, including re-humanization, lowering of salience of opposing groups, and creation of shared identity is one of the fundamental necessary steps in transformation of conflict.

Re-humanization of the other group, creation of a shared group identity or a shared future on one territory is filed under soft approaches commonly left to post-peace agreement long-term local reconciliation efforts. However, the type of external intervention and the type of peace agreement may hinder eventual transformation. The type of international intervention process and strategies may contribute to transforming or hardening differences between groups. Supporting particular leadership, taking sides in a conflict, backing opposing groups in conflict or designing institutions that cement rather than transform differences may all contribute towards building walls rather than bridges between groups. Group transformation, however, is generally left out of official peace discussions and institutional designs and filed under post-conflict "people to people" encounters that will gradually with time remove some of barriers. But what happens when the type of international process or the type of institutional group identity strategy, regardless of intention, prevents long-term group transformation?

Group identity and conflict transformation

As argued in this chapter, group identities are constantly changing and adjusting. This is not to say that people change their identities or convert to the "other side" in deeply divided societies. Instead, I argue that the meanings of the categories are constantly renegotiated internally, within the group, and externally between groups. Perceptions of self and others change, and inclusive and exclusive nature of group identities change, shared identities can blossom or disintegrate and all of these have a dramatic impact on the potential for a lasting peace. With or without intention, external intervention has an impact on the potential of group transformation. The question is, when intervening in a violent conflict, does the international intervention contribute to the long-term transformation or reification of the salience of conflicting group identities?

The potential for identity transformation at a group level as a consequence of external intervention in conflict has not been adequately examined. Nancy Frazer used a helpful typology of "affirmative" and "transformative" group strategies to discuss the politics of recognition versus redistribution (Fraser 1997). According to her definition, affirmative remedies propose "to redress disrespect by revaluing unjustly devalued group identities, while leaving intact both the contents of those identities and the group differentiations that underlie them" (Fraser 1997). On the other hand, transformative remedies "redress disrespect by transforming the underlying cultural–valuational structure. By destabilizing existing group identities and differentiations, these remedies would not only raise the self-esteem of members of currently disrespected groups, they would change everyone's sense of self" (Fraser 1997).

There are advantages and challenges inherent in both strategies. In the affirmative approach, the group's homogeneous structure is recognized and may be institutionalized. Affirmative approaches may include dialogues between groups, promotion of civil society along group lines and institutionalization of power sharing arrangements that strengthen participation of disadvantaged groups. On the other hand, transformative strategies seek to abolish the underlying cause of differentiations and destabilize or blur some of the differences between the conflicting groups. This might include promotion of individual human rights, ending discrimination and the cultivation of other identities that cut across the groups in conflict. An example would be strategies that promote identities that decrease group boundaries, such as development of communal linkages or supra-identities.

Affirmative strategies are aimed at addressing grievances by affirming the attributes of a particular group. The group's homogeneous structure is recognized, and may be institutionalized into an unchanging framework (Smithey and Kurtz 2003). Affirmative strategies may include concrete steps to promote group participation or otherwise address some of the concrete grievances of a specific group. At a political level, affirmative strategies promote the institutionalization of group rights within a state framework that may be needed to guarantee expanded or equal participation. Following violent conflicts or severe discrimination, affirmative group strategies have frequently been deemed as necessary to address inequalities and past grievances such as exclusion. Affirmative strategies can also be described under the rubric of accommodation, which will be discussed in depth in Chapter 3.

Transformative strategies seek to abolish the underlying cause of the differentiations and destabilize or blur some of the differences between conflicting groups. This might include cultivating other identities across groups in conflict, for example, cutting across ethnic lines through the promotion of other common identities, such as gender, nationhood, profession, religion or ideology (Keane et al. 1997). Other transformative approaches include the promotion of identities that may lower group boundaries, for instance developing communal linkages or supra and national identities (Jesse and Williams 2006). Another key aspect of this approach includes the transformation of the meanings of the group identities. Transformation strategies do not attempt to undermine the existing categories but rather aspire to gradually change their meaning and the relationship between them. This also includes re-humanization and the transformation of how each group categorizes the other and identifies itself.

The dual typology is narrow and thus this book will introduce another element relevant to intervention strategies in violent conflict: the *reification* of conflicting group identities. Reification refers to the hardening or solidification of group identity along conflict lines. It implies strategies that, whether intended or not, result in the building of psychological or physical walls between groups which may prevent or hinder their transformation. Thus the existing conflicting group lines, whether along religious, ethnic, linguistic or other criteria, become more rigid and locked along conflicting lines. As will be discussed in the subsequent chapters, although it may not be the intended result of the external interveners, strategies such as consociational institutional frameworks along specific conflicting group lines, territorial separation and segregation along group lines, and the promotion or support of exclusive leadership may contribute to reification of the identities of the conflicting groups. Reification of group identities may also stem from domestic factors; however, in this book, the focus is on external interventions that may inhibit or stimulate group identity reification or transformation.

Despite the vast literature on intervention and conflict, few authors have examined external intervention and group identity and only a handful emphasized the importance of the transformation of the salience of conflicting group identity. Most studies of violent internal conflict have been analyzed from the perspective of historical, domestic, ethnic, religious or other cultural group divisions (Gurr 2002; Horowitz 2000). The majority of studies of conflicts have focused on historical animosities between groups, frequently leading to ontological assumptions about cultural and historical differences at work behind violent conflicts. Ontological analyses are problematic because of two misleading assumptions. First, there is the assumption that conflict is constituted in history. Rather, as noted by David Campbell, conflict is constituted in the present and history becomes a resource in a contemporary violent struggle (Campbell 1998). Ontological constructions are also misleading because they presume a linear and deterministic understanding of conflict. Instead, violent conflicts arise from differing narratives with constructed chronologies and justifications for the violence. The constructed framing or narrative tends to emphasize the victimhood of one's own group and the aggressive/perpetrator status of the other. Violence is also not a determined consequence or sequence from the past, since historical disputes can be managed in a non-violent manner.

Certain historical and ontological analyses have also been plagued by simplistic "ancient hatreds" generalizations, based on negative regional stereotypes and on racist or ignorant assumptions about particular groups. This has been well discussed by Edward Said in *Orientalism* and in more critical studies of the "Balkan" region (Campbell 1998; Said 1978). As will be discussed in Chapter 3, the prognosis of conflicts as based on ancient ethnic hatred and ontological understandings of conflict can lead to prescriptions of physical separation between groups. The formation of a nexus between group identity and territory is problematic for several reasons. Divisions between groups, which are not as solid and unchanging as frequently presumed, are complicated. Group identities are multi-layered and dynamic and thus it is never clear-cut who is to be included within the group and who decides the qualification of inclusion and exclusion. Thus the nexus between identity and territory is ambiguous and attempts at achieving absolute clarity can incite more conflict, violence or ethnic cleansing.

The promotion of identity shifts within groups is a delicate but vital and essential ingredient in conflict transformation. As noted by Jennifer Todd,

> Identity shifts, it may be argued, make the difference between peace settlements and interim truces, between settling out on a path to peace and a readiness to return to war. One might suggest that identity shifts make the difference between successful and failed settlement processes.
>
> (Todd 2008)

However, identity transformations are a tall order and raise challenging questions of causality: does identity shift lead to settlement or does settlement lead to identity shift? Arguably, the answer lies in both, since group identities are dynamic and the two are not mutually exclusive. Identity shifts may contribute to a peace settlement, and, if well designed and implemented, a peace settlement may contribute to a "positive" or a constructive group transformation. However, this is dependent on the type of process and type of strategies integral to the peace agreement.

A common theoretical framework of analysis used in conflict resolution literature presupposes the examination of conflicts in terms of stages, as follows: latent or hidden conflict, conflict emergence, escalation, war, stalemate, de-escalation, resolution/settlement and post-conflict peace building (Kriesberg 1998; Ramsbotham et al. 2005). Intervention is generally identified according to the appropriate mechanisms for each particular stage of the conflict. For example, peace-building measures, such as civil society development and reconciliation, are subsequent to the peace-making stage (Crocker et al. 1999). The different stages in the conflict are, at times, also related to the type and robustness of the external intervention. Fisher and Keashly distinguish between four levels of escalation: discussion, polarization, segregation and destruction (Fisher 2001, Fisher and Keashly 1990). Their argument is that the higher the level of escalation, the more forceful the type of intervention that may be required. The justification is that a fiercer conflict requires more external muscle.

Group identity transformation, if addressed at all, is left to the initial escalation or to the final reconciliation stage of conflict. Group identity is most closely researched during the escalation of conflicts, such as studies that examine demonization. For example, Nahi Alon analyzes group identity and shifts in identities as negative factors, such as demonization, polarization, and exclusion, which all contribute to the conflict emergence and to its escalation (Alon and Omer 2005). Alternatively group identity strategies are left to the post-resolution stage of intervention. The detrimental side of advocating identity transformation strategies after the peace-making stage is that the particular type of strategies achieved during an earlier phase could prevent or hinder the subsequent stage of transformation. For example, official mediation, which is the most common way of bringing conflicts to a resolution, often ignores issues related to group identity or presumes conflicting group identities to be a permanent and unchanging element in a conflict.

In international mediation, the outside actor(s) assist conflicting groups to come to some mutually beneficial outcome. Mediation can take on many forms, but can be divided into two separate schools that perceive group identities in a very different light. The first focuses on settlement and is most closely related to law, rational choice, and game theory. The second emphasizes relationship, has its roots in psychology and is associated with unofficial dispute resolution and transformation. The settlement approach prioritizes the reaching of a settlement which may come from bargaining, principled negotiation (Fisher and Uri 1981), creative problem solving (Pruitt and Rubin 1986), trade-offs and conciliations whose primary goal is to create a peace agreement based on a compromise between the conflicting groups. The settlement approach may include power mediation or coercion in the form of promised rewards and punishments (Fisher et al. 1996). The settlement approach may also be focused on dividing territory and other resources between conflicting groups.

Mediation has also been commonly categorized into official mediation between top leadership (track 1) and unofficial or behind closed doors discussions between middle leadership (track 2). The official mediation or track 1 process has tended to focus on settlements such as distributing power, land and other resources between what are commonly presumed to be hostile and unchanging groups. Unofficial or track 2 efforts have tended to focus on recognition, small group problem solving, and ritual reconciliation and generally takes place between middle range leadership. When attempted, the transformation of identities has generally been relegated to the track 2 or unofficial mediation processes. Although track 2 is considered vital in helping the parties move towards an agreement, transformation strategies have commonly been avoided or left out of the official peace-making processes.

Much of the settlement and official mediation literature and practice focuses on positions and interests and ignores the complex, multi-layered and fluid nature of group identity. Identity groups are considered to be on opposing sides and need to be pressured into a compromise with no emphasis placed on transformation. In general, the settlement approach tackles group identity issues in a more affirmative manner focusing on dividing power and resources between the presumably solid groups. On the other hand, transformative mediation is a relationship-oriented process that centers on empowerment, recognition and the long-term improvement of the relationship between conflicting groups (Bush and Folger 1994; Folger et al. 2010). Transformative mediation has been part of unofficial or track 2 mediation, involving middle range leadership prior to track 1 or official mediation. Problem-solving workshops, developed by John Burton and Herbert Kelman, were put into practice in several disputes, such as in Oslo in the Israeli–Palestinian conflict, aiming to establish common understanding and perceptions in a conflict (Kelman 1998; Burton 1987). Unlike the settlement approach, which focuses on ways of dividing power and resources between groups, transformative mediation attempts "interaction[s] that change attitudes and perceptions and allow parties to explore options and develop solutions outside of the charged arena of formal negotiations" (Fisher 2007, 311). Transformation can be pursued using different tools, such as the fulfillment of basic human needs, which focuses on the transformation of goals and behavior based on the attainment of all basic human needs for the conflicting parties.

Although a few official mediators have borrowed from the transformative approach, most international mediators focus on settlement or divisions of goods and the establishment of power sharing between groups. For example, as will be discussed in subsequent chapters, one may draw a comparison between Richard Holbrook's coercive settlement mediation process at Dayton to end the conflict in BiH, and George Mitchell's conciliatory and more transformative approach in Northern Ireland. As noted by Daniel Curran, although George Mitchell's prolonged approach may not have necessarily been the right process for Bosnia, as a strategy, it focused more on transforming the relationship between the leadership of the groups and resulted in an arguably more just, acceptable and workable agreement (Curran et al. 2004). It is unsurprising that the settlement or bargaining form of mediation, which pegs one group against the other, may create walls between groups and, on certain occasions, may even heighten rather than resolve a conflict. However, a transformative approach is commonly downgraded to medium range leadership and is not attempted in official mediation.

Another aspect of group strategies, in which international mediators commonly play a significant yet unrecognized role, is in the selection or legitimization of participants in official mediation. During a violent conflict, it is commonly extremists who come to power and end up playing a substantial role in the negotiation and design of a peace agreement that is commonly tied to the future institutional frameworks. Although group representation in mediation may be dependent on domestic group preferences and conditions such as the possibility of elections, international and regional mediators commonly play a significant role in advocating, legitimizing and at times imposing the conditions of mediation, which include agreement on who will sit around the mediation table. Representatives of conflicting groups are commonly invited, based on a compromise of external and internal priorities of representation. There is a significant distinction between groups or states represented by elected leadership and groups represented by leaders of paramilitary or military groups. External mediators can play a role ensuring a more complete representation of moderates, women, and minorities in addition to potential spoilers. UN Resolution 1325 urged all actors to increase the participation of women in the resolution of conflicts, including within peace negotiations; however, thus far, the role of women has been marginal. Not only are women commonly excluded within peace negotiations, thus far, most of the international mediators have been male. In the midst of a violent conflict, the common focus has been on appeasing potential spoilers, which has come at the expense of moderates, women and other groups and tends to hinder the future functioning of the state and the potential for group transformation.

Until recently, most studies have presumed a constant salience, or equality of dynamism, which individuals maintain within particular groups. However, salience that individuals attach to group identity varies as a result of choice, incentives and/or manipulation (Chandra 2006). According to recent findings, ethnic salience, or the importance that individuals attach to a singular ethnic identity, is also a fundamental determinant of the intensity of conflict. Bhavnani and Midownik, note that "if the importance individuals attach to their ethnic identities is a key determinant of conflict, then shifts in ethnic salience should assume center stage in explanations that link ethnicity to conflict" (Bhavnani and Miodownik 2009). However, this has been omitted in both literature and in practice where groups are viewed as constant unchanging phenomena. As noted by Brubaker, "[b]oundary-strengthening, group-making projects *within* ethnic groups are almost always central to violent conflicts *between* groups, but these crucial intra group processes are obscured by international relations-inspired approaches that treat ethnic groups as unitary actors" (Brubaker and Laitin 1998, 438).

The lessening of boundaries and transformation strategies between groups also needs to take place during the process of peace making. According to Lisa Schirch, "transformation of identity is necessary to reconciliation. Those people who have expanded their understanding of their own and their adversaries' identities and are able to find some shared identities seem to become the peacemakers" (Schirch 2000, 152). Identity shifts are, however, difficult to track as well as to attribute since they can have numerous causes. Group identity shifts can be linked to changing power relations, new institutions, globalization or changing circumstances on the ground such as increase or decrease in violence or negotiations towards peace. Although challenging to monitor and perilous to manipulate, identity change is a key in the success of conflict transformation.

Moving beyond the peace-making stage, one can note three key possibilities of long-term shifts in group identities; bottom up, top down and middle out. First, there can be a populist or a grassroots shift among a particular group of the meanings of their group identity as it pertains to the membership of their own group(s) and in relations to others. This can be thought of as a bottom-up approach since it is a populist sentiment arising from a shift of public opinion pertaining to the group. Second, there can be a shift among the elite or leadership of a group in positions, election strategies, the jargon/language or the means that is used to gain support from the public and various groups. Beginning with the leadership, this can be thought of as a top-down transformation process.

The two approaches, "bottom up" versus "top down," are intertwined and dynamic particularly when leadership is dependent on gaining votes from across the group membership. The third shift can take place within the middle range of the representation of the group, for example, among civil society or influential representatives of NGOs. The middle range can be influential either on the leadership or on the population of the various groups. During reconciliation, a simultaneous change involving both the public and the leadership is said to be the most effective. As noted by Danny Bar Tal,

> while reconciliation may begin with the leaders or the grassroots, to be effective it must always proceed top-down and bottom-up simultaneously. This entails that while, on the one hand, the psychological change of leaders, especially from the mainstream, greatly influences the society members, on the other hand, the evolvement of mass movement that embraces the psychological change has an effect on the position of the leaders.
>
> (Bar-Tal and Bennick 2004, 20)

The above-mentioned aspects of group transformation – bottom-up, middle-out or top-down – can be impacted by events, through changed realities or the perception of new realities from within the group. The transformation can also be as a consequence of actions or change in the perceptions of reality by an opposing conflicting group or by interventions from parties outside of the conflict. Although external interveners, whether mediators or governments of other countries, could intentionally or unintentionally have influence at the grassroots level, their direct effect is most likely at the middle and top levels. Group identities are most impacted by international process, which is the road interveners take to attempt to end the conflict, and international strategies that are the accepted, proposed or at times imposed conflict resolution tools.

Group identity transformation and international intervention process and strategies

Whether intentional or not, external intervention process and strategies have a long-term impact on group identities. The fundamental question is under which conditions external processes and strategies include elements that promote transformation of group identities and the type of external process and type of strategies that harden or reify divisions between conflicting groups. There has been little scholarly research examining group identity and external intervention. Part of the reason for this is that group identity has been commonly studied in micro studies, while external intervention is commonly examined at a macro level. In addition, group identity is generally examined within the domestic context, which is presumed to be sheltered from the international arena by the state. However, a violent conflict within a state opens up opportunities and at times obligations for external intervention. First, the intervention process, "how" international actors intervene in domestic conflicts, impacts on the domestic conflict and on the dynamics between the conflicting groups. Second, intervention strategies, "what" institutional arrangements are proposed and at times imposed by external players, also impacts on the long-term dynamics between the groups.

The type of strategy can be inclusive or exclusive towards groups commonly marginalized and vulnerable during a violent conflict, including women, minorities, and individuals outside the dominant groups. Despite UN Security Council Resolution 1325, women are continuously excluded in prevention, brokering peace and within the rebuilding phase. Brokering peace is commonly left to those who were participants in the conflict and special prominence is given to ex-combatants, who tend to be men. A UNIFEM study found that only 2.5 percent of signatories of peace agreements have been women and no women have been designated as chief mediators (UNIFEM 2010). Other groups outside of the dominant conflicting divisions are also commonly excluded.

International interveners are commonly in the position to influence or decide whether the conflicting groups can live together or whether the divisions justify secession or partitioning. External interveners are also in a position to influence and legitimize a dividing line along solid group contours. Intervention policies in favor of a particular ethnic or religious group over another are often based on the presumption that group salience is solid and unchanging. However, the dividing line in conflicts is often between moderates and extremists rather than between ethnic or religious groups. As will be noted in the case studies, extremists not only kill members of other groups but also attack the moderates of their own group. Extremists and profiteers from different groups may also adopt measures of cooperation between themselves. For example immediately following the BiH conflict, the level of cooperation between Serb, Croat and Bosnians was much higher among the smugglers and criminals than between police officers. The question is whether international intervention strategies are promoting moderates over extremists, and inclusionists over exclusionists?

The two elements of external process, or the manner in which external players intervene, and the external strategies, or the types of intervention, contribute towards reification or the transformation of group identities (see Figure 1.2). I

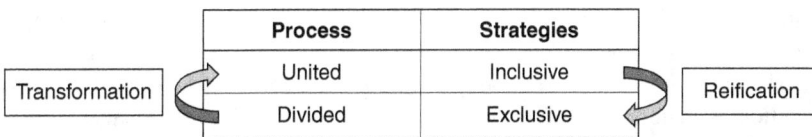

	Process	Strategies	
Transformation	United	Inclusive	Reification
	Divided	Exclusive	

Figure 1.2 International intervention and group strategies.

hypothesize that united intervention contributes towards transformation, while divided intervention contributes towards reification of group identities. The complexities of external process, including neutral versus partisan process, will be discussed in Chapter 2. I also hypothesize that exclusive strategies, such as partisan intervention along ethnic lines or accommodation along exclusive principles, contribute towards reification, while inclusive strategies, including inclusive integration, contribute towards transformation.

As will be discussed in the subsequent chapters, the type of external process – united, divided, neutral and partisan – can contribute to lessening or deepening divisions between conflicting groups. The type of intervention process raises several crucial questions. Although the impact of a divided versus united intervention is evident, the impact of neutral versus partisan intervention is case specific. What is the impact of neutral versus partisan intervention on groups in conflict? Under what conditions may external interveners use a partisan or a neutral intervention effectively?

External group strategies play an unrecognized role in contributing towards reification or transformation of group identities. International mediators play a powerful role in proposing, drafting and at times imposing peace agreements on groups in conflict. The terms of peace agreements include strategies towards partitioning, integration or accommodation within the future internal constitutional order of the conflicting state(s). There are several fundamental questions related to international strategies that will be analyzed in Chapter 3 and within the case studies. First, do the international strategies determine group identities as permanent and unchanging or as dynamic, with the capacity to change? Second, are institutions that accommodate group differences, created in a flexible or a cementing manner? Third, are institutions made with inclusive or exclusive notions of group identity? Fourth do external strategies include mixed identities and overlapping identities? These questions will be addressed within the subsequent theoretical chapters and the case studies.

Conclusion

Considering the distortion of group identities as a result of violent conflict, I argue that the purpose of conflict resolution strategies and external intervention should by definition entail attempts at group identity transformation. Manufacturing or promoting "positive" or "constructive" identity shifts may include encouraging inclusive identities, replacing ethnic identity with civic identity, promoting common or supra identities and engaging in the de-rigidification of group identities. Admittedly, these are challenging for local actors, not to mention international ones. The transformation of group identities, particularly addressing the salience of ethnic or religious identities, has seldom been consciously attempted by international interveners. Identity formation and transformation is generally thought to be firmly in the hands of national or group leadership or the state. However, international intervention and process including the formulation of peace agreements, designing future institutions, and peace and nation building efforts, impact on group identities. Whether with intention or not, when intervening in conflicts, external parties play a major role in reification or transformation of group identities.

What is vital to analyze is whether external intervention, both the type of process and the type of strategies, allows for and encourages transformation or reification of group identities. Transformative strategies may be visualized as attempts to build bridges between the groups. Transformative strategies may not satisfy demands of nationalistic, threatened or severely aggrieved groups; they may be challenging to promote and could also be hindered, obstructed or violently opposed by nationalist or extremist leadership. Although at times necessary, the affirmative or accommodative strategies may reify the difference and promote further segregation or collusion along conflicting lines. Indeed, accommodative strategies implemented during official external intervention at times entrench and institutionalize antagonistic group relationships and hamper future reconciliation. In other words, when intervening in violent conflict is the international community contributing to building walls or bridges between the conflicting groups?

References

Adelman, Howard, ed. 2005. "The Theories of Genocide: Rwanda." In *Genocide at the Millennium*, ed. Samuel Totten. London: Transaction. 31–54.
Alon, Nahi and Haim Omer. 2005. *The Psychology of Demonization: Promoting Acceptance and Reducing Conflict*. London: Routledge.
Aspinall, Edward. 2007. The Construction of Grievance; Natural Resources and Identity in a Separatist Conflict. *Journal of Conflict Resolution* 51 (6): 950–972.
Bar-Tal, Daniel and Gemma H. Bennick. 2004. "Nature of Reconciliation as an Outcome and as a Process." In *From Conflict Resolution to Reconciliation*, ed. Bar Siman Tov. Oxford: Oxford University Press. 11–38.
Bhavnani, Ravi and Dan Miodownik. 2009. Ethnic Polarization, Ethnic Salience and Civil War. *Journal of Conflict Resolution* 53 (1): 30–49.
Birch, Anthony. 1989. *Nationalism and National Integration*. London: Routledge.
Brass, Paul R. 1991. *Ethnicity and Nationalism: Theory and Comparison*. New Delhi: Sage Publications.
Brubaker, Rogers. 2000. Beyond "Identity." *Theory and Society* 29: 1–47.
Brubaker, Rogers. 2002. Ethnicity without groups. *European Journal of Sociology* 43 (2): 163–189.
Brubaker, Rogers and David S Laitin. 1998. Ethnic and Nationalist Violence. *Annual Review of Sociology* 24: 423–452.
Burton, John W. 1987. *Resolving Deep Rooted Conflict: A Handbook*. Lanham MD: University Press of America.
Bush, R. A. B. and J. P. Folger. 1994. *The Promise of Mediation*. San Francisco: Jossey Bass.
Campbell, David. 1998. *National Deconstruction: Violence, Identity, and Justice in Bosnia*. Minneapolis MN: University of Minnesota Press.
Chandra, Kanchan. 2006. What is ethnic identity and does it matter? *Annual Review of Political Science* 9: 397–424.

Crocker, Chester A., Fen Osler Hampson and Pamela Aall, eds. 1999. *Herding Cats: Multiparty Mediation in a Complex World*. Washington DC: United States Institute of Peace Press.

Cohen, Gili. 2014. "Reservists from elite IDF intel unit refuse to serve over Palestinian 'persecution'." In *Haaretz*, September 12.

Collier, Paul. 2000. Rebellion as a Quasi-Criminal Activity. *Journal of Conflict Resolution* 44 (6): 839–853.

Cornell, Stephen E. and Douglas Hartmann. 1998. *Ethnicity and Race: Making Identities in a Changing World*. London: Pine Forge Press.

Curran, Daniel, James Sebernius and Michael Watkins. 2004. Case Analysis: Two Paths to Peace, Contrasting George Mitchell in Northern Ireland with Richard Holbrooke in Bosnia. *Negotiation Journal* 20 (4): 513–537.

Deutsch, Morton. 1973. *The Resolution of Conflict*. New Haven CT: Yale University Press.

Fearon, James D. and David D. Latin. 2000. Review: Violence and Social Construction of Ethnic Identity. *International Organization* 54 (4): 845–877.

Fisher, J. Ronald 2001. "Methods of Third Party Intervention." In *Berghof Handbook for Conflict Transformation*, Norbert Ropers, Martina Fischer and Eric Manten. Berlin: Berghof Research Centre.

Fisher, R. J. and L. Keashly. 1990. "A Contingency Approach in Third Party Intervention." In *The Social Psychology of Intergroup and International Conflict Resolution*, ed. R. J. Fisher. New York: Springer-Verlag.

Fisher, R. J. 2007. Assessing the contingency model of third-party intervention in successful cases of prenegotiation. *Journal of Peace Research* 44 (3).

Fisher, Roger and William Uri. 1981. *Getting to Yes*. London: Penguin Books.

Fisher, Roger, Elizabeth Kopelman and Andrea Kupfer Schneider. 1996. *Beyond Machiavelli: Tools for Coping with Conflict*. London: Penguin Books.

Folger, Joseph P., Robert A. Baruch Bush, and Dorothy J. Della Noce, eds. 2010. *Transformative mediation: A Sourcebook*. Belfast: Association for Conflict Resolution and the Institute for the Study of Conflict Resolution.

Fraser, Nancy. 1997. *Justice Interruptus*. London: Routledge.

Galtung, Johan. 1996. *Peace by Peaceful Means: Peace and Conflict, Development and Civilization*. London: Sage.

Gellner, Ernest. 1983. *Nations and Nationalism*. New York: Cornell University Press.

Gurr, Ted Robert. 1996. "Minorities, Nationalists, and Ethnopolitical Conflict." In *Managing Global Chaos; Sources of and Responses to International Conflict*, eds. Chester A Crocker, Fen Osler Hampson, and Pamela Aall. Washington: United States Institute of Peace.

Gurr, Ted Robert, ed. 2002. *Peoples versus States, Minorities at Risk in the New Century*. Washington DC: United States Institute of Peace

Horowitz, Donald L. 2000. *Ethnic Groups In Conflict*. Berkeley CA: University of California Press.

Huntington, Samuel P. 1998. *The Clash of Civilizations and the Remaking of World Order*. New York: Simon and Schuster.

Jesse, Neal G. and Kristen P. Williams. 2006. *Identity and Institutions; Conflict Resolution in Divided Societies*. Albany NY: State University of New York Press.

Keane, Margaret C., David N. Livingstone and F. W. Boal. 1997. *Them and Us?* Belfast: Institute of Irish Studies.

Kelman, Herbert. 1998. Interactive Problem Solving: An Approach to Conflict Resolution and its Application in the Middle East. *Political Science and Politics* 31 (1): 190–198.

Kreidie, Lina Haddad and Khristen Renwick Monroe. 2002. The Dilemmas of Political Identity and Ethnic Violence. *International Journal of Politics, Culture and Society* 16 (1): 5–36.

Kriesberg, Louis. 1998. *Constructive Conflicts, From Escalation to Resolution*. Lanham MD: Rowman & Littlefield Publishers.

Kriesberg, Louis. 2003. " 'Us' versus 'Them'." *Beyond Intractibility*. www.beyondintractibility.org.

Pruitt, D. G. and J. Z. Rubin. 1986. *Social Conflict: Escalation, Stalemate and Settlement*. New York: Random House.

Ramsbotham, Oliver, Tom Woodhouse, and Hugh Miall. 2005. *Contemporary Conflict Resolution: The Prevention, Management and Transformation of Deadly Conflicts*. Cambridge UK: Polity Press.

Ritchie, Jason. 2010. How do you say "come out of the closet" in Arabic? Queer Activism and the Politics of Visibility in Israel-Palestine. *Journal of Gay and Lesbian Studies* 16 (4): 557–576.

Rothman, Jay. 1997. *Resolving Identity-Based Conflicts in Nations, Organizations and Communities*. San Francisco: Jossey-Based Publishers.

Said, Edward. 1978. *Orientalism*. New York: Pantheon Books.

Schirch, Lisa. 2000. "Ritual Reconciliation: Transforming Identity/Reframing Conflict." In *Reconciliation, Justice and Coexistence: Theory and Practice*, ed. Mohammed Abu-Nimer. Lanham MD: Lexington Books.

Smith, Anthony D. 2009. *Ethnic Origin of Nations*. Oxford: Wiley-Blackwell.

Smithey, Lee A. and Lester R. Kurtz. 2002. "Parading persuasion: nonviolent collective action as discourse in Northern Ireland." In *Consensus Decision Making, Northern Ireland and Indigenous Movements (Research in Social Movements, Conflicts and Change, Volume 24)*, ed. Patrick G. Coy. Bradford, UK: Emerald Group Publishing Limited.

Tailor, Rupert and Mark Orkin. 2001. "The Politics of Social Science Research." In *Race, Ethnicity and Social Change*, ed. Peter Ratcliffe. London: Palgrave Macmillan.

Tajfel, Henri. 1978. *The Social Psychology of Minorities*. London: Minority Rights Group.

Tajfel, Henri and John Turner. 1979. "An Integrative Theory of Intergroup Conflict." In *The Social Psychology of Intergroup Relations*, eds. G. William and Stephen Worchel Austin. Monterey CA: Brooks-Cole.

Taras, Raymond C. and Rajat Ganguly. 2002. *Understanding Ethnic Conflict, the International Dimention*. New York: Longman.

Taylor, Donald M. and Falthaly M. Moghaddam. 1987. *Theories of Intergroup Relations, International Social Psychological Perspectives*. New York: Praeger.

Todd, Jennifer. 2008. "Identity Shift in Settlement Process: The Northern Ireland Case." In *Failure of the Middle East Peace Process: A Comparative Analysis of Peace Implementation in Israel/Palestine, Northern Ireland and South Africa*, ed. Guy Ben-Porat. London: Palgrave Macmillan.

UNIFEM. 2010. *Women's Participation in Peace Negotiations: Connections between Presence and Influence*. www.unwomen.org/~/media/headquarters/media/publications/unifem/0302_womensparticipationinpeacenegotiations_en.pdf.

Volkan, Vamik. 1997. *Blood Lines, From Ethnic Pride to Ethnic Terrorism*. Boulder CO: Westview Press.

2 International intervention process

United, divided, neutral and partisan interventions

Imagine a rock fight between groups of kids in two separate schools. In the first school, peers trained as mediators break the fight, agree on what is to be done and attempt to work with the kids to find a long-term solution to the conflict. In the second school, peers disagree who is at fault and what is to be done and attempt to help their friends by providing rocks or joining the fight to assist one or both of the sides in the conflict. Clearly, regardless of intention, the outcome will likely be very different. Although the international arena is far more complex than a schoolyard, the type of intervention – united, divided, neutral or partisan – has an underappreciated impact on the groups in conflict. This chapter examines the impact of four interlinked types of intervention processes: united, divided, neutral, and partisan. I argue that the type of international intervention process not only affects the outcome of the conflict but also impacts on the identity of the groups in conflict. Under what conditions do external intervention processes include elements that promote a positive shift between conflicting group identities and under what conditions does the international intervention process contribute to hardening conflicting group identities?

International interventions in internal conflicts are increasingly conducted not by single but rather by multiple external actors (Crocker et al. 1999). Multiparty mediation adds a complex dimension that needs to be addressed. Multiple interveners, regardless of intention, can contribute to resolution or escalation of a conflict. There are contradicting claims regarding the effects of multilateral intervention. Crocker et al. note that multiparty mediation may lead to serious coordination problems (Crocker et al. 1999). As noted by Crocker, organizing international mediators in a conflict is a lot like herding cats (Crocker et al. 1999). A coalition of interveners can increase the complexity of the mediation process, which can undermine the effectiveness of an intervention (Böhmelt 2011). At the same time, multilateral mediators are able to create synergy due to their combined efforts and can potentially be more effective than a single party (Böhmelt 2011). Böhmelt's research notes an inverted "U-shape" relationship between the size of the mediation coalition and mediation effectiveness (Böhmelt 2011). I suggest a focus is needed not on the number of mediators but rather the degree of consensus among the mediators, most notably on whether there is agreement on the type of intervention, which is vital in the success of a complex multiparty intervention.

In a multiparty intervention, an essential differentiation must be made between divided and united intervention. United intervention takes place when key influential external parties intervene neutrally or on behalf of the same group or state. On the other hand, divided intervention is when significant states intervene in a partisan manner on behalf of opposing sides in the conflict. Several studies have noted that the most effective and successful type of external intervention is united (Nalbandov 2009; Regan 2002). Unlike divided intervention, where external players support opposing sides, thus adding fuel to a fire, a united international intervention can potentially have a transformative impact on the conflicting parties. Although studies have demonstrated the benefits of united intervention, the impact of the united versus divided intervention on groups in conflict has been undervalued. My contention, which will be discussed in this chapter and examined in the case studies, is that a united intervention contributes towards group transformation, while a divided external intervention contributes towards solidification of group identities, deepening barriers between conflicting groups.

The impact of neutral versus partisan intervention is far more complex and has been the source of much debate among scholars as well as practitioners. In a neutral intervention, the external actor(s) intervene in an impartial manner. This may include diplomacy, humanitarian assistance or peacekeeping. In a partisan intervention, the external intervener purposely favors or disfavors a specific group at the expense of the opposing group(s). Partisan intervention may include diplomatic, economic or military support, or sanctions and boycotts against a state or a conflicting group. The debates on the benefits and perils of partisan versus neutral intervention have been prevalent among many academics (Nalbandov 2009; Regan 2002; Svensson 2007; Yoshihara 2010). Mediation literature has tended to emphasize the importance of impartiality of the external party (Crocker et al. 1999; Fisher et al. 1996). However, neutral interventions have been noted to be ineffective against powerful, uncooperative or aggressive actors (Krain 2005). Partisan interventions have been seen to be more effective against powerful uncooperative actors but can also escalate a conflict (Ryan 1995). Partisan interventions may forcibly end the conflict; however, they may not necessarily result in conflict transformation.

Whether the international intervention process is neutral or made on behalf of a particular group has an impact on the groups in conflict. A united multiparty intervention necessitates a consensus on the type of intervention. In many cases, reaching a consensus among multiparty mediators on a neutral or a partisan intervention can be the largest challenge but is a fundamental step for a more effective intervention. As will be discussed in the next section, impartial interventions, such as numerous UN peacekeeping operations, have come under strong criticism after failing to stop genocides in conflicts such as Rwanda and Bosnia and Herzegovina. On the other hand, partisan interventions have come under attack for adding fuel to the fire and failing to resolve conflicts. Interventions where powerful countries support opposing sides have been the most significant hindrance to conflict resolution. I emphasize the importance of reaching a consensus among international interveners on a united–neutral or, when deemed necessary to protect lives of civilians, a united–partisan intervention.

Focusing on American, European and UN intervention policies, what are the common key motivations for a neutral or a partisan intervention? Are the reasons due to elements external to the conflict, such as domestic factors, intervener bias towards a group or government, or the crossing of red lines when the situation on the ground is deemed critical enough to necessitate a partisan intervention? What impact does the type of external intervention process have on group identities and on the violent conflict? The subsequent section will examine how the type of international intervention impacts on the relationship between the groups and the potential success or failure of an externally led peace process.

Neutral, partisan, united versus divided intervention process

The type of external intervention process has an impact on conflicting parties and their identities. Regardless of intention, this impact can be positive or negative, moving the parties towards or away from resolution. The main question addressed is the conditions under which external processes include elements that contribute towards building bridges between conflicting groups and the conditions under which the international intervention process contributes towards hardening group identities. I contend that reaching a consensus among principal mediators on either a united–neutral or a united–partisan intervention process in a conflict is a key to a successful intervention. However, this has not been possible in many conflicts. Divided intervention has not only hindered resolution, it has heightened divisions between groups. This section will outline the key types of international intervention processes – neutral, partisan, united and divided – and discuss some of the causes behind the type of intervention and the impact on groups in conflict.

External intervention is a broad term encompassing diplomacy, humanitarian assistance, international mediation, arbitration, economic pressure or incentives, covert and overt military action as well as the threat of sanctions or the promise of rewards. The focus of this study is on diplomatic or international mediation efforts to end a violent conflict. However, when international diplomatic and mediation efforts are accompanied by military or other measures, these will also be addressed. Recent international mediation attempts have commonly been supplemented with economic, military, legal or other measures. In complex international interventions such as in Bosnia and Herzegovina (BiH), the international community used multi-faceted intervention that included diplomatic, humanitarian, economic and military measures, all with varying degrees of success and failure. Presuming the official intention of the external intervener is altruistic – to facilitate a resolution – the emphasis is on mediation, as military and economic interventions can be assessed in either contributing to or hindering diplomatic efforts to end a conflict.

Although in decline since the 1990s, violent conflicts continue to break out within states, providing external actors with opportunities and obligations for intervention (Kriesberg 2009). According the Uppsala Conflict Data Base (UCDP), since World War II there have been 228 armed conflicts throughout the world, the highest number (51 conflicts) occurring in 1991 and 1992 (Harbom and Wallensteen 2005). The overwhelming majority of them have been internal and took place in developing countries, particularly in Africa and Asia. Wallensteen and Sollenberg noted that, of the 108 conflicts that took place between 1989 and 1998, 92 were intrastate (Wallensteen and Sollenberg 2000). Although categorized as internal, external interveners frequently play a role whether in mediation, supplying weapons, providing financial assistance or sanctions. Since the end of the Cold War, external actors provided some type of military or economic support in 80 out of 111 conflicts (Harbom and Wallensteen 2005). In 2013, UCDP recorded 33 armed conflicts and six signed peace agreements (Themner and Wallensteen 2014). As noted by Lotta Themner and Peter Wallensteen, external mediators played an important role in all of the signed peace agreements.

In this chapter, I outline and examine four types of international intervention processes: united–neutral, united–partisan, divided–partisan and divided-neutral/partisan (See Figure 2.1). In a *united–neutral* intervention process, key international interveners intercede neutrally. In a *united–partisan* intervention process, key interveners intercede on behalf of the same side. In a *divided–partisan* intervention, key actors intervene on opposing sides of a conflict. Lastly, in a *divided–neutral/partisan* intervention, some of the key interveners intercede in a neutral manner while others intercede in support of a group in a conflict.

Practitioners and scholars alike agree on the importance of a united intervention. As noted by Crocker, "Experience in such varied places as the former Yugoslavia, Somalia, Cyprus, Mozambique, Central America, and Central Africa points to the growing need for comprehensive thinking and coherence or unity of action" (Crocker et al. 1999, 695). Research has demonstrated that, by empowering opposite sides, a divided intervention heightens a conflict (Regan 1996). Not surprisingly, united interventions are empirically more likely to succeed than divided interventions, where external players, supporting different sides, tend to exacerbate the conflict. Reagan and Abouharb note that "the worst possible condition for an intervention is when there are interventions already supporting the opposing party" (Regan and Abouharb 2002, 53).

While united intervention is clearly preferable to divided intervention, there is an unresolved debate among scholars and practitioners on the merits of neutral versus partisan intervention. The impact of neutral versus partisan intervention is complex since it is more firmly dependent on the nature of the conflict and the already existing power dynamics between the conflicting groups. A united–neutral intervention may contribute to transformation in cases when neither group is behaving in an uncooperative and aggressive manner. A neutral intervention against an uncooperative and aggressive group may have little impact on the behavior of the aggressive leadership of the group. In the case of an aggressive group, a united–partisan intervention process may have a transformative impact on the groups in conflict. However, partisan intervention against a group may also increase the salience of the said group, since the group will feel under threat.

Thus, although a united–partisan intervention may end a conflict, it may not have the desired group identity transformation.

The type of intervention process – united–neutral, united–partisan, divided–neutral/partisan or divided–partisan – not only affects the success of the intervention but also the relations between groups. Based on the above argument, I suggest that a united–neutral external process contributes towards group identity transformation under conditions in which neither party is behaving in an aggressive or an uncooperative manner. A united–partisan intervention may contribute towards transformation under certain conditions such as legitimacy. Thus, a shift from a united to a divided intervention is likely to deepen a conflict between groups, while a shift from a divided to a united intervention can be a contributor to transformation. However, a united intervention necessitates an agreement on a neutral or a partisan intervention. A neutral intervention against an uncooperative and aggressive group may have little impact on the behavior of hostile leadership of the group. In case of an aggressive group, a united–partisan intervention process can have a transformative impact on the groups in conflict. However, partisan intervention against a group may also increase the salience of the said group, since the group will feel under threat. Divided partisan intervention is not only likely to have little constructive input in a conflict; it may widen the divides between the conflicting groups. The following section will examine some of the causes and consequences of neutral versus partisan interventions.

Neutral versus partisan intervention process

Whether to intervene in a neutral versus partisan manner is a conundrum for scholars and practitioners alike. The impact of partisan versus neutral intervention on groups in conflict is complex, since it heavily depends on the context and the already established relations between the conflicting groups. In a neutral intervention, the external actor makes an effort not to take sides in the conflict. Neutral intervention may include non-coercive mediation, humanitarian assistance or peacekeeping. In a partisan intervention, the external intervener purposely favors or disfavors a specific group at the expense of an opposing group in the conflict. Partisan intervention may include coercive mediation, military intervention, economic or military support or sanctions and boycotts against a state or one of the conflicting groups. The causes of neutral versus partisan intervention are multifold but the most significant distinction may be made between *exogenous* or *endogenous* factors. Exogenous factors are related to the intervener while the endogenous factors are related to the conflict.

Whether intervention is partisan or neutral is not always clear due to different perceptions and clandestine support. The distinction between neutral and partisan intervention may be dependent on perceptions, since a state or a mediator may claim to intervene neutrally but be perceived as partisan. There may also be differences between what is agreed on in principle and in practice. I suggest that the scope of neutral versus partisan intervention may be distinguished by three elements: *principles, practice and perceptions* (PPP). Intervention may be neutral in principle, but partisan in practice. For instance, countries may agree on united–neutral diplomatic intervention in principle but be covertly supporting one of the sides. Intervention may also be neutral in principle and in practice but still be perceived as partisan by the conflicting groups. This is a common phenomenon in violent conflicts when warring parties are immersed in the psychology of self-justification and victimhood and perceive most external interveners as biased against them. For example, analysis of media coverage in conflicts shows that it is common for both conflicting parties to perceive identical stories as biased against them (Maoz 1999).

The effectiveness of neutral and partisan intervention is widely debated. Much of the mediation literature tends to emphasize the importance of impartiality of the third party since, through a partisan intervention, a third party can exacerbate a conflict (Fisher et al. 1996; Crocker et al. 1999). Arguments in favor of partisan intervention note that biased third parties may mitigate the commitment problems between parties, by serving as guarantors for the weaker side (Fearon 1998). Partisan intervention may also take place in support of the stronger side, challenging the prospect of the mediator balancing unequal power relations between the conflicting groups. Isak Svensson notes that the success of biased mediation is "not so much about using power to push the parties to a settlement but more about enhancing the credibility of their commitments" (Svensson 2007, 191).

Debates on neutral versus partisan intervention are commonly related to specific connections between the intervener and the target point of intervention, such as military, cultural, ethnic, religious, economic, strategic or ideological links. Stephen Saideman argues that ethnic politics influence which states support which groups (Saideman 1997). First, ethnic ties between the intervener and one of the groups in conflict increase the chances of external intervention. Secondly, regardless of their goals, groups are better situated to bargain or fight if they have external allies (Saideman 2002). Rupen Cetinyan likewise argues that groups that are perceived to have powerful ethnic guarantors take advantage of mediation to increase their bargaining power if they anticipate external support (Cetinyan 2002).

As visualized in Figure 2.1, international actors may intervene in a neutral or a partisan manner for multiple interrelated reasons. The first is the interpretation of the conflict by the external actor. The interpretation of the conflict by a state representative or a mediator draws a map of the current and expected behavior of the groups in conflict. It may be related to ideology, international politics and perceptions of the groups in conflict. Interpretation of the conflict, I would argue, is a critical reason for a neutral or a partisan intervention but is generally overlooked as a factor in determining the type of intervention. States, international organizations and leaders diagnose a conflict based on their interpretations of group identities and the construction of the reality as presented by the conflicting groups or other involved players. In essence, violent internal conflicts expose a competition between the contesting realities of groups that, lacking sufficient private resources, may attempt to lure external interveners to their sides. Interveners may decide between the competing contested realities, or interpret the conflict in a manner different to that presented by either conflicting party. External agents may also construct their interpretation of the conflict according to their respective interests, influenced by the dominant groups or ideology. The framing of a discourse may be constructed in a manner that allows the promotion of the type of intervention to a domestic and an international audience.

The second reason is the relationship between the intervener and the parties in conflict. The relationship between the intervener and the group is a vital factor and is commonly discussed as a primary reason for a neutral or a partisan intervention. Bias in favor or against a group can stem from closeness or distance to one of the conflicting groups. Donald Black notes that parties in conflict create a gravitational pull that attracts with a strength proportional to their nearness to a conflicting party and distance from the opponent (Black 1998). Arie Nadler argues that intervention to aid another reflects a cost/reward analysis, in which the costs and the rewards are affected by empathy with the other's sufferings and the perceived similarity between oneself and the victim (Nadler 2002). The similarity between an intervener and the group may include a common ethnic or cultural heritage, shared ideology or a shared historical background. The relationship between the conflicting party and the intervener affects the interpretation of the conflict as well as the presumed expected behavior of the conflicting groups.

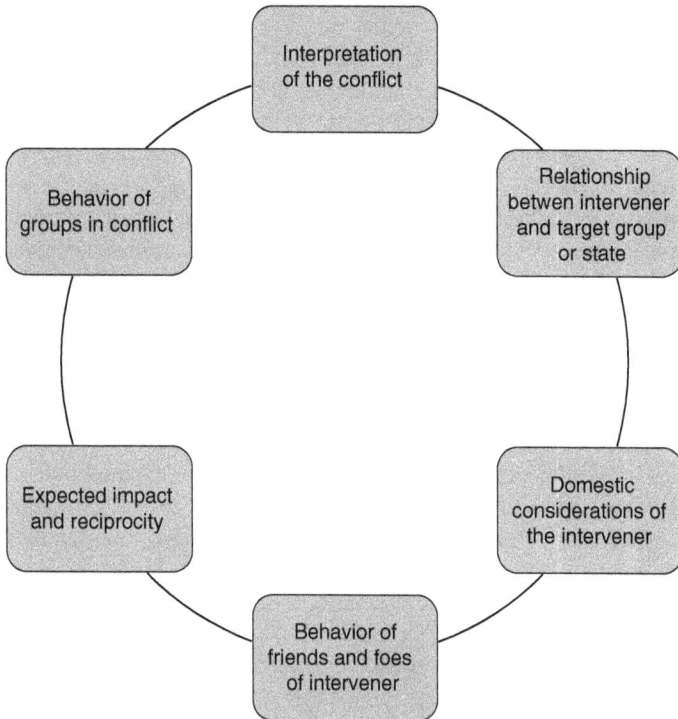

Figure 2.1 Causes of the type of intervention.

The third set of reasons is the domestic considerations of the intervener. Domestic reasons may be related to public popularity, domestic pressure groups or other domestic political or economic factors. The external intervener's consideration may also be related to the expected costs of the intervention, including perceived potential benefits and risks. The decision to intervene is also affected by the perceived benefits in intervention versus the costs of non-intervention. These considerations may be heightened during times of elections and power struggles.

The fourth set of reasons is the behavior of the friends and foes of the intervener. Research has shown that many interveners disregard the context and behavior of the group or state and intervene according to interventions by friends and foes. Renato Corbetta determined that major powers intervene not on the basis of their relationship with the warring parties, but rather because of the antagonism or rivalry between the major intervening states (Corbetta and Dixon 2005). Rivalries between major states frequently have a gravitational effect in which major powers pull each other into conflicts in order to assist or oppose other interveners (Corbetta and Dixon 2005). Research carried out by Corbetta and Dixon, examining 1809 diplomatic, military and economic interventions in disputes since World War II, noted that the entry into a conflict by a major state significantly increased the chances that other major powers would join the conflict as well (Corbetta and Dixon 2005). This was the case for both military and non-military interventions. Studies by Findley and Teo confirmed that when a powerful state has already intervened on the side of the government, the likelihood of intervention by the rival power on the side of the opposition increases by over 1100 percent (Findley and Teo 2006).

The first four reasons are related to exogenous factors tied to the intervener. The final two reasons – fifth, the behavior of the groups in conflict and sixth, the expected impact of neutral versus partisan intervention – are related to the endogenous or internal factors of the conflict. Endogenous factors, however, are subject to interpretations that can vary considerably. Interpretations of endogenous factors may justify a type of intervention preferred by external states. The decision to intervene in a neutral versus partisan intervention should ideally be made on an endogenous and not an exogenous basis. Bias related to exogenous factors is far less likely to gain international legitimacy than bias related to endogenous elements. Partisan intervention that is related to the circumstances of the conflict is also far more likely to gain consensus among interveners than partisan intervention related to the domestic preferences of the intervener.

It is critical to highlight that countries that support particular groups in other countries because of ethnic, ideological or other ties may, however, play either a beneficial or a detrimental role. Sean Byrne notes that external "ethno guarantors," or those who support external groups on a basis of a similar ethnic identity, can play a destructive as well as a constructive role (Byrne 2000). Commonly pulled into an alignment with internal co-nationals, ethno guarantors have often been the cause as well as the cure in conflicts. If choosing to play a constructive role, ethno guarantors, as will be discussed in the Northern Ireland case study, may have a transformative impact on internal group identities.

A final fundamental issue linked to the motivations of the intervener is to gauge the expected impact of partisan versus neutral intervention. Neutral interventions have been noted to be ineffective against powerful and aggressive actors. According to Matthew Krain, in the case of a very aggressive and powerful party, neutral interventions do not appear to have much of an effect and might even exacerbate the killing (Krain 2005). In his examination of the effect of neutral military interventions in slowing or stopping ongoing instances of genocide or politicide, Krain determined that neutral interventions have no impact on the severity of the conflict. According to his study, in the case of one-sided atrocities, only interventions that directly challenge the perpetrator or aid the target appear to reduce the severity of the killings (Krain 2005). The question is whether there is a red line that, once crossed, means that a partisan intervention becomes necessary to protect the civilian population.

Partisan intervention, particular multiparty intervention, contains serious elements of risks. Stephen Ryan notes that biased or partisan interventions introduce new issues into the conflict, which are likely to escalate the conflict, particularly when there are instrumental reasons for the intervention (Ryan 1995). On the other hand, if powerful enough, and particularly if they are in favor of the stronger party, biased interventions may rapidly end a conflict through an outright victory (Ryan 1995, 65). According to some quantitative studies, interventions supporting one side are associated with shorter conflicts relative to neutral interventions (Regan 1996). Ending a conflict quickly however, does not necessarily entail a sustainable resolution. These studies have failed to address whether the partisan intervention, which ended the conflict in a more efficient manner, ended it with a sustainable resolution. As noted by Gurr, "The nature of international engagement is a major determinant of whether ethnopolitical conflicts are of short duration or long and of whether they end in a negotiated settlement or a humanitarian disasters" (Gurr 1996, 70). In the long term, in order to enhance group transformation, successful resolution must address core issues and lead to a just resolution; otherwise conflicts are likely to spring back to life.

An emphasis on a sustainable resolution has been noted by much scholarly research. In investigating international intervention in genocides and politicides, Matthew Krain discards empirical findings, such as Regan's, in which the success of the intervention is based on whether the intervention lengthened or shortened the conflict (Krain 2005). Interventions can shorten a conflict but might hasten perpetrators to ramp up their genocidal policy during that time frame. On the other hand, interventions might lengthen the conflict but force perpetrators to curtail mass killings of civilians and non-combatants. Thus, rather than only focusing on the duration of a conflict, one should also examine the effects of the type of intervention on the severity of the conflict and the strategies and the behavior of the conflicting parties (Krain 2005). One may also examine how neutral versus partisan intervention contributes to general well-being of groups, in particular related to the safety of civilians.

Brown notes the vital distinction between intervening when parties are ready to stop fighting and are receptive to international involvement and when the same parties are not ready to end the conflict. "The track record of international efforts to bring fighting to an end is good in the former, bad in the latter and truly awful when the line about the terms of international engagement is blurred" (Brown 1996, 616). International engagement in cases where the justification for a partisan intervention and the good will of the intervener are widely questioned, such as was the case with US intervention in Iraq, tend to be the least successful type of interventions.

The debate on the impact of neutral versus partisan intervention is explored in the theory of reciprocity, which deals with the impact of external parties on the behavior of one conflicting party towards the other. According to Joseph S. Goldstein, when it comes to aggressive states or groups, there is a tendency for the aggressive party to adopt an inverse response to an outside force rather than a reciprocal one (Goldstein and Pevehouse 1997). In other words, when faced with hostile actions by an outsider, an aggressive actor will become more cooperative towards his opponent and will become more hostile when faced by a cooperative outside power. Thus, the aggressive state or group will take advantage of cooperative external actions, but start to cooperate in response to hostile external actions (Goldstein and Pevehouse 1997). Determining whether one of the groups or the state is behaving in an aggressive fashion, however, also depends on the interpretation of the conflict and the relationship between the intervener and the conflicting groups. However, international law, including conventions on genocide and norms on responsibility to protect (R2P), offer some standards on the protection of civilians and the need of a partisan intervention.

The majority of scholarly findings on the effectiveness of neutral versus partisan intervention neglect ethical considerations, disregard issues related to legitimacy and are removed from literature related to human rights or responsibility to protect civilians based on international law (Kathman and Wood 2011; Wood and Kathman 2012). One notable exception is Hafner-Burton, who makes a crucial point that human rights should be part of the decision on whether and how to intervene. Hafner, however, makes a strong claim on the side of neutral intervention. "One of the most important lessons learned is that for third-party interventions to improve human rights, impartiality is essential" (Hafner-Burton 2014). As has already been discussed, neutral interventions are not always sufficient to end severe human atrocities. The challenge for both scholars and practitioners is reaching a consensus on the red line, beyond which partisan intervention is necessary to protect the lives of civilians.

Neutral and united–partisan interventions can both be effective, depending on the circumstances of the conflict and consensus among interveners in a given case. Partisan military intervention has the potential to create more harm and unintended effects. Recent research has pointed to the greater effectiveness of non-military coercion tools such as sanctions and "naming," "blaming" and "shaming." As noted by Amanda Murdie and Dursun Peksen, many human rights organizations target a regime in the popular press "mobilizing others to take actions to protect a repressed population from ongoing abuse" (Murdie and Peksen 2014). The essential element is reaching a consensus on the location of the red line, or the point at which neutral intervention is insufficient to prevent atrocities and partisan intervention is necessary to protect the lives of civilians. Although reaching a consensus on the type of intervention based on international norms is ideal, in practice, this can be challenge.

United versus divided intervention process

Divided external intervention is a consequence of many factors including strategic, ideological, economic and political divisions between the intervening states. States may be strategically motivated to weaken or strengthen an opposing group or state. States may also support a particular group in order to weaken an enemy state. Divided intervention was common during the Cold War, when the US and the Soviet Union commonly intervened on opposing sides, generally heightening a conflict (Khachikian 1999). Opposing dominant ideologies and discourses frequently paved the road of a divided intervention. Although the Cold War ended, it has not eroded divisions between the main intervening states, which have continued to fuel divided interventions.

During the Cold War, conflicts were often defined and constructed in polarized, ideological and socio-economic terms. For the US, internal violent power struggles were categorized as conflicts between the left communist and undemocratic forces that were aligned with the Soviet Union versus the groups/states on the right, which were deemed by the US as pro-democratic and pro-capitalist. In numerous conflicts, particularly from the 1950s to the end of 1980s, in South America, Asia, and the Middle East, the US sided with a state or group, regardless of the context or how repressive they were, in order to prevent a left-oriented group with real or perceived ties to the Soviet Union from attaining power. American deposition of Chilean Marxist President Salvador Allende in favor of the brutal regime of Pinochet and the US support for the violent paramilitary groups in El Salvador, Guatemala and Nicaragua are just few examples. Support of some groups, such as US support of the Taliban in Afghanistan, was also a direct attempt to weaken the opposing superpower rather than decided on ideological grounds. Likewise the USSR used its troops to squash domestic rebellions in Eastern Europe such as the 1969 Prague Spring, deposing local reformist politicians in favor of pro-Soviet apparatchiks.

The Cold War rivalry did not only lead to divided intervention but, in order to gain attention and support from one of the superpowers, identities of groups in conflict were often altered. Regardless of ethnic or religious ties, most violent groups defined themselves as belonging to the ideological sphere of the right, supported by the US, or of the left, supported by the USSR. Rebel groups, for example Peru's *Sendero Luminoso* (the Shining Path), were inspired by Communist and Maoist ideas of agrarian reform. Moscow gave support to numerous national liberation movements and Marxist regimes, while Washington supported anti-communist rebels and states ideologically and economically linked to the US. Not only was the Cold War a period of much divided external intervention, the constructed interpretations of conflicts as ideologically based had a direct impact on the identities of groups in conflict. Indeed, the identities of groups were frequently altered in line with one of the dominant external powers, deepening the divides between the domestic conflicting groups.

Although the thawing of relations between the superpowers did not end all conflicts, it lessened the number of divided interventions and impacted on the amount of partisan support for particular groups. Numerous conflicts in South America, Asia and Africa were essentially proxy wars between the two super-powers seeking to expand their spheres of influence (Holmqvist 2006). The decrease in hostility between the opposing superpowers meant less support for some of the violent groups. Numerous violent groups including the Sendero Luminoso, the PLO, Afghani Muhajadin, and Contras were affected by the change. Losing financial or military support from one of the superpowers was a major blow to opposition groups. In order to sustain themselves economically, some groups had to resort to extortion, theft and drugs. The change also affected the nature and the interpretation of the causes of the violence.

The end of the Cold War did not bring an end to violence, but a different interpretation of the source of the violence. Some internal power struggles became more "ethnic" in character, as groups moved away from left and/or right ideological focus to gain the attention and the needed support. More groups gained attention from external interveners by focusing on historical grievances and inability to coexist. The option of having a state offered leaders of ambitious groups greater potential than an ideological alignment with a weakened super-power. The end of the Cold War also created greater possibilities for united external interventions. A shift from a divided to a more united intervention removed some of the contributing arsenal from many conflicts but gave a rise to others. The terrorist attack on the US in September, 2001 launched a "global war on terror" and the creation of a new existential enemy, deepening perceptions of divides along religious fault lines. The thaw between the US and Russia was short lived, giving rise to more divided interventions.

In the post-September 11 period, the perceived group identity divisions have remained, for the most part, based on cultural differences, with a heightened emphasis on differing world-views, liberal democracy, the threat of terrorism and religion. Samuel Huntington in his famous *Clash of Civilizations* reflected this sen-timent (Huntington 1998). American foreign policies under the George W. Bush administration have been driven by "existential" threats from "rogue states," such as Iran, Syria, Libya and North Korea, and the rise of non-state terrorist move-ments, such as Al-Qaeda. The new threat shifted the focus to the creation of a pre-ferred world-order that is free from terrorist organizations and governed by liberal and democratic principles. As exemplified by former US President George W. Bush: "We are in a conflict between good and evil … In this way our struggle is similar to the Cold War. Now, as then, our enemies are totalitarians, holding a creed of power with no place for human dignity" (Bush 2002). Many groups and countries shifted their policies and grievances against or in line with the new world order, established by the US, which emphasizes the establishment of liberal demo-cracy, the combating of terrorism and the marginalization of the "axis of evil."

The election of Barack Obama as the president of the US toned down some of the "us" versus "them" rhetoric and shifted American support of particular groups and states. The Arab "awakening" of 2011 led to a partial shift of international support from the Middle East dictators to opposition leaders, in defiance of the corrupt and authoritarian regimes. The first peaceful Egyptian protesters were deemed to be heroes not only by the American administration but also the American public, which found inspiration in the Egyptian populist uprisings. However as the country stumbled in its new-formed democracy, group divisions become more prominent increasing incidents of violence. The US overtures to the Muslim Brotherhood, which was effectively pushed out of power and outlawed in Egypt following the 2013 coup that ousted elected President Mohamed Morsi, was an illustration of a modification of American policy. The US shift in policy against the Egyptian military regime has, however, led to some Egyptian leadership calls for renewal of ties to Russia (*World Tribune* 2013). However both the US and Russia have been cautious in support of any group in a dynamic environment like Egypt at a risk of losing influence.

Divided intervention has become common and more troublesome in recent years with ongoing intergroup conflicts in Iraq, Afghanistan, Yemen, Syria, and Ukraine. American intervention in Iraq and Afghanistan clearly heightened tensions and divisions between the different groups (Aitken 2007). Support of particular groups, such as the arming of Shia militants in Iraq, had been justified in the short term as beneficial to gaining US backing in Iraq but in the long term deepened the divides, contributing to building walls between the conflicting groups. The majority of Iraqis are Shias, but Sunnis tended to dominate under Saddam Hussein. The American invasion and support for the Shia contributed to the sectarian conflict. The pseudo-democracy empowered the Shia majority with support from Washington. The support and the arming of Kurdish rebel groups will also be likely to have long-term regional impact. The tension between Shia and Sunnis has also become a powerful recruiting tool for the establishment of a new insurgent terrorist organization, the Daesh or the Islamic State in Iraq and Syria (ISIS).

The ongoing conflict in Syria is another example where the international community has intervened by supporting opposing groups and is deeply divided, backing conflicting sides. While Americans and Europeans have supported opposition groups against the Assad regime, Russia and China has continued to support the Assad government. The divided intervention has been the greatest hindrance to resolving the conflict, serving to throw fuel on the fire. In 2012, former UN Secretary General Kofi Annan resigned as the UN Special Envoy for the Syrian crisis, noting that

> without serious, purposeful and united international pressure, including from the powers in the region, it is impossible for me, or anyone, to compel the Syrian government in the first place and also the opposition, to take the steps necessary to begin a political process.
>
> (Annan, quoted in Greig 2013)

Regardless of the intention of interveners including the US, divided-partisan intervention in Iraq and Syria has only escalated the conflicts. It has resulted in millions of refugees and the countries becoming the launching pad for extremist groups such as ISIS. In 2014, the US mobilized a powerful coalition of more than 50 countries including the UK, France, Canada, Saudi Arabia, Bahrain and Jordan, in its fight against ISIS. Obama justified its lead in the coalition against ISIS noting:

> America leads. We are the indispensable nation.... We have capacity no one else has. Our military is the best in the history of the world. And when trouble comes up anywhere in the world, they don't call Beijing. They don't call Moscow. They call us.
>
> (Obama 2014)

However the intervention has not been united and is far from effective. The arming of particular groups such as opposition groups in Syria and the Kurds in Iraq will likely have long-term regional consequences that will play out after the end of this conflict. American and Russian rivalries have also served to heighten the conflict in Ukraine. The citizens of Ukraine are the latest victims in the rivalry between Russia and the US and NATO to taste the consequences of divided partisan intervention.

Reaching a consensus on a type of intervention

The type of intervention process – united–neutral, united–partisan, divided– neutral/partisan or divided–partisan – not only impacts on the effectiveness of the intervention but also on long-term relations between groups. I emphasize the importance of a united intervention and highlight it as the primary condition under which multilateral mediators may effectively employ a partisan intervention. It is argued here that united intervention is a first necessary step for a constructive external contribution towards the transformation of a conflict between groups. However, the decision to intervene in a partisan versus a neutral manner goes beyond effectiveness and cannot be void of context or international norms. The long-term sustainability and impact of neutral versus partisan intervention is the subject of much debate. A fundamental question is under what conditions can or should interveners switch from a neutral to a partisan intervention? Is there a red line beyond which a partisan intervention becomes necessary?

The optimal strategy of an effective and sustainable multiparty intervention is a *united–neutral* intervention (see Figure 2.2). Neutral intervention ensures that external interveners are not supporting opposite sides and thus not escalating the conflict. A neutral intervention precludes the support of "friendly" armed groups, which in the long term may destabilize a region. A neutral multilateral intervention is more likely to attain consensus and international legitimacy, based on international law and authorizations by international bodies such as the United Nations. As noted by scholarly findings, neutral interventions are also less likely

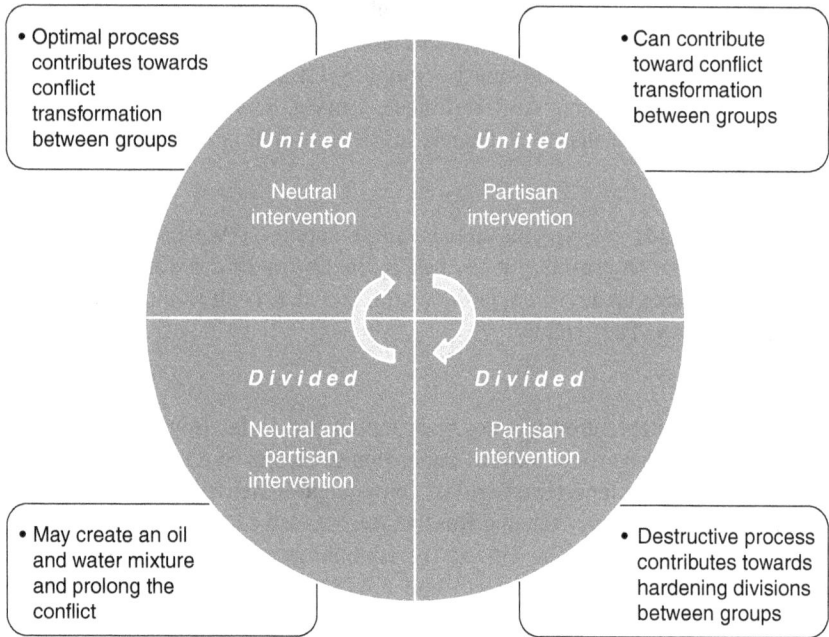

Figure 2.2 Intervention strategies.

to contribute to adding to civilian casualties and more likely to improve human rights (Hafner-Burton 2014). However, in disagreement with scholars such as Hafner-Burton, neutral intervention may not be sufficient to end every conflict. The challenge with a neutral intervention is that, in the case of a powerful, unco-operative group or state, a neutral intervention may not be forceful enough to end serious atrocities.

The potential effectiveness of a united–neutral intervention is largely dependent on the ability and the willingness of a leadership of conflicting parties to prevent atrocities against civilians and play a constructive role in transforming their own conflict. As argued by scholars examining severe cases of atrocities and genocide, neutral intervention has little impact on powerful, non-cooperative actors. United–neutral intervention was sufficient to end numerous conflicts including Mozambique, Ecuador/Peru and Northern Ireland. Northern Ireland, as will be discussed in the second case study, was a case where the eventual united–neutral mediation effort by the US, Great Britain and Ireland was sufficient to transform the conflict. The leaderships of the conflicting sides had lost their partisan support from their respective ethno-guarantors and were subsequently convinced by key internal and international mediators from Great Britain, Ireland, and the US that transformation was the only alternative. However, neutral intervention may be insufficient to end every conflict.

In a multilateral intervention, a partisan intervention by an intervener risks a *divided–partisan* intervention (See Figure 2.2). A multilateral partisan intervention, in which interveners are not united, leads to the most destructive type of process: a divided–partisan intervention. As already discussed, in the case of multiparty intervention, the support of opposite sides in the conflict, regardless of intention, will contribute to fuelling a conflict. A divided intervention process is the least optimal intervention type and is most likely to contribute towards deepening of divisions between conflicting groups. Divided international intervention weakens the intention of the intervention, in addition to affirming or hardening the identities of the conflicting groups. Supported by opposing sides, conflicting parties feel no need to transform their goals, positions or narratives.

Lack of consensus on a partisan or a neutral intervention may lead to a divided–neutral/partisan intervention. The challenges of a divided–neutral/partisan intervention go beyond problems related to coordination. A mixture of neutral and partisan intervention may create an oil and water situation where one type of intervention undermines the effectiveness of the other. As will be discussed in the Bosnia chapter, this was the case during the height of the conflict where UN troops were deployed simultaneously as NATO launched its airstrikes. Not only did this place the lightly armed troops at risk, it also opened the door to kidnapping of international personnel, undermining the effectiveness of a partisan intervention. A divided–neutral/partisan intervention may also limit the force of a partisan intervention, thus prolonging the conflict.

The first condition of a successful *united–partisan* intervention is reaching a consensus among the main mediators on the need to take strong measures against one of the groups or states in the conflict. Reaching a consensus on a united–partisan intervention is not an easy feat. Examples of successful united–partisan interventions have included international sanctions against the South African regime, the 1995 intervention in Bosnia and Herzegovina and international intervention to depose the former President of Liberia Charles Tailor. However, a consensus on a united–partisan intervention is not the only measure of success.

Scholarly debate on effectiveness of neutral versus partisan intervention has focused on measuring the length of conflict or reaching a settlement (Regan 2002). However, a "successful" united–partisan intervention cannot exist outside of normative and ethical considerations. A successful intervention, it is argued here, should not only contribute to ending the violence but also enhance the transformation of the relations between the conflicting groups. Ideally, a successful intervention should be in line with global legal principles and international law, and contribute towards ending or at the least reducing atrocities again civilians. An optimum base of a consensus among international interveners is legitimacy based on endogenous factors and international law. According to Bruce Cronin, states consider collective actions to be legitimate when they have met the following conditions:

> first, that the common good clearly outweighs a state's territorial integrity; second, that there is a broad consensus around the principles under which

multilateral intervention is undertaken; and third, that the actions taken are consistent with the limits established by international law and broadly supported multilateral treaties.

(Cronin 2002, 157)

For a partisan intervention to be united and effective in the long term, it must obtain international legitimacy and be based on international normative standards. Responsibility to Protect (R2P) norms provide a potential working tool to draw a red line between a neutral intervention and the need for a partisan intervention. The R2P, enshrined in a UN charter in 2005 and 2009, paves the way for collective international action when a state fails to provide protection for its people threatened by the most grave human rights crimes. As noted by Bellamy, R2P is a label that can be attached to a particular crisis in order to generate the will and consensus necessary to mobilize a decisive international response (Bellamy 2010, 159). The norms can be used to distinguish between the mishandled invasion of Iraq and broadly accepted interventions such as in BiH. The appropriate application of the R2P norm is, however, subject to much debate.

Conclusion

This chapter suggests a framework under which international mediators may more effectively employ a neutral or a partisan intervention. International actors may intervene in a neutral or a biased manner because of their own domestic or internal issues, due to a biased preference for one of the groups in the conflict or because red lines have been crossed by one of the parties within the conflict, making a partisan intervention necessary. While the first two may be common causes behind a neutral or a partisan intervention, I suggest that only the last one has the potential for the full international legitimacy required for a united multilateral partisan intervention.

External interveners may heighten or lesson divisions between groups, depending on the type of intervention process. United–neutral intervention can contribute towards constructive group transformation. On the other hand, divided–partisan intervention contributes to the solidification of the group identities of the conflicting parties. The impact of partisan versus neutral intervention depends on the power dynamics between groups. A shift from divided–partisan towards united–neutral intervention, where parties are relatively equally powerful and cooperative, is likely to have a transformative impact on groups. Also, a shift from a united–neutral or a divided–neutral intervention to a united–partisan intervention against an uncooperative and aggressive group or state may have a transformative impact on the said group or state. The above propositions will be analyzed in the case studies.

References

Aitken, Rob. 2007. Cementing Divisions? An Assesment of the Impact of International Inverventions and Peace-building Policies on Ethnic Identities and Divisions. *Policy Studies* 28 (3): 247–267.

Bellamy, Alex J. 2010. The Responsibility to Protect – Five Years On. *Ethics and International Affairs* 24 (2): 143–169.

Black, Donald. 1998. *The Social Structure of Right and Wrong*. San Diego CA: Academic Press.

Böhmelt, Tobias. 2011. Disaggregating Mediations: The Impact of Multiparty Mediation. *British Journal of Political Science* 41 (4): 859–881.

Brown, Michael E. 1996. *International Dimensions of Internal Conflict*. Cambridge: Centre for Science and International Affairs.

Bush, George W. 2002. "President Bush Delivers Remarks at West Point." CNN.com.

Byrne, Sean. 2000. Power Politics as Usual: Divided Islands and the Roles of External Ethno-Guarantors. *Nationalism and Ethno Politics* 6 (1): 1–24.

Cetinyan, Rupen. 2002. Ethnic Bargaining in the Shadow of Third-Party Intervention. *International Organization* 56 (3): 645–677.

Crocker, Chester A., Fen Osler Hampson, and Pamela Aall, eds. 1999. *Herding Cats: Multiparty Mediation in a Complex World*. Washington DC: United States Institute of Peace Press.

Corbetta, Renato and William J. Dixon. 2005. Danger Beyond Dyads: Third Party Participants in Militarized Interstate Disputes. *Conflict Management and Peace Science* 22: 39–61.

Cronin, Bruce. 2002. "Multilateral Intervention and the International Community." In *International Intervention: Sovereignty versus Responsibility*, eds. Michael Keren and Donald A. Sylvan. London: Frank Cass Publishers.

Fearon, James D. 1998. "Commitment problems and the Spread of Ethnic Conflict." In *The International Spread of Ethnic Conflict*, eds. David A. Lake and Donald Rothchild. Princeton NJ: Princeton University Press. 107–126.

Findley, Michael G. and Tze Kwang Teo. 2006. Rethinking Third-Party Interventions into Civil Wars: An Actor-Centric Approach. *The Journal of Politics* 68 (4): 828–837.

Fisher, Roger, Andrea Kupfer Schneider, Elizabeth Borqwardt and Brian Ganson eds. 1996. *Coping with International Conflict: A Systematic Approach to Influence in International Negotiation*. Upper Saddle River NJ: Prentice Hall.

Goldstein, Joshua S. and Jon C. Pevehouse. 1997. Reciprocity, Bullying and International Cooperation: Time-series Analysis of the Bosnian Conflict. *The American Political Science Review* 91 (3): 515–559.

Greig, J. Michael. 2013. Intractable Syria? Insights from the Scholarly Literature on the Failure of Mediation. *Journal of Law and International Affairs* 2 (1): 48–56.

Gurr, Ted Robert. 1996. "Minorities, Nationalists, and Ethnopolitical Conflict." In *Managing Global Chaos; Sources of and Responses to International Conflict*, eds. Chester A. Crocker, Fen Osler Hampson, and Pamela Aall. Washington DC: United States Institute of Peace.

Hafner-Burton, Emilie M. 2014. A Social Science of Human Rights. *Journal of Peace Research* 51 (2): 273–286.

Harbom, Lotta and Peter Wallensteen. 2005. Armed Conflict and Its International Dimensions, 1945–2004. *Journal of Peace Research* 42 (5): 623–635.

Holmqvist, Caroline. 2006. "Major Armed Conflicts." In *Patterns of Major Armed Conflict, 1990–2005*, eds. Lotta Harbom and Peter Wallensteen. Oxford: Oxford University Press.

Huntington, Samuel P. 1998. *The Clash of Civilizations and the Remaking of World Order*. New York: Simon and Schuster.

Kathman, Jacob D. and Reed M. Wood. 2011. Managing Threat, Cost, and Incentive to Kill: The Short-and Long-Term Effects of Intervention in Mass Killings. *Journal of Conflict Resolution* 55 (5): 735–760.

Khachikian, Arthur. 1999. *Great Powers and Collective Intervention in Multipolar International Systems*. Stanford CA: Stanford University Press.

Krain, Matthew. 2005. International Intervention and the Severity of Genocides and Policides. *International Studies Quarterly* 49: 363–387.

Kriesberg, Louis. 2009. Changing conflict asymmetries constructively. *Dynamics of Asymmetric Conflict* 2 (1): 4–22.

Maoz, Ifat. 1999. The Impact of Third Party: Communications on the Israeli–Palestinian Negotiations. *The Harvard International Journal of Press Politics* 4 (3): 11–25.

Murdie, Amanda and Dursun Peksen. 2014. The Impact of Human Rights INGO Shaming on Humanitarian Interventions. *Journal of Politics* 76 (1): 215–228.

Nadler, Arie. 2002. "When Intervention is Likely?" In *International Intervention: Sovereignty versus Responsibility*, eds Michael Keren and Donald A. Sylvan. London: Frank Cass.

Nalbandov, Robert. 2009. *Foreign Interventions in Ethnic Conflicts: Global Security in a Changing World*. Farnham, UK: Ashgate Publishing.

Obama, Barak. 2014. "President Obama: What Makes Us American." In *60 Minutes*.

Regan, Patrick M. 1996 Conditions of Successful Third-Party Intervention in Interstate Conflicts. *The Journal of Conflict Resolution* 40 (2): 336–359.

Regan, Patrick M. 2002. *Civil Wars and Foreign Powers; Outside Intervention in Intrastate Conflict*. Ann Arbor, MI: University of Michigan Press.

Regan, Patrick and Rodwan Abouharb. 2002. Interventions and Civil Conflicts. *World Affairs* 165 (1).

Ryan, Stephen. 1995. *Ethnic Conflict and International Relations*. London: Dartmouth Publishing Group.

Saideman, Stephen M. 1997. Explaining the International Relations of Secessionist Conflicts: Vulnerability versus Ethnic Ties. *International Organization* 51 (4): 721–753.

Saideman, Stephen M. 2002. Discrimination in International Relations: Analysing External Support for Ethnic Groups. *Journal of Peace Research* 31 (1).

Svensson, Isak. 2007. Bargaining, Bias and Peace Brokers: How Rebels Commit to Peace. *Journal of Peace Research* 44 (2): 177–194.

Themner, Lotta and Peter Wallensteen. 2014. Armed Conflicts, 1946–2013. *Journal of Peace Research* 51 (4): 541–554.

Wallensteen, Peter and Margareta Sollenberg. 2000. Armed Conflict, 1989–99. *Journal of Peace Research* 36 (5): 593–606.

Wood, Reed M. and Jacob D. Kathman. 2012. Armed Intervention and Civilian Victimization in Intrastate Conflicts. *Journal of Conflict Resolution* 49 (5): 647–660.

World Tribune. 2013. "Report: By supporting Muslim Brotherhood, Obama drove Egypt to Russia, China." *World Tribune.com*.

Yoshihara, Susan. 2010. *Waging War to Make Peace; US Intervention in Global Conflicts*. Westport CT: Praeger.

3 International intervention strategies

Integration, accommodation and partitioning

International actors and states have a toolbox from which to choose a strategy to deal with conflicting groups. Determining that groups can live together, external interveners can promote a strategy ranging from integration to accommodation, or where they cannot, propose or legitimize partitioning solutions. Advocating and legitimizing a particular type of institutional arrangement has a profound and long-term impact on the conflict and on the potential of group transformation. The type of international strategy may be dependent on domestic preferences, external interests, interpretation of the conflict and presumptions on whether the groups in conflict are perceived to be able to coincide. Integration policies tend to favor the state; accommodation balances between rights of group and state; and partitioning along conflicting group lines prioritizes the rights of the group over the rights of state. Although integration is the normatively preferred arrangement for minorities within the state, when it comes to resolving violent conflicts, internationally sponsored solutions have been commonly found within accommodative frameworks (Berg and Porat 2008; Hoddie and Hartzell 2003).

Since the 1990s, accommodative institutional frameworks, most notably consociational arrangements, have become the "tool of choice" both within scholarly debate and among practitioners in internal violent conflict (Hoddie and Hartzell 2003; Taylor 2009; Wolff 2011). In all but a handful of cases of violent intergroup conflict, accommodation has been the prescribed strategy, with partitioning as its default alternative. Rupert Taylor emphasized a "new wave" of contemporary accommodative consociational agreements, driven by international intervention (Taylor 2009). These include Bosnia and Herzegovina (1995), Burundi (1998), Northern Ireland (1998), Macedonia (2000), Afghanistan (2004), Iraq (2005), and Kenya (2008). Many scholars including Wolff, Hartzell and Hoddie, and McGarry and O'Leary have offered support for the use of accommodative consociational institutional frameworks as prescriptions for post-conflict divided societies (Hoddie and Hartzell 2003; McGarry and O'Leary 2006; Wolff et al. 2011).

Although accommodative frameworks have been commonly utilized tools to end violence and appease hostile groups, what are the long-term implications of an accommodation strategy on groups in conflict? Does accommodation foster group transformation or does it cement divisions between conflicting groups, setting up divisive institutional frameworks that pave the way towards separation or eventual partitioning? Are there elements of accommodation that foster equal integration and potential transformation and are there elements that harden divisions between conflicting groups? How does accommodation compare to alternative strategies, namely integration or partitioning? Finally, why is accommodation the current tool of choice? Is it due to endogenous, exogenous or normative factors?

Partitioning, accommodation and integration are the three main types of potential prescriptive international strategies for groups engaged in a violent conflict (see Figure 3.1). There are also several non-prescriptive group strategies that are for the most part shunned by international interveners, including segregation, occupation, ethnic cleansing, assimilation and exclusion. Accommodation seeks to accommodate diversity through power sharing arrangements or minority-specific institutions (Kymlicka 2008). Accommodation entails the recognition of the group, promotion of group rights and the inclusion of a group within an institutional type of power sharing arrangement. Accommodation, however, can come in many shapes and forms, which can include federalism, corporate or liberal consociationalism, or some type of group power sharing within a political and institutional framework (Lijphart 2007). Accommodation and integration, depending on their level of inclusion, may both foster democratic equality and give space for some recognition of group rights within the state. The latter, however, is a more integrative strategy where groups may gain some specific protection such as cultural recognition but are integrated within a state as part of a multicultural, liberal or a civic framework. Integration policies seek to integrate all citizens, ideally on a non-discriminatory basis, into shared institutions.

Partitioning entails territorial division or the formal separation along group or non-group lines towards the eventual creation of new states. Separation or partitioning can be fought for, forced, coerced or voluntary, stemming from a mutual agreement. Partitioning options along ethnic lines, particularly when forced, have tended to incite ethnic cleansing and in most cases have not been visibly professed as the preferred international option for the improvement of relations between conflicting groups. Partitioning and accommodation tend to favor rights of the group over those of states. On the other hand, integration strategies tend to favor interests of the state over the groups (Figure 3.1).

Since the 1980s, the majority of internal conflicts or civil wars have ended through a negotiated agreement (Hoddie and Hartzell 2003). Peace agreements between parties are often the road map towards the creation of new structures that favor some type of power-sharing arrangement meant to resolve the conflict. The terms of peace agreements generally include policies or guidelines towards separation, integration or accommodation within the future internal constitutional order of the conflicting state. Most peace agreements favor accommodation, thereby increasing the strength of the groups. As noted by Isak Swenson, peace agreements, which generally include some new form of power sharing, have the tendency to strengthen the group and weaken the state (Svensson 2007).

Self-Determination / Federalism / Multiculturalism / Civic State

Autonomy / Consociationalism / Centripetalism

Partitioning   Accommodation   Integration

⟸ Towards separation of Groups   Towards integration within the State ⟹

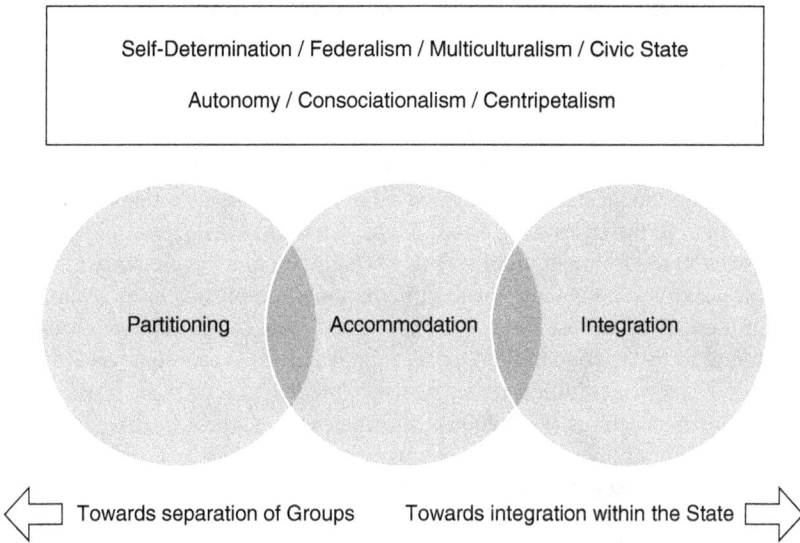

Figure 3.1 International toolbox of group identity strategies.

Peace agreements can vary according to their outcome, as to whether conflicts over sovereignty, statehood and identity are completely resolved, partially postponed or completely postponed (Bell 2006). For example, both the Good Friday Agreement and the Dayton Agreement left major unsolvable issues for the future. The Good Friday Agreement left the partitioning option open for a possible future referendum. The Dayton Agreement left the difficult issue of Brčko for international arbitration to be decided a year after signing of the agreement. Peace agreements can be signed by elected representatives of conflicting parties, armed opposition groups, states, international bodies, and thus often legitimate certain leadership or groups. Often, under pressure from and enforcement by the international community, they provide the constitutional blueprints for long-term group relations and the future functioning of the state.

Accommodation, partitioning and integration contain advantages, disadvantages and potential dangers. The purpose of the next section is not to highlight a particular approach that is appropriate for all conflicts, but rather to examine some of the advantages and challenges within the differing approaches. Depending on the level of inclusion and exclusion, integration, accommodation and partitioning can all harden differences between groups or provide opportunities for identity transformation. There are several factors that should be taken into consideration. First, it is important to note within the strategies that are commonly integrated into a peace agreement whether group identities are deemed as permanent and unchanging or as dynamic, with the capacity to change. As argued in this book, the former builds walls while the latter can potentially build bridges between groups. Second, are the new post-conflict institutions, particularly institutions that accommodate group differences, created in a flexible, or a cementing manner? Third, are the strategies made with inclusive or exclusive notions of group identity? Do the strategies take account of mixed group identities and overlapping identities?

Peace making has commonly been closely tied to constitutional designs. Constitution brokering can come under the guidance of the Security Council Resolutions, individual states or even non-governmental organizations. Christine Bell noted that, in the cases of Kosovo, Afghanistan and East Timor, the process was achieved in the following four stages: (1) adoption of a UN Security Council resolution providing a mandate for the international establishment of an interim administration; (2) establishment of an appointed local transitional government in an attempt to foster cooperation; to pave the way for (3) elections; and (4) the drafting of a new constitution to replace the interim structures of governance with permanent structures (Bell 2006). In some cases, such as in BiH, elections took place following the drafting of a new constitution that was essentially the internationally imposed peace agreement. Since the 1990s, more than half of civil wars have ended through peace agreements and in most cases, the international community had taken an active role in their design and implementation. More than half of peace agreements have failed and some agreements have even been blamed for subsequent violence (Bell 2006). For example, the Arusha Accords, mediated by US and France, have been blamed for facilitating genocide in Rwanda after changing the political and military power balance between the conflicting groups. The accords produced an agreement that favored the Rwandese Patriotic Front, and the 1994 shooting down of the Presidential plane served as a catalyst for the violence since the government blamed the RPF.

International interveners are often in the position to influence and legitimize whether the conflicting groups can live together or whether the divisions are so deep as to justify secession or partitioning. Their decisions often reflect their perceptions on group identity and its potential for transformation. The following sections examine the different types of strategies, outlining some of the reasoning behind the choice of strategies and their potential impact. The selection of strategies can be based on international norms, or domestic circumstances within the conflicting state or the intervener's interests. The sections will elaborate further on the three main options within the international toolbox of resolving conflicts between groups: integration, accommodation and partitioning.

International interveners, including states and mediators, are commonly in a powerful position to influence, justify and legitimize strategies of integration, accommodation and/or partitioning. Weak states can be dysfunctional and may result in state failure. In turn, failed states have been noted as one of the primary causes of conflicts (Goldstone 2008). Under what conditions do international interveners including states and mediators advocate integration, accommodation and partitioning solutions? What are the international justifications for a particular type of strategy? Are those related to international norms, endogenous factors connected to the conflict or exogenous factors linked to the preferences of the intervener? Finally, what impact does each strategy have on group identities in conflict?

Accommodation

Accommodation is the most common internationally sanctioned strategy of dealing with conflicting groups in a violent dispute. Accommodation can include territorial federation, consociational arrangements, or some type of group power-sharing arrangement as agreed in the terms of a peace agreement. Accommodation may be demanded by groups and legitimized by external interveners; however, it is not an internationally recognized right. Accommodation, in line with international norms, is presently an international right only for natives or aboriginals (Kymlicka 1996). Currently, the right of self-determination also applies to colonial territories but not to disputed territories or self-proclaimed national groups (Berg and Porat 2008). However, in practice, external interveners in violent conflicts tend to favour accommodation. Among the 38 negotiated peace settlements analysed by Hartzell and Hoddie, all except one contained some form of power sharing arrangement (Hoddie and Hartzell 2003).

The most common form of accommodation that has in recent years become the "tool of choice" for an institutional framework subsequent to a violent conflict is consociationalism (Taylor 2009). According to its scholarly founder Lijphart, consociational democracy may be defined in terms of four basic principles: grand coalition or power sharing, mutual veto, proportionality and segmental autonomy, which implies that decision making is delegated as much as possible to the separate groups (Lijphart 1979). Federalism, like consociationalism, was designed as an "antithesis of majoritarianism" and generally implies a territorial division of power within a state (Lijphart 1979). The main principles focus on proportionality in the public and economic sectors and on power sharing commonly prescribed for deeply divided societies. Power sharing between groups may include: executive power sharing, autonomy or self-government, grand coalition, proportionality and veto-rights (McGarry and O'Leary 2004). The role of power sharing between groups is to ensure that key decisions, including elections to significant posts, are taken on a cross community basis.

Much has been written on the benefits and perils of consociational arrangements. Many theorists defend the consociational approach as being necessary both as a protection against domination by a more powerful group and as something demanded by minorities. As argued by John McGarry, most aggrieved minorities want far-reaching institutional group recognition of their national identity and would not be satisfied with individual equality. Therefore, substantive institutional recognition of national minorities might "bring out the benign characteristics of rival identities and to marginalize chauvinists more effectively than unwanted inclusion projects" (McGarry 2001, 127). However, is accommodation a remedy to ensure inclusion of all groups and address questions of exclusion, or is it a way of appeasing violent conflicting groups?

Through institutionalizing permanent group divisions, does it not become a hurdle towards long-term group transformation?

Several recent scholars, including Rob Aitken, Sven Gunnar Simonsen and Rupert Taylor, have criticized the consociational approach as exaggerating the depth and permeability of social categorizations and institutionalizing them in marble (Aitken 2007; Goldstone 2008; Simonsen 2005). According to its critics, first, the consociational approach overemphasizes the primacy and the permanency of ethnic divisions. As noted by Simonsen, institutionalization of ethnicity has become an important hindrance to peace building (Simonsen 2005). Second, it actively excludes other social categories, such as gender and class, that crosscut ethnic divisions. As noted by Rupert Taylor, "It is neither obvious nor logical that ethno-nationalism can be cured by prescribing more of it through constitutional engineering" (Taylor 2001, 38). Accommodation has also resulted in many dysfunctional and failed states.

So why has accommodation been the tool of choice? The primary reason given by most scholars is that groups in violent conflict demand accommodation. However, leadership in the midst of violent conflicts is generally not moderate and may make many demands that may be deemed as unacceptable, including an independent state, expulsion and exclusion of other groups. Accommodation is seldom advised or recommended in non-ethnic conflicts. Today, it would be considered inappropriate to set up distinct governing institutions divided along other group lines such as race or class.

Still, accommodation may contain arrangements that do not suffer from the same challenges. Recent studies have distinguished between liberal and corporate types of consociational arrangement. As noted by Alison McCulloch, corporate consociation accommodates groups according to an ascriptive criterion such as ethnicity or religion (McCulloch 2014). On the other hand, liberal accommodation rewards whatever salient political identities emerge in democratic elections. In recent years, McCulloch and other prominent scholars including McGarry and Brendan O'Leary eschew corporate formulas in favour of more liberal models (Goldstone 2008; Lijphart 2007; McCulloch 2014). Corporate consociational arrangements such as in BiH and Lebanon have been subject to much more criticism than the more liberal arrangements such as in Northern Ireland and Malaysia. However, as noted by McCulloch, both have had the ability to create gridlock in governance and have the tendency to entrench divisive identities (McCulloch 2014). Centripetalism has been advocated by some scholars, including Donald Horowitz, as a more consensus-building strategy that fosters cooperation across group lines (Horowitz 2014). Centripetalism lies closer to integration, somewhere between consociationalism and multiculturalism, since it uses the political and/or electoral system to promote cooperation between different groups. By its design, centripetalism encourages political representatives to look for support from outside of their own group, thereby encouraging cooperation between groups (Briey 2005). Centripetalism also may not suffer from the type of gridlock and disfunctionality of a consociational arrangement.

Indeed, even if one removes violence from the equation, one encounters few cases of long-term functioning accommodation and many cases of dysfunctional states. Belgium, which is based on a corporate accommodation formula, has been paralyzed subsequent to the 2007 and 2010 elections, breaking world records for being 541 days without a government. Consociational arrangements in former communist states, including Czechoslovakia and Yugoslavia, contributed to their disintegration. Czechoslovakia, which underwent a peaceful breakup, was paralyzed for more than a year before the leadership decided to throw in the towel and move towards partitioning. Canada and Switzerland are unique in creating a long-term stability, though independence of Quebec from the rest of Canada has never completely left the agenda. Afghanistan and Iraq, ostensibly based on a liberal consociational formula, have both spiralled into sectarian violence.

Are there aspects of accommodation that may be necessary to counter cultural or political domination? Alan Patten distinguishes between two forms of accommodation: *cultural preservation* and *equality of status* (Patten 2008). Under the rubric of cultural preservation, the state actively supports vulnerable cultures and identities by providing them with rights and resources. One example would be Quebec, where the Canadian government permits the French-speaking province to set up its own language and immigration policies in order to rectify what is perceived to be an unfair disadvantage. Another example would be Northern Ireland, where, as part of the Good Friday Agreement, under "rights, safeguards and equality of opportunity," provisions were made not only seeking to end any restrictions on the public use of Gaelic, but also for the active promotion of it, including providing financial support for Gaelic film and television production in Northern Ireland.

The second type of accommodation comes under the rubric of equality of status within the state. Under this approach, the state promotes an even-handed recognition of various ethnic, language and religious groups. For example, when dealing with religion and education, rather than choosing a dominant religion, or keeping religion out of schools, "all religions would be afforded roughly comparable time or space in the curriculum or school system" (Patten 2008). Bosnia is a good example, since the Dayton Agreement allowed the three recognized groups to set up their own schools, curriculum and religious education. Although the agreement provided for equality between groups, it institutionalized a separation between the groups, giving little space for integration or inclusion of individuals from mixed backgrounds. Thus while cultural preservation may work to protect vulnerable minorities from domination, equality of status strategies may be a precursor to segregation.

Accommodation arrangements can also differ with regards to being inclusive or exclusive of other non-dominant groups and individuals belonging to complex or mixed group identities. A critical question in accommodation subsequent to a violent conflict is whether the strategies harden or soften differences between conflicting groups. Consociationalism arrangements, which fall under the rubric of equality of status, offer a guarantee of political participation to the key groups.

These power-sharing arrangements, however, often entrench divisions, privilege conflicting group identities and give additional power to ethnocentric elites (Berg and Porat 2008). A key difference lies between institutions that are inclusive, flexible and accommodate identity change and those that are exclusive, cement divisions and hinder transformation. In addition, if the institutions are not functional, they can result in government paralysis, state collapse and be a precursor to partitioning.

Partitioning

When accommodation fails or is not deemed possible, the common substitute prescription is partitioning. Although the partitioning option lacks broadly accepted international institutional norms, it has been and continues to be advocated and realized in numerous "ethnic" violent conflicts. Partitioning has been an option of external interveners in some of the most challenging violent conflicts, most commonly with devastating results. Partitioning has also been an endorsed option when external parties intervened on opposing sides or favored division based on strategic interests. More often than not, partitioning furthered violence rather than resolved the conflict. The partitioning of Ireland (1921), the partitioning of India (1947), the partitioning of Palestine (1947), the break up or the partitioning of Yugoslavia (1991–92) all had dire, violent consequences and did not resolve the conflicts they sought to end. There have been few successful cases of partitions of states along group lines that did not result in ethnic cleansing or the creation of exclusive states.

Strategic interest to break up enemy states has historically been one of the primary causes of active external support for partitioning. Following World War I, official international intervention by the great powers was framed on the grounds of the creation of nation states. Former US President Woodrow Wilson championed the self-determination of nations living within multi-ethnic states, claiming that dissatisfied "nationalities," deprived of their own state, would be a major threat to world peace. This policy resulted in the carving up of empires and the creation of numerous "nation states," including Austria, Finland, Estonia, Latvia, Lithuania, Czechoslovakia and the Kingdom of Serbs, Croats and Slovenes. Although the concept of "nation state" was evoked, many of the states created were far from being dominated by a single nation or without significant minorities. Leadership of many groups utilized self-determination to gain power over territory. For the external interveners, the nation-state concept was an instrumental and very successful tool used to disintegrate empires and strengthen the position of the allies. There were also no shortages of groups willing to play this nation-state card.

Supporting the national aspirations of a particular group in order to justify the collapse of an enemy state was not limited to post World War I policy. It became a useful tool abused by Adolph Hitler prior to and during World War II. The empowerment of the nationalistic leadership of ethnic groups such as the Slovaks and the Croats at the expense of Czechoslovakia and Yugoslavia respectively was used very successfully by Hitler to rally support and weaken opposition to the Nazi takeover of Europe. Following World War II, ideological rivalries between the two superpowers, the US and the Soviet Union, were extremely influential in shaping external intervention in conflicts and determining which superpower would support a particular state or group. Satellite states under the influence of the Soviet Union, such as Poland, Hungary, Czechoslovakia and East Germany, were forced to follow the Communist agenda.

Partitioning has commonly been justified under the rubric of self-determination and the creation of the nation state. The creation of the nation state is not a new phenomenon. As noted by Emanuel Adler, "In the beginning, Europe created the modern sovereign state and later, the nation state. And it saw that it was good – but only for three hundred years" (Adler 1992, 287). Although the majority of the states are not "nation states", the modern global system continues to be dominated by the nation state framework of analysis. In reality, the nation-state system was originally unique to Western Europe and was used by Western countries to break up empires and later free groups from colonial rule. The creation of nation states within a framework of resolution for groups in conflict is a questionable approach for groups engaged in territorial disputes.

In practice, countries continue to be created under the principle of one nation per state. In 2008, the United States and major European countries recognized the autonomous region of Kosovo against the fierce objections of Serbia. There is no doubt that Serbia's policies in its autonomous region of Kosovo under the Milosevic regime were indeed atrocious. NATO, however, intervened militarily in 1999 and, with a fierce bombing campaign against Serbia, ended the Serbian aggression in Kosovo. Serbia subsequently sent Milosevic off to be tried to The Hague and the Serbian people voted in a more moderate leadership that transformed the formerly fiercely nationalistic country. Thus, international recognition that gradually gave legitimacy to the creation of a new "nation" state, forcefully carving up Serbia against its wishes, was based on past behavior rather than current policy. The recognition was given without an agreement with the dwindling Serbian minority within Kosovo, which fiercely objected to being included in the new state, opening up new sources of grievances not only with Serbia but also with the Serb minority. Thus the partitioning has become another area of contention, with long-term international involvement in ensuring a functional state.

Although numerous states have been partitioned on the "nation-state" principle, in practice the nation state is a misnomer, since it rarely exists. In fact, less than one-third of the countries today could arguably be described as "nation states" and none are completely homogeneous. According to Gurr, out of 164 states studied, only 45 could be described as single nation group states in which 95–100 percent of the population come from a single national group (Gurr 2002). This data did not take into account multiple identities. However, instances of violent, messy partitions along group lines, such as within the former Yugoslavia, have been on the decline. In his study of *People Versus States*, Ted Robert Gurr noted that a comparison of "ethnic conflicts" during the 1990s showed a modest decline, from 115 to 95 groups in open conflict. Trends were noted in de-escalation of conflicts, as well as fewer new episodes of conflict and a steep decline in secessionist wars. According to Gurr, by the end of 1999, 18 secessionist wars were being fought, fewer than at any time since 1970 (Gurr 2002, 276). In recent years, secessionist wars have been replaced with violent internal disputes and proxy wars such as in Syria, Iraq and Yemen.

The policy of redrawing borders along group lines as an appropriate remedy to internal group conflict has been questioned by a number of scholars. First, as noted by Fearon, there is the faulty premise that internal violence stems from incompatible cultures and badly drawn borders (Fearon 2001). There is little evidence that partitioning according to ethnic or religious criteria decreases the level of violence. Second, it is a questionable premise that the world is made up of homogeneous groups that can, with the proper alteration of borders, be separated into distinct units based on cultural/religious/ethnic similarities and differences (Fearon 2001). Considering the dynamics of group identities, mixed groups, overlapping groups, intermarriage, globalization, immigration, and the fundamental international right for individuals not to belong to a particular group, this is impossible.

Most fundamentally, there is a questionable but presumed infinite link between group identity and territory. There is a large difference between claiming that a group or people belong to a land and a land belongs to a single group (Bashir Bashir, from discussions with the author in Jerusalem in 2011). A group may belong to a land or feel it has strong linkages to a particular land, but it is not an exclusive or infinite concept, since the territory may be shared by many groups. Land belonging to a particular group is an exclusive concept not conducive towards conflict resolution and long-term sustainability. The nexus between group identity and territory has been supported under the principle of the nation state. Although self-determination may be a positive concept, in practice the carving of the world into distinct ethnic, religious or other groups is simply impossible. The first question is who will decide on the physical boundaries of each group. As Wallenstein noted: "On the surface it seemed reasonable: let the people decide. It was in fact ridiculous because the people cannot decide until someone decides who are the people" (Wallerstein 1996, 485). In addition, the notion according to which, after proper redrawing of borders, there will be a nation which will be justly in charge of its own affairs without interference from others is also not realistic. Instead, any new line drawn to separate populations will almost always be problematic since it will leave fearful groups on one or both sides (Fearon 2001). As noted by Kelman, "ethnic pluralism is most consistent with the principles of democracy and human rights ... because the establishment of new, ethnically based states could become a threat to ethnic minorities within new borders" (Kelman 1997, 329). Indeed, if partitioning is done under the umbrella of exclusion of other groups, it will likely heighten rather than resolve a conflict.

Still, distinction can be made between partitions along ethnic or religious group lines and partitions of a state that do not involve presumably fixed group identities but rather the creation of two or more states with inclusive identities. The carving of states along presumably fixed group lines is a result of the way identity issues are formulated and interpreted. Self-determination and the creation of the nation-states concept has commonly been utilized to carve mixed states. The creation of nation states can be problematic not only due to difficulties in ethical implementation but also to policies of exclusion. The resolving of group conflicts based on the principle of nation states has in many cases meant violent separations of mixed populations. However, even if the process is assisted by international actors and done "ethically" with no violence as suggested by supporters of partitioning such as Kauffman, one has to question the logic of the strategy (Kauffman 1996).

There are, however, a handful of cases of peaceful partitioning along non-exclusive group lines from which one can draw deductions of the minimum requirements for a successful partition. The 1992 peaceful partitioning of Czechoslovakia had created two functional democracies and lowered the salience of the identity of conflicting groups. Subsequent to the velvet revolution, Slovak national leadership used political and economic grievance in the Slovak region to block the functioning of the consociational Federation. Unable to find a compromise, and blocked by a dysfunctional accommodative framework, Czech and Slovak politicians moved towards the creation of two states. Although neither the Czech Republic nor Slovakia can be looked at as an ideal case study in their treatment of other minorities, particularly the Roma, the partitioning improved the relations between the Czechs and the Slovaks.

There were a few reasons for this. All citizens in Czechoslovakia, whether Czech, Slovak, mixed or other, were given the choice of living within either one of the breakaway countries, regardless of which group they belonged to. Thus, the partitioning did not involve any territorial disputes, forced ethnic cleansing or induced settlements to the other country. Second, neither Slovaks nor Czechs are discriminated against or excluded in the Czech Republic or Slovakia. Indeed, prominent personalities including politicians of the non-dominant group are active members in both countries. Third, the self-determination of the Slovaks put an end to inter-ethnic rivalry and claims of economic injustice, shifting the blame and focus to other directions. Still, the public was not consulted since the breakup took place with no referendum and the partitioning far from resolved issues related to discrimination of other minorities living within the two states. The nation-state framework in both countries has been used to justify policies of discrimination against groups that are not perceived as belonging to the dominant groups of the respective states.

Partitioning options have commonly been accepted under the rubric of support for a nation state. Although there are many virtues of self-determination, partitioning along ethnic/religions lines and policies of exclusion have not led to long-term viable resolutions of violent conflicts. Although easy to propose, partitioning is not simple to implement and remains questionable as the ultimate solution to many of today's violent conflicts. Still there is a fundamental difference between partitioning along presumably permanent group lines and partitioning territory with the purpose of creating two or more inclusive territories.

One can argue that partitioning may be a potential option when its design is not exclusive, is negotiated, is validated by the public and is not coerced or imposed. Herbert Kelman proposes that a group's national identity and right to self-determination must be negotiated with those who are affected by it (Kelman 1997). To be inclusive, partitioning cannot succumb to the creation of exclusive territories linked to specific group identities. The newly created states must offer a viable home for all individuals and groups residing in the territory. As noted by Kelman, an independent national state is not entitled to international legitimacy unless it provides absolute guarantees for the protection of minority rights and the fulfillment of other obligations. A new state cannot be an ethnically pure state, nor claim to strive to become one (Kelman 1997). Lastly, and rather obviously, a viable partitioning option cannot include forced or coerced transfer of civilians since this violates basic human rights and can spark an escalation of violence and further ethnic cleansing.

Partitioning in the midst or subsequent to a violent conflict is far from the ideal solution and could heighten a conflict. Indeed it is questionable whether accommodation or partitioning along fixed group lines are the appropriate strategies towards long term transformation of relations between groups in a violent conflict. Can accommodative and partitioning solutions, legitimized in internationally mediated peace agreements, eventually result in some type of inclusive integration? As in multiple cases such as the case of Czechoslovakia, partitioning can come about as a consequence of a dysfunctional accommodative framework. Although integration is the normative right for groups internationally, should it or can it be on the mediation menu for groups in the midst of a violent conflict?

Integration

In line with international law, all groups have rights and protection under the umbrella of integration. Within integration, groups may gain specific guarantees such as cultural recognition but are integrated within a state as part of a multicultural, liberal or civic framework. International norms dictate that all ethnic, religious, linguistic and other groups or minorities within a state have rights under the umbrella of integration (Kymlicka 2008). According to international norms as outlined by the Charter of the United Nations, integration is the official policy for managing groups within a state. The emphasis is on human rights for all, non-discrimination and the protection of cultural rights. The 1992 *Declaration on the Rights of Persons Belonging to National, Ethnic, Religious and Linguistic Minorities* reaffirms its purpose as "to achieve international cooperation in promoting and encouraging respect for human rights and for fundamental freedoms for all without distinction as to race, sex, language or religion" (UN/RES/47/135 1992). Its first article notes that "states shall protect the existence and the national or ethnic, cultural, religious and linguistic identity of minorities within their respective territories and shall encourage conditions for the promotion of that identity." Article Two states that persons belonging to national or ethnic, religious and linguistic minorities (hereinafter referred to as persons belonging to minorities) have the right to enjoy their own culture, to profess and practice their own religion, and to use their own language, in private and in public, freely and without interference or any form of discrimination.

(UN/RES/47/135 1992)

It further notes the rights of minorities to participate fully in the state, politically and economically, without any discrimination.

These policies are evident in the 1992 UN *Declaration on the Rights of Persons Belonging to National, Ethnic, Religious and Linguistic Minorities*, which adopted an integrationist approach for minorities, focusing on non-discrimination and civil rights policies. According to current international norms, accommodation is reserved as a right for indigenous or aboriginal groups only (Kymlicka 2008). The *UN Declaration on the Rights of Indigenous Peoples* focuses on self-government and institutional autonomy. The distinction between the rights of integration for minorities and accommodation for natives is outlined by the UN's *Working Group on Minorities and Working Group on Indigenous Populations*.

The United Nation policy is pretty clear in its current principled approach. Groups, whether national, ethnic, religious, or linguistic, living within a state, are protected against discrimination, but do not necessarily have any power-sharing or sovereign rights. Article 8 of the declaration specifically states that "Nothing in the present declaration may be construed as permitting any activity contrary to the purposes and principles of the United Nations, including sovereign equality, territorial integrity and political independence of States" (UN/RES/47/135 1992). In theory, integration espouses the model of "universalism," focusing on common liberal rights of citizenship. In practice, integration can range from nation building, multiculturalism, assimilation, to exclusion. The question of exclusion and inclusion is one of the foremost issues subsequent to a violent conflict.

The legitimacy of integration depends on the inclusion of all groups, protection against cultural assimilation, and the removal of discrimination and other barriers against members of particular groups. During a violent conflict the term integration is often feared to be a cover for assimilation. In distinguishing between integration and assimilation, Adrian Guelke notes assimilation occurs when hypothetical group A joins group B, simply enlarging one group through the convergence of another group (Guelke 2012). Integration on the other hand, ideally produces a new entity, Group A + Group B. As noted by Nagle and Clancy, the importance is the creation of a shared society where "the complex determinants of social identity are not constrained by a single communal narrative; individual identities are numerous and they cross-cut multiple cleavages" (Nagle and Clancy 2010, 2).

Alan Patten distinguishes between two forms of integration: *disembolishment* and *nation building*. In disembolishment, the state becomes blind to group differences and makes "no attempt to acknowledge, accommodate, or assist the variety of different cultures and identities to which citizens are attached in a diverse society" (Patten 2008). Arguments in favor of disembolishment include its neutral stance towards different groups. This is challenging in practice in certain spheres, since the state for example must have a language and education policy, which prioritizes certain language(s) or cultures over others. Within the nation-building type of integration, the state promotes a particular common form of national identity among all of its citizens. It is indifferent to different groups, seeking to converge all groups and citizens to a single national identity. France is a classic case of nation-building policy, promoting political and social equality under a French national identity.

Nation-building policies are built on the notion of group identity transformation. A critical question is whether the nation-building policies are formulated and implemented with the principles of *inclusion* or *exclusion*. How much transformation is required for a group to be incorporated into the collective national identity? One can differentiate between the US type of nation building which, despite its history and current divisions, is in principle accepting of all differences, and the French model that requires some group adaptation (for example, when it comes to visible religious groups). Arguably, nation-building policies that are more inclusive and tolerant of difference have a greater chance of being accepted by all groups. This is particularly the case in an already volatile or violent environment. Nation-building strategies that do not protect the rights of individuals to practice their culture and beliefs may be interpreted as forced assimilation that can heighten a conflict.

Highlighting issues related to inclusion and exclusion, Oren Yiftachel distinguishes between three different types of state strategies towards integration of its citizens:

(a) a civic homeland, which regards all citizens as fully belonging regardless of their ethnic background; (b) cultural homeland, which conditions full membership on cultural assimilation; and (c) an ethnocratic homeland, which claims the state to be the homeland of one group only.

(Yiftachel 2006)

As noted by Yiftachel, the first two have the potential to create an inclusive sense of identity while the third, "is driven by an opposing force, a desired seizure of the entire territory by one ethnic group at the exclusion or inferior incorporation of minorities and immigrants" (Yiftachel 2006, 45). Subsequent to a violent conflict where groups are already engaged in a hostile relationship, the creation of a "cultural homeland" is also likely to antagonize those groups whose culture is not represented by the state. Although it may be possible for a country such as France to integrate groups into one dominant culture, though not without problems, it will likely raise many objections and heighten conflict in a country where groups are already engaged in a violent conflict. Clearly, an ethnocracy where the non-dominant group(s) are purposely excluded would serve as a cause contributing to deepening divisions between groups.

Although integration, where individuals are subject to equal rights and non-discrimination, is an accepted part of international norms, when it comes to a violent conflict, the current conflict resolution strategies are most commonly found within group accommodation. As noted by scholarly research, almost all peace agreements contain some elements of power sharing between conflicting groups. As discussed in the previous section, policies of accommodation, which are currently most frequently recommended by scholars and implemented in the midst of a violent conflict, have been known to freeze conflicting group identities and hinder conflict transformation. Attempts at integration, subsequent to violence, are indeed challenging since they may be feared and resisted by national leadership. When intervening in a violent conflict, do international mediators advise or advocate integration? Is integration not on the table because of endogeneous or also exogeneous factors?

Between accommodative, partitioning and integrative strategies

The majority of peace agreements feature some type of accommodation of group rights or power-sharing arrangements. An accommodative framework may be designed as a temporary measure with the intent to contribute towards eventual inclusive integration and transformation, or be designed along permanent fault lines, which, regardless of intention, may contribute towards hardening divisions between groups. Much of this depends on the level of inclusion and exclusion. Integration, accommodation or partitioning, depending on the type of approach, each offers inclusive or exclusive solutions to group identity that may either harden differences or soften divisions between conflicting groups. A crucial element that requires further elaboration in the case studies is why a particular strategy is selected and how the type of strategy affects group identities. Externally proposed group identity strategies may reify, or transform, group identities in conflict. Certain external group identity strategies may strengthen moderates and weaken extremists or vice versa.

The level of inclusion and exclusion refers to all groups. The emphasis on a specific fault line during a violent conflict has commonly led to the exclusion of other groups, such as other minorities or women. Women, for example, have commonly been excluded during the peace making as well as within power-sharing strategies. As noted by Siobhan Byrne and Allison McCulloch, "While gender inequality is not unique to power sharing, the overarching emphasis on one specific kind of identity – ethno-national – in need of inclusion, makes power-sharing practice particularly vulnerable to the exclusion of women" (Byrne and McCulloch 2012).

Integration, accommodation and partitioning strategies, as visualized in Figure 3.2, each contains potential elements of inclusion or exclusion. Partitioning can be conducted along solid group lines, which could incite ethnic cleansing and heighten divisions between groups. Alternatively, partitioning could be a democratically agreed separation of a state into two or more inclusive states. Accommodation may include short-term protective group measures such as

	Partitioning	Accommodation	Integration	
Exclusion	Democratic separation along non-fixed group lines	Affirmative action	Civic state	Inclusion
	Self-determination/ ending occupation	Cultural preservation	Multiculturalism	
	Creation of new nation states	Equality of status	Nation state/ cultural homeland	
	Partitioning along solid group lines, ethnic expulsion	Ethnic segregation	Ethnocracy	

Figure 3.2 Group identity strategies.

cultural preservation or affirmative action or create strategies that may cement group divisions along territorial or institutional lines. Finally, integration could be to a civic state, a multicultural state, a nation state or an ethnocracy. The exclusive options for all three strategies are far worse than the inclusive strategies of any of the options. There are also strategies far worse than accommodation, integration or even partitioning including occupation, ethnic cleansing, assimilation and genocide.

Much of official international intervention in "ethnic" violent conflicts has been based on primordial understanding of groups as ancient, solid and unchanging, resulting in solutions that build walls rather than bridges between groups. As noted in Chapter 1, primordial interpretations have often fostered policies or the promotion of a single group living within a particular state or territory. Numerous official mediation efforts have focused on primarily territorial, resource and power divisions between what have been perceived as solid and unchanging hostile groups. International interventions, including in Yugoslavia, Cyprus, Iraq, and Israel-Palestine, have been based on primordial interpretation of group identity and the subsequent partitioning strategies of states that have led to cementing rather than transforming hostile group identities. Interpretation of violent intergroup conflicts based on ethnic hatreds or primordial group identity have commonly lead to exclusive accommodation and partitioning solutions.

Conclusion

The type of international intervention strategies depends on several factors, including on how external interveners perceive group identities, and on endogenous and exogenous interests. Are group identities perceived as solid primordial units or are they perceived as dynamic with the capacity to transform? As is argued within this book, group identities can change and the type of intervention proposed following a violent conflict should ideally be made with the prospect of eventual group identity transformation. Currently much of the international intervention falling under the umbrella of accommodation and partitioning does not envision or enhance the potential of group transformation. In academic analysis as well as in practice, however, there has been little attempt to examine the potential of identity transformation such as attempts to de-ethicize a conflict and create flexible and inclusive institutions.

The subsequent chapters will analyze the external intervention process, their strategies and their impact in three divergent and influential conflicts: Northern Ireland, Israel-Palestine, and Bosnia and Herzegovina (BiH). International intervention process and strategies will be examined for their contribution to the goals and behavior of the groups in conflict. Following a brief historical overview, the analysis will focus on external intervention from the 1990s until today.

References

Adler, Emanuel. 1992. "Europe's New Security Order: A Pluralistic Security Community." In *The Future of European Security*, ed. Beverly Crawford. Berkeley CA: International and Area Studies.

Aitken, Rob. 2007. Cementing Divisions? An assesment of the impact of international inverventions and peace-building policies on ethnic identities and divisions. *Policy Studies* 28 (3): 247–267.

Bell, Christine. 2006. Peace Agreements: Their Nature and Legal Status. *American Journal of International Law* 100: 373–412.

Berg, Eiki and Guy Ben Porat. 2008. Introduction: Partition vs. Power Sharing? *Nations and Nationalism* 14 (1): 29–37.

Briey, Laurent de. 2005. "Centripetalism in Consociational Democracy: The Multiple Proportional Vote." Université Catholique de Louvain.

Byrne, Siobhan and Allison McCulloch. 2012. Gender, Representation and Power-Sharing in Post-Conflict Institutions. *International Peacekeeping* 19 (5): 565–580.

Fearon, James D. 2001. Separatist Wars, Partition and World Order. *The Leonard Davis Institute* (88): 1–26.

Goldstone, Jack A. 2008. Pathways to State Failure. *Conflict Management and Peace Science* 25: 285–296.

Guelke, Adrian. 2012. *Politics in Deeply Divided Societies*. Cambridge: Polity Press.

Gurr, Ted Robert, ed. 2002. *Peoples versus States, Minorities at Risk in the New Century*. Washington DC: United States Institute of Peace.

Hoddie, Matthew and Caroline Hartzell. 2003. Civil War Settlements and the Implementation of Military Power-Sharing Arrangements. *Journal of Peace Research* 40 (3): 303–320.

Horowitz, Donald L. 2014. Ethnic Power Sharing: Three Big Problems. *Journal of Democracy* 25 (2): 5–20.

Kauffman, Chaim D. 1996. Possible and Impossible Solutions to Ethnic Conflict. *International Security* 20 (4): 136–175.

Kelman, Herbert C. 1997. Negotiating National Identity and Self Determination in Ethnic Conflicts: Choice Between Pluralism and Ethnic Cleansing. *Negotiation Journal* 13 (4): 327–340.

Kymlicka, Will. 1996. *Multicultural Citizenship*. Oxford: Oxford University Press.

Kymlicka, Will. 2008. The Internationalization of Minority Rights. *International Journal of Constitutional Law* 6 (1): 1–32.

Lijphart, Arend. 1979. Consociation and Federation: Conceptual and Empirical Links. *Canadian Journal of Political Science* 12 (3): 495–515.

Lijphart, Arend. 2007. *Thinking about Democracy: Power Sharing and Majority Rule in Theory and Practice*. London: Routledge.

McCulloch, Allison. 2014. Consociational Settlements in Deeply Divided Societies: the Liberal Corporate Distinction. *Democratization* 21 (3): 501–518.

McGarry, John. 2001. "Northern Ireland, Civic Nationalism and the Good Friday Agreement." In *Northern Ireland and the Divided World, Post Agreement Northern Ireland in Comparative Perspective*, ed. John McGarry. Oxford: Oxford University Press.

McGarry, John and Brendan O'Leary. 2004. *Northern Ireland Conflict: Consociational Engagement*. Oxford: Oxford University Press.

McGarry, John and Brendan O'Leary. 2006. Consociational Theory, Northern Ireland's Conflict, and its Agreement. Part 1. What Consociationalists can learn from Northern Ireland. *Government and Opposition* 41 (1): 43–63.

Nagle, John and Mary Alice C. Clancy. 2010. *Shared Society or Benign Apartheid? Understanding Peace Building in Divided Societies*. Basingstoke UK: Palgrave Macmillan.

Patten, Alan. 2008. "Beyond the dichotomy of universalism and difference: Four responses to cultural diversity." In *Constitutional Design for Divided Societies*, ed. Sujit Choudhry. Oxford: Oxford University Press.

Simonsen, Sven Gunnar. 2005. Addressing Ethnic Divisions in Post Conflict Institution-Building: Lessons from Recent Cases. *Security Dialogue* 36 (3): 297–318.

Svensson, Isak. 2007. Bargaining, Bias and Peace Brokers: How Rebels Commit to Peace. *Journal of Peace Research* 44 (2): 177–194.

Taylor, Rupert. 2009. "The Promise of Consociational Theory." In *Consociational Theory, McGarry and O'Leary and the Northern Ireland Conflict*, ed. Rupert Taylor. London: Routledge.

Taylor, Rupert 2001. "Northern Ireland: Consociation or Social Transformation." In *Northern Ireland and the Divided World, Post-Agreement Northern Ireland in Comparative Perspective*, ed. John Mcgarry. Oxford: Oxford University Press.

UN/RES/47/135. 1992. "Declaration on the Rights of Persons Belonging to National or Ethnic, Religious and Linguistic Minorities." Adopted by the UN General Assembly at its 92nd Plenary Meeting on December 18, 1992.

Wallerstein, Immanuel. 1996. "National Development and the World System at the End of the Cold War." In *Comparing Nations and Cultures; Readings in a Cross-Disciplinary Perspective*, ed. Alex and Masamichi Sasaki Inkeles. New York: Simon and Schuster.

Wolff, Stefan. 2011. Post-Conflict State Building: the debate on institutional choice. *Third World Quarterly* 32 (10).

Yiftachel, Oren. 2006. *Ethnocracy: Land and Identity Politics in Israel/Palestine*. Philadelphia PA: University of Philadelphia Press.

4 Bosnia and Herzegovina

Catch-22 in international nation
building

In my first few months working in Sarajevo for the UN just after the war ended,
I spent time meeting the local leadership of the Bosniacs, Bosnian Serbs, and
Bosnian Croats and there was a phrase I heard from all three of them: "ti si nasa"
(you are one of us). The comment was said as a compliment and meant "you
come from Czechoslovakia, you are a Slav, you understand." At the time it perplexed me how I could be part of all of "their groups," and yet they were not part
of each other's. Nationalism, extremism and opportunism served to cut deep
divides between the formerly mixed groups. Despite some progress, 20 years
after the signing of the peace agreement, the group divisions have solidified
within the corporate accommodative framework.

Despite an international intervention, which "successfully" terminated the
violent conflict, Bosnia and Herzegovina (hereafter: BiH) remains a thorny issue
for American and particularly European policy makers whose member countries
continue to spend billions of dollars to preserve the peace. The ethnically divisive policies institutionalized through the 1995 Dayton Peace Agreement created
a dysfunctional state, solidifying the differences between the groups and, at the
same time, made the international community a permanent part of the makeup of
BiH. Although most policy makers agree that BiH is a fragile state requiring
additional solutions, they disagree on the causes of the problem and consequently on the solutions required.

The differences over interpretations of the conflict by policy makers goes back
to the beginning of the violence in BiH and the subsequent type of intervention
process. The initial interpretation of the conflict in BiH by European interveners
as an internal ethnic civil war based on ancient group rivalries within Bosnia
resulted in the European-led intervention being neutral, limited and focused on
partitioning solutions. The deepening US engagement and a gradual switch of
interpretation from "ethnic civil war" to a war of aggression initiated and orchestrated by paramilitary groups and nationalistic extremists sponsored by neighboring Serbia facilitated a switch from a neutral to a partisan intervention. The
transformation to a partisan intervention forcefully brought an end to the conflict.
For many policy makers, however, the emphasis remained on ethnic division and,
at the Dayton peace talks, the international community formulated solutions of
internal partitioning, institutionalizing group divisions along ethnic lines.

Discussions on the external intervention in BiH are varied, with radically different opinions on the relative success or failure. Rory Stewart and Gerard Knaus in *Can Intervention Work?* hailed the international intervention in BiH as a successful case study (Stewart and Knaus 2011, 156). Other analyses of the realities in BiH are far less positive. Christopher Bennett in *Bosnian Paralyzed Peace* pointed out the evident failures in international attempts to restructure BiH (Bennett 2012). The differences in interpretation of current and past realities in BiH reflect different solutions to the problems. There are a few analysts today who prescribe the abandoning of the multi-ethnic exercise in favor of partitioning BiH, arguing that changing borders and ethnic division will resolve the conflict (Kauffman 1996). They take this position despite the fact that partitioning would consolidate and reward ethnic cleansing and could likely result in further violence. What is more troublesome about the above-mentioned partitioning option is that it had been the primary solution suggested by the international community (IC) from the beginning of the violence in the former Yugoslavia. It also reflects the manner in which many policy makers in the IC perceived group identities in BiH, as primordial, unchanging and unable to coexist.

This chapter will analyze the international intervention in BiH, from the initial eruption of the conflict in the former Yugoslavia until today, focusing on the external process and group identity strategies. It will examine the consequences of the interpretation of the conflict on the type of intervention, as well as the impact of the said intervention on the conflict and the identities of the groups. The chapter will analyze the change from divided to united intervention and the shift from a neutral to a partisan international intervention against the wartime Bosnian Serb Republic (Republika Srbska, hereafter: RS). Finally, it will examine the way the international community dealt with, and is continuing to deal with, group identity politics. In essence, the framework created at Dayton was one of soft partitioning with a consociational power-sharing democracy based on ethnic differences. The institutions that were designed favored strong ethnically based entities and a very weak central state. Since the signing of the Agreement, the IC has been directly engaged in restructuring, guiding and propping up the ineffective state, paradoxically hindered by the framework it imposed at Dayton.

This chapter argues that, although a united–partisan international intervention process was sufficient to terminate the violence in BiH, the group identity strategies – namely the accommodative institutions designed at Dayton – were far from ideal for the creation of an effective state. The building of an effective state might have benefitted from the construction of flexible and inclusive institutions, not only for the management of but also for the transformation of group identities. This is something the Dayton Peace Agreement not only failed to do but also hinders. Although there has been little violence and some progress, almost 20 years after the signing of the Dayton Peace Agreement, BiH remains essentially a failed state. The Dayton Agreement stopped the war; however, the IC is still required to keep the peace, both with troops and through imposed internal governing structures. Without significant transformation or continuous international propping up, the institutional framework designed at Dayton continues to be essentially unworkable and is unlikely to be sustainable in the long term.

Some fundamental questions need to be asked regarding the international intervention process as well as strategies. How did the IC eventually come to a consensus on a united–partisan intervention? What was the IC's role in the selection of the corporate accommodation strategies for Bosnia? Was it the only available solution on the table? The contention of this chapter is that the interpretation of primordial hatred, which the IC understood to be the key cause of the conflict, was not only present at the start of the conflict but remained active during the negotiations at Dayton and contributed to the institutionalizing of ethnic divisions. The interpretation of ethnic realities affected both the international intervention process and the strategies. International processes and strategies resulted in further hardening of divisions along ethnic lines and prevented reconciliation and transformation.

Although there is currently an increasing willingness on the part of the main international governing body in BiH, the Office of the High Representative, to bypass, overcome, and transform Dayton's institutional designs, the process is not simple. The necessity for institutional change places the leading international bodies in BiH in a very awkward position. On the one hand, they have been assigned the task of implementing the Dayton Peace Agreement; on the other hand, the Agreement itself hinders the peace process, and needs to be changed. This catch-22 has been a fundamental obstacle to transformation and reconciliation. Although there is resistance from the national politicians, much of the population within all communities supports the need for change.

The background to the conflict

In effect, there are two diametrically opposed interpretations of the causes of the war in Bosnia. The first sees Bosnia as an ethnic or a civil war, while the second depicts the international conflict as stemming from planned aggression from neighboring Serbia. The ethnic/civil war explanation focuses on historical divisions between the three ethno/religious groups of Bosniacs (Muslims), Serbians (Orthodox) and Croats (Catholics) that culminated in a vicious three-sided war. It stresses the history of divisions and conflict, particularly the brutal nature of World War II in the former Yugoslavia, as well as the ancient ethnic hatred that Tito managed to keep in check with the "Yugoslav brotherhood" policy. In line with this interpretation, subsequent to the death of Tito, the lid on the ethnic hatreds was opened, unleashing the vicious conflict. Numerous academics and practitioners have accepted this interpretation, particularly at the beginning of the conflict. For example, Coles notes that "[t]he Balkans have been primarily linked with a static ethnic essentialism, with a secondary status given to the more traditional essentialist representations of fragmentation, barbarism, tribalism or reversion to pre-civilization" (Coles 2007, 259). This interpretation helped to formulate the first international intervention policies, specifically neutral humanitarian international intervention, as well as the legitimacy of division along ethnic lines.

The second interpretation of the conflict sees the violence in Bosnia as an international conflict stemming from Serbian aggression. It emphasizes hundreds of years of peace in Bosnia and regards the brutalities committed during World War II as an exception rather than a reflection of Bosnian history. It focuses on the collapse of the state of Yugoslavia and its key institutions, most importantly the Yugoslavian army, which resulted in the creation of brutal, self-serving, private militias that were responsible for the greatest share of violence and destruction. Much of the blame for what occurred in Bosnia is placed on the Serbian nationalism and extremism that supported the private militias, and the desire of Serbian President Slobodan Milosevic and Croatian President Franjo Tudjman to carve out a Greater Serbia and a Greater Croatia at the expense of the newly formed Bosnia. By the end of 1994, this interpretation mostly overtook the IC's understanding of the conflict as a civil/ethnic war and was responsible for the shift from a neutral to a more robust partisan international intervention.

The two views reflect starkly different interpretations of the history of the region and of the Bosnian conflict, which is a mixture of complexities. In line with the second interpretation, this chapter asserts that the hostilities that resulted in the brutal violence beginning in 1992 were for the most part not native to BiH but were exported from outside. Although the war in Bosnia was a regional conflict and erupted from regional dynamics, Bosnia had specific characteristics that made it unique. First and foremost, it was ethnically and religiously the most mixed area in the region, with inhabitants from Serbian, Croatian, Turkish and other diverse cultural and religious roots. Prior to 1992, the mixed population in BiH did not experience very tense or hostile relations. Mixed marriages were very common in the area (Fine 1993). Regionally, BiH had the highest number of mixed marriages, stemming from centuries of coexistence. This was particularly the case in the main cities such as Sarajevo, Banja Luka, Mostar and Tuzla. In Sarajevo, it would indeed be difficult to find one family that did not have at least one member that came from another ethnic or religious group.

Bosnia sat in the midst of diverse cultures, particularly Croat and Serb, and as such tended to shift its allegiance depending on economic and political benefits. The first independent Bosnian state emerged in 1180 and, due to its rugged terrain, was largely left alone by its more powerful neighbors until the invasion of the Ottoman Turks in 1388 (Malcolm 1994). The Ottoman rule had lasting consequences, one of the most important being a large number of religious conversions to Islam, which left much of the population of Bosnia Muslim. Although the history should by no means be idealized, the people in Bosnia lived relatively free from any major wars or internal, ethnic, or religious hostilities. Most accounts of ancient hatreds and ethnic rivalries are the results of modern day myths rather than historical realities. In the famous battle at Kosovo Polje in 1389, Bosnian troops fought alongside Serbs against the Turks. Later, the more ingrained local Muslims fought against the Ottomans, establishing themselves as loyal subjects of the Austro-Hungarian Empire.

Yugoslavia was created following World War I from the rubble of the disintegrated Hungarian and Ottoman Empires, which controlled much of the Balkan territory. Like Czechoslovakia, it was created based on US President Woodrow Wilson's nation-state principle that one nation should be in charge of one state. The creation of "nation states" served the purpose of undermining the fabric of the European-based empires of the nineteenth and twentieth centuries far more than providing a specific territory to particular ethnic or national groups. As the cases of Czechoslovakia and Yugoslavia demonstrated, one nation within one state was a falsehood. However, in both cases, the new republics became centralized and dominated by the main ethnic group, in the case of Czechoslovakia, by the Czechs and, in Yugoslavia, by the Serbs. To justify the falsehood, supra national identities were created: "Czechoslovaks" and "Yugoslavs." The principle of "one nation-one territory," which stood behind their creation, however, ensured that other groups were not given any recognition and in both countries this became a source of grievance and contention.

During World War II, Adolf Hitler was able to take advantage of the grievances of the minorities and used the promise of statehood for minorities to gain Nazi support. World War II was particularly brutal in Yugoslavia, as different groups took opposing sides or ended up fighting each other. The Croatian leadership, eager to regain its statehood, became a Nazi republic and separated itself from Serbian-dominated Yugoslavia. The Croatian governing Fascist movement Ustase was particularly violent, killing Jews, Roma, Serbs, and Muslims and setting up massive and brutal concentration camps. In its traditional uncertainty, the Bosnian leadership wavered between allegiance to Nazi Croatia and an alliance with Allied Serbia, ending up at times used and, at times, attacked by both. The Serbian nationalistic movement "Chetniks" had an official policy of supporting the Allies but, in practice, collaborated also with the Nazis and killed or ethnically expelled thousands of Muslims (Malcolm 1994). Although suspicious of Communism, and having closer ties to Croatia, in the end, many Bosniacs ended up joining the Partisans. After the death of more than one million people, the Communist Partisans won in Yugoslavia and Josef Broz Tito in 1945 united the republics in a Communist Yugoslavia. President Tito imposed a non-tolerant view of nationalist and religious practices. Islam and Islamic cultural and educational institutions were particularly not tolerated, since the religion was perceived as backward (Malcolm 1994).

However, in accordance with the new Yugoslav Constitution, minorities received more autonomy within the new state structure, which was divided into six republics and two autonomous regions. The six republics were Croatia, Slovenia, Serbia, Montenegro, Macedonia and Bosnia. Vojvodina and Kosovo received a lesser autonomous status. Since the Communist party controlled the state, the autonomy for the republics and autonomous provinces was largely symbolic. The status of the republics increased in 1974 when they were granted greater control and autonomy by the Communist regime.

Under Communist leadership, the division of Bosnia was discussed by Serb and Croat politicians but was deemed impossible by the new Communist state. The status of the Bosniacs and of Bosnia was evident in the First Communist Party Congress which stated: "Bosnia cannot be divided between Serbia and

Croatia, not only because Serbs and Croats live mixed together on the whole territory, but also because the territory is inhabited by Muslims who have not yet decided on their national identity" (Malcolm 1994, 199). This implied that the Bosniacs were not a recognized group and had to choose to be either Serb or Croat. However, many Muslim Bosnians wished to be recognized, not according to their religion, but as a distinct national group.

The push to recognize Bosniacs as having a national identity came from numerous Bosniac intellectuals, particularly in the 1960s and 1970s. In 1971, Muslims were recognized as a religious group, but not as a nation. In reaction to the constitutional change, former Bosnian President Hamdija Pozderac stated: "They don't allow Bosnianhood but they offered Muslimhood. We shall accept their offer, although the name is wrong, but with it we'll start the process" (Malcolm 1994). Recognition of a Bosnian identity was an important concept since many Bosniacs were not religious but felt tied to a Bosniac or Muslim identity rather than a religious one. As noted by Banac, "The peculiarities of Bosnian Muslim socialist nationhood, whereby one can be a Muslim by nationality and a Jehovah's Witness by religion (this is not a bizarre invention but a commonplace in the town of Zavidovici) became fully accepted by the Bosnian Muslim Community" (Banac 1993, 146). State intolerance towards the Muslim religion continued, however. A clampdown on Bosniac activists took place in 1983, in which 13 people, including the future president of BiH Alija Izetbegovic, were tried and jailed for "hostile and counter-revolutionary acts derived from Muslim nationalism" (Malcolm 1994, 208). Izetbegovic, who became the wartime president of BiH, was also accused of advocating Western-style parliamentary democracy.

The rise and spread of nationalism across Yugoslavia in the late 1980s was linked to many factors including failing economics, the demise of the Communist party, the death of Tito, which left a power vacuum, and the end of the Cold War, which left Yugoslavia without external support. Also vital was the significant imbalance between the rich Yugoslav Republics and the struggling Republics or regions in the state, the leaders of which began to pull in different directions. Yugoslavia, as a state, became weak, while increasingly powerful and rich regional governments, particularly Croatia and Slovenia, demanded greater autonomy. The Communist party also became fragmented along national lines, as Serbia favored increased centralization, whereas Slovenia and Croatia pushed for further decentralization. Economic problems played a strong hand in heightening the grievances and increasing the tensions. By the late 1980s inflation was up to 1200 percent and per capita income dropped by half. The wealthier republics of Croatia and Slovenia, which desired rapid shift to market economics, became resentful of carrying the economic burdens of the poorer republics and pushed towards independence. The original aim of Serb nationalism was to increase authority and recentralize the state power. In 1989, Slobodan Milosevic, the leader of the Serb Communist Party, used the centralization pretext to topple the governments of Vojvodina, Montenegro and Kosovo. Threatened by increasing nationalism in Serbia, and the toppling of other regional governments, Slovenia and Croatia seized the opportunity and, in 1990 and 1991, held referendums and voted for independence. The independence led to a minor scuffle with Slovenia and a lengthy war with Croatia over the Serb-dominated region of Krajina.

The dissolution of Yugoslavia and the conflict between Serbia and Croatia left a large question over the future status of Bosnia unanswered, creating the anticipation of a potentially larger, more violent conflict. The mixed population of BiH should have made the territorial separation of BiH a questionable option. According to the 1991 census, the last one to be conducted before the war, among the four million-plus population of BiH, about 43.5 percent of the population had registered themselves as "Muslims," 31 percent as Serb, 17 percent as Croat, 5 percent as Yugoslavs and 2 percent as others (Census 1991). The groups were mixed territorially and even within families, due to the large amount of intermarriage. Indeed, there was little nexus between territory and identity. Most of the population lived in mixed regions where the majority group formed less than 66 percent of the population. The large cities were particularly mixed, some with as much as 50 percent of marriages involving different religions or ethnic groups.

Despite this reality, ethnic territorial partitioning was deemed the best solution by many Croatian and Serbian nationalists and by key mediators from the IC. Unsurprisingly, the decision on which group belonged to which territory was challenging and volatile. Hard-line nationalists made historical claims to all of the land. According to the notorious extremist Radwan Karadzic, presently on trial in the Hague, "Serbs have a right to territory not only where they're now living but also where they're buried, since the earth they lie in was taken unjustly from them" (Zimmermann 1999, 175). When asked by former US Ambassador Zimmerman if he would accept parallel claims on behalf of Croats and Muslims he replied "of course not ... because Croats are fascists and Muslims are Islamic fanatics" (Zimmermann 1999). In 1991, Karadzic became the President of the newly created Republika Srbska. The tragedy of BiH stemmed not only from the reality that extremists were able to take charge particularly in the RS but also from the fact that the IC ignored the moderate voices and considered the extremists to be the representatives of particular ethnic groups. International mediators readily accepted ethnic partitioning solutions, advocated by extremists and paramilitaries, as the only solutions to the problem. As noted by Campbell, "peacemakers of the international community were in an alliance of political logic with some of the paramilitaries, and thus failed to provide space for, let alone encourage, non-nationalist forms of social and political life" (Campbell 1998, 14).

The conflict in BiH was bloody, complicated, and involved three different sides, but its origin had little to do with ancient hatreds. The reasons for the conflict were linked to economic opportunism and external attempts, mainly Serbian, to divide the country. Although there was internal support for division, the violence and ethnic cleansing could not have taken place without the support of Serbia. The organized violence was conducted externally and then promoted locally. Most scholars today view the conflict in BiH as international aggression rather than a civil or an ethnic war (Woodward 1995). When the conflict first erupted, however, the interpretation was that it was a civil war based on ancient hatreds. As noted by Campbell: "Rendered as a civil war, Bosnia invites different strategies than those that might be involved if it were to be cast as international aggression" (Campbell 1998, 157). The IC's proposed strategies involving ethnic partitioning had devastating effects. Despite what may have been good intentions, the interpretation by the IC of the conflict as an ethnic civil war resulted in detrimental intervention strategies, with ongoing consequences.

International intervention process – from divided–neutral/partisan to a united–partisan intervention

From the initial violence in BiH, international intervention was divided on principles but was neutral in practice. Early presumptions about group identities of the conflicting parties molded the international interpretation of the conflict in BiH as either an internal ethnic conflict or as an act of international aggression, orchestrated by outside national extremists. Both interpretations led towards what was presumed to be the required solution. Differing interpretations of the causes of the conflict translated into key international players supporting different types of external process. In principle, the United States advocated a partisan approach, but for the first three years abstained from active involvement in the conflict. In practice, the main external interveners in the conflict, the EU and the UN, adopted a neutral approach. In effect, this created a divided neutral/partisan intervention, which, in the first three years, did little to impede the violence. This section examines the shift of external approach from a divided neutral/partisan to a united–partisan intervention that forcefully helped to terminate the conflict.

From the beginning of the war in BiH, there was a wide difference between the way American and European policy makers perceived the conflict and the manner in which they envisioned its termination (Bildt 1999). Under George W. Bush, the American administration was first within the key US/EU/UN international intervention triangle to advocate a principled partisan approach. Yet, it did not act on it until years into President Clinton's administration, more than three years into the violent conflict. Although American leadership was not immune to using the "ethnic hatred" narrative to publicly justify an initial non-intervention policy, there was a clear preference for a partisan approach against Serbia. In principle, American leadership favored a military campaign in line with what was interpreted in Washington as Serbian aggression, but, in practice, they were uninterested in becoming actively engaged. The 1991 infamous quote by James Baker, "we do not have a dog in the fight," was quite reflective of the initial American lack of interest in the Yugoslav conflict. In line with the ethnic war interpretation, Europeans and the UN promoted and embarked on neutral diplomatic solutions that focused on humanitarian assistance, ceasefires, and on ways to partition Bosnia along ethnic lines. The transition from a neutral to a partisan international intervention in BiH was a gradual and difficult process, reflecting an arduous diplomatic battle between American, European and UN diplomats and policy makers.

Neutral intervention or non-intervention by the international community was what was hoped for by neighboring nationalist leaderships, who wished to carve BiH between Croatia and Serbia. In March 1991, the President of Croatia Franjo Tudjman and the Serbian President Slobodan Milosevic secretly met to discuss the partitioning of BiH (Little and Silber 1996). The Bosnian government, fearing being divided between Croatia and Serbia or absorbed into what was left of Yugoslavia, organized a referendum for independence. BiH President Izetbegovic hoped independence would deter regional violence or provoke an external intervention in case of an overt attack. In anticipation of looming Bosnian independence, President Milosevic decided to preempt the independence and deter international intervention by organizing a covert military involvement. Realizing the attack would need to be orchestrated by special forces since the Yugoslavian National Army (JNA) had essentially disintegrated as many soldiers dodged the draft, mutinied or deserted on mass, the solution was either the creation of a special Bosnian Serb national army or the use of paramilitaries (Mueller 2000). Milosevic chose both options. By transferring all nationalists or volunteering Bosnian Serbs to BiH and removing those who were not, Milosevic created a Bosnian Serb Army. The new Bosnian Serb Army gained access to all JNA weapons and was unofficially commanded from Belgrade. Having learned from his experience in Croatia, Milosevic saw this as insufficient and also recruited paramilitary forces. It was the paramilitaries who committed most of the atrocities.

In March 1992, immediately following the referendum and the declaration of Bosnia's independence, paramilitaries trained in Serbia crossed into BiH and began a vicious campaign of ethnic cleansing (Little and Silber 1996). The paramilitaries went directly after the Bosniac civilians, or, since there were no distinguishing visual or linguistic characteristics, those whose identities were determined as Muslim on the basis of having an identity card with a Muslim sounding name. With no Bosniac army, the civilians were left at the mercy of local police, who managed to put up a resistance in some of the towns. The vast inequality of arms at the beginning of the war created a disproportionate imbalance that left the Bosnian civilians vulnerable to expulsions and murder. Prior to the war "it was estimated that they [Bosniacs] possessed two tanks and two armored carriers (APCs) while the Serb Army in Bosnia had 300 tanks, 200 APCs 800 artillery pieces and 40 aircrafts" (Malcolm 1994, 243). Through military superiority in the first six weeks of the war, the newly formed Serbian Bosnian Army equipped by JNA and supported by the paramilitaries managed to take over 60 percent of BiH, forcibly removing most of the Bosniac civilians from the territory. The United Nations Security Council Report on Special Forces investigation committee found that most of the brutal violence, death and atrocities committed in Bosnia were conducted by paramilitaries against ordinary citizens. As noted in the report, "The ethnic cleansing included massacres, rapes, destruction of property, organized extortions, looting and the forcible removal of hundreds of thousand Muslim civilians" (UNSC 1994). The violence spiraled across the territory, inciting mobilization and violent retributions by other groups that were formed from police, criminals and new recruits.

Although paramilitary units operated throughout Bosnia and beyond, the UN listed the most active paramilitary groups operating in the conflict to be under the command of "Arkan" Zeljko Raznatovic and Vojislav Seselj, who both had direct ties to Milosevic. Vojislav Seselj created the "white eagles," heavily composed of criminals and mercenary opportunists. In an interview, Vojislav Seselj noted that "Milošević organized everything. We gathered the volunteers and he gave us special barracks, … all our uniforms, arms, military technology and buses" (LeBor 2004, 191). Zeljko Raznatovic (Arkan) was a renowned Serbian criminal from Belgrade, on the top ten list of wanted men by Interpol during the 1970s and 1980s for committing numerous European bank robberies and murders. With backing from the Serbian secret service and supplied and equipped by reserves of the Serbian police, Arkan created and led a paramilitary unit made up of Serbian criminals and thugs. As investigated by the War Crimes Tribunal, the Arkan Tigers were directly responsible for numerous war crimes including murder, rape, pillaging and ethnically cleansing Eastern Bosnia of Muslims.[1]

Although criminality is often part and parcel of war, in the case of BiH it played a prominent role. One of the ironic tragedies of the war was that the motive of most of the paramilitary units was not fighting the "enemy," but rather robbery and looting civilians, as most paramilitaries were common criminals released from jails in Serbia and recruited for the task. The majority of ordinary civilians, including local leaders, whether Serb, Croat, Bosniac or other, tended to be the victims and not the perpetrators of the violence. Even after incitement to violence by extremist politicians, much of the local leadership in BiH, including most mayors regardless of ethnic background, refused to cooperate with paramilitary units and allow ethnic cleansing and tried to protect civilians of all ethnic backgrounds. Thus, extreme politicians in Serbia found it necessary to recruit more thugs and hooligans for the job, empting jails of thieves, murderers and common criminals (Mueller 2000). The most frequently reported violations were the killing of civilians, torture, rape, destruction of property, and looting which were inspired more by greed than by local extremism.[2] As noted by Mueller, "The violence that erupted in Yugoslavia principally derived not from a frenzy of nationalism – whether ancient or newly inspired – but rather from actions of recently empowered and unpoliced thugs" (Mueller 2000, 47).

For the extreme nationalist politicians in Serbia, ethnic cleansing was the essential goal of the organized attack and not an unintentional by-product of the war (Cigar 2000). The paramilitary groups sent to BiH from Serbia were given specific orders to clear the Eastern Region of BiH, or the two-thirds of Bosnia neighboring Serbia, of Muslims. Some of the violence was staged in order to heighten fear and encourage residents to flee. A common method was to select the most prominent Bosniac politicians and leaders, kill them in a brutal and visible way and then drag them through the streets, suggesting all "Muslims to immediately leave". As the conflict progressed, other newly created paramilitary groups were given similar instructions to cleanse regions of undesired minorities or majorities, whether Serbs, Croats, or Bosniacs (Muslims). Approximately

100,000 people, the majority of whom were civilians, died during the violent conflict in BiH. Almost 2.5 million people, or about half of the population of BiH, were forced from their homes and became displaced internally or as refugees abroad.

The disparity between what was happening inside BiH and discussions within European capitals was very wide. The interpretation in Europe was that this was a civil war based on ethnic hatreds and the sides were equally guilty, thus necessitating a neutral diplomatic intervention. When violence broke out, EC mediator Lord Carrington placed equal blame on everyone and focused on attaining cease-fire arrangements. "Everybody is to blame for what is happening in Bosnia and Herzegovina, and as soon as we get a cease fire there will be no need to blame anybody" said Carrington (Malcolm 1994, 242). Between the eruption of violence in 1991 and the height of the BiH war in 1994, the EC and UN were the main sponsors of the various peace efforts. More than 100 cease-fire arrangements were made and broken during the first year of the war. The March 1992 Lisbon Agreement, negotiated by EC representative Lord Carrington and Portuguese Ambassador Jose Cutileiro, was a final attempt to prevent BiH from sliding into violence. Signed by BiH President Aliya Izetbegovic, Bosnian Serb representative Radovan Karadzic, and Croatian Bosnian representative Mate Boban, the agreement proposed ethnic power sharing and the devolution of the central government. However, with encouragement from the US government, which promised recognition to an independent BiH, Bosnian and Croatian representatives backed away from the plan (Gibbs 2009). For European policy makers, US meddling was perceived as unhelpful and damaging to European peace efforts.

Although the US in principle supported the BiH government and called for a partisan intervention against Serbia, it failed to take any practical steps to assist the new country. In line with the ethnic civil war interpretation, Europeans treated the sides as equally guilty of causing the violence and called for cease-fires that were ignored. Despite BiH's state of defenselessness against the organized onslaught from Belgrade, partisan proposals, favored by the Americans, were viewed with disdain. According to chief EU representative Lord Owen:

> In late June 1992 the US government had argued for effectively "taking sides" in favor of the legitimate government of Bosnia and Herzegovina and of those representatives of Bosnia's Muslims, Serbs and Croats who favored a viable multi-ethnic Bosnia Herzegovina and opposed the violent strategy and tactics of what they called the "terrorist wing" of Karadzic's Serbian Democratic Party of Bosnia...
>
> (Owen 1997, 49)

Owen opposed this strategy calling it "unrealistic." Although acknowledging Izetbegovic as a legitimate President, he felt European policies had to reflect the new "reality that Izetbegovic was in control of only about 11 percent of the country," given the extent of ethnic cleansing and military power (Owen 1997, 51).

Despite President Bill Clinton's 1992 election campaign, which criticized President George Bush for ignoring Bosnia and promised action, the US Democrats were also hesitant about becoming involved in what was publicly referred to by the new Secretary of State Warren Christopher as a "problem from hell" (Holbrooke 1998, 55). Richard Holbrooke, who eventually became America's top peace envoy and the person most credited for the end of the violence and for the Dayton Agreement, was disappointed by the lack of action. From the beginning of the war in Bosnia, Holbrooke placed the largest share of the blame on Belgrade's military support of Nationalist Serb politicians in Pale. Holbrooke advocated an aggressive partisan policy and was thwarted by what he viewed as inaction from both Washington and Europe. Hoping that there would be a change of policy after the election of President Clinton, Holbrooke wrote a memorandum to the new administration suggesting strong policy changes including lifting the arms embargo against Bosnia, allowing covert arms supply to Bosnia so that Bosnian support came not only from Islamic nations, and using direct force against the Serb militants. "Bombing the Bosnian Serbs and even Serbia proper if necessary would send the proper message. However, the actions must be effective, both militarily and politically!" (Holbrooke 1998, 52). The January 1993 memo went ignored as the Clinton administration took a back seat to the Europeans, hoping they would solve the problem in their own back yard. According to Holbrooke, the lack of US involvement made further Serb aggression inevitable. "As the chances of American involvement visibly declined, the Serbs became bolder," noted Holbrooke (Holbrooke 1998, 55).

Although the US administration would have preferred an aggressive policy against the Serb regime in Belgrade, the US government was not eager to jump into the BiH conflict. The October 1993 fiasco in Somalia, where the US lost 18 soldiers in an ill-fated humanitarian attempt, had a profound effect on the lack of enthusiasm for direct US involvement in Bosnia. Still, the interpretation of the Bosnian conflict in Washington was clearly different than the one advanced in the key European capitals. In June 1993, US Secretary of State Warren Christopher traveled to London, Paris and Bonn, proposing to lift the arms embargo against Bosnia and conduct air strikes against the Bosnian Serbs. As noted by Holbooke, "the European reaction was, predictably, negative" (Holbrooke 1998, 55). Public condemnation by US officials of European inaction only added fuel to the fire, widening the divisions between the continents.

David Owen, the designated co-chairman of the Steering Committee of the International Conference on the Former Yugoslavia, condemned the Americans for their "unconstructive meddling and criticism." "From the spring of 1993 to the summer of 1995, in my judgment, the effect of US policy, despite being called 'containment', was to prolong the war...." (Owen 1997, 365). This, he argued, was especially due to Washington's lack of enthusiasm for some of the peace agreements negotiated by the EU. According to Owen, the Clinton administration, for example, encouraged Bosnian Muslims to reject the Vance–Owen Peace plan without offering the Bosniacs any concrete military help. Owen lamented that "had the Clinton's administration supported the Vance–Owen Peace Plan, we would have been able to carry it out" (Owen 1997, 38).

By 1993, the failure of the ceasefires, the extent of the violence against civilians, and the reliance on UN humanitarian assistance, referred to disparagingly in the media as a "band-aid for a gun wound," was becoming increasingly embarrassing for the EU and the UN. During the Vance–Owen negotiations, as a chief aide to Cyrus Vance, US diplomat Herbert Okun pushed for a more forceful approach, lamenting that "diplomacy without a threat of force is like baseball without a bat." In hindsight, Okun told the *New York Times*, what was always necessary "was sufficient peacekeeping or the threat of force. But the international community was not willing to cough up the troops. The international community was not unanimous."[3]

In light of evidence of the atrocities committed by mainly Serb paramilitary forces, NGOs on the ground, the international media and the public began pressuring the IC towards a more partisan approach (HelsinkiWatch 1993, 7). In April 1993, the UN Security Council voted to make the town of Srebrenica, a formerly majority Bosniac town in Eastern Bosnia, "a safe haven." The decision came after a visit by UN's commander in Bosnia General Philippe Morillon to Srebrenica, where tens of thousands of Bosniac civilians had been under siege for close to a year with virtually no food or medical supplies. Besieged by panicked crowds who prevented him from leaving, General Morillon, to the shock and disbelief of UN headquarters, declared Srebrenica "under UN protection" (Silber and Little 1997). Although the UN decided to honor the declaration, it was largely symbolic and placed not only the UN troops but also the affected civilians in a vulnerable position. In May 1993, the designation of a safe area was extended to five other majority-populated Bosniac towns still under Bosniac control to which most of the refugees fled: Sarajevo, Tuzla, Zepa, Gorazde and Bihac. In effect, the mostly unarmed Muslim civilians were being herded into deadly, densely populated, isolated urban pockets surrounded by the Serbian army. Since there was no enforcement of "the safe areas," these designated cities became the least safe and bore witness to some of the worst atrocities in the war. Through formalizing areas for the protection of only Bosniac Muslim civilians, the UN effectively took sides in the conflict and became completely ineffective in protecting the Bosniacs, countering the paramilitaries, or providing security for its own personnel.

With the UN forces being stretched beyond their limits, the pressure increased on the EU to control the increasingly deteriorating conflict in its hemisphere. Part of the reason the EU was unable to come up with a common policy beyond humanitarian assistance and ceasefire agreements, was its new institutions and an internal paralysis. As noted by Juncos, "the inability to act or even to agree on a common line during the first stages of the crisis in former Yugoslavia showed the limitations of the newly created CFSP [Common Foreign and Security Policy]" (Juncos 2005, 95). In 1993, none of the European institutions, nor the sleeping giant NATO, was prepared to interfere in what was perceived as an internal ethnic conflict. The inability of the Europeans to have a functional policy in BiH drew strong criticism that highlighted its incapability of dealing with the post-cold war reality. David Rieff noted that,

> What has taken place in Bosnia has revealed the bankruptcy of every European security institution, from the North American Treaty Organization to the Council on Security and Cooperation in Europe, exposed the fact that nowhere in these great structures was there either intellectual preparedness or moral fortitude for dealing with the crisis of the post-Cold War world or for coming to terms with the likelihood that in the future a great many wars will take place not between states but within states.
>
> (Rieff 1995, 22)

The international inaction in BiH meant that the IC became immersed in a blame game. The United States blamed the Europeans, the Europeans blamed the United Nations and the UN blamed the world for its inability to work together to end the conflict.

The establishment of the Contact Group in 1994 was designed to formulate a common international policy on BiH and for the Americans to become actively engaged and sideline the EU and UN. The Contact Group included representatives of the United States, Germany, Britain and France, which all increasingly favored a more partisan approach against Serbia and the Bosnian Serbs in Pale. Russia, the fifth member of the Contact Group, was against a partisan approach against Serbia, but with the collapse of the Soviet Union had its focus elsewhere. The Contact Group became quickly engaged in territorial debates with the focus of forcing the Bosnian Serb leadership to withdraw from large sections of territory they had taken over. Agreed to by all Foreign Ministers, the Contact Group Plan had divided Bosnia into two entities: 49 percent of the land was to remain in the hands of the Bosnian Serbs and 51 percent given to the Croat–Muslim Federation. This was the basis of the plan that would be permanently formalized at Dayton and dependent on rolling back some of the Serb takeover and strengthening ties between the Croats and Bosniacs in Bosnia. By 1994, there was also a growing consensus between the EU and the US on the benefits of using NATO airpower. Fearing its potential collapse following the end of the Cold War, North American and many European policy makers agreed that NATO's role should be widened and strengthened. As was noted by David Owen, "I was to become even more convinced over the next few months that NATO should be the main forum for Bosnian discussions because it involved not only Canada and the US but also Turkey, which was important for our credibility with the Islamic nations" (Owen 1997, 225). In its first military engagement in BiH at the beginning of 1994, NATO shot down four Serbian war planes, lifting the organization from its defunct post-cold war status.

The common fear of an Islamic threat in the midst of Europe played a significant role in the change of policy for both Europeans and the Americans and the formulation of a united policy. Abandoned by Europe and the US, the Bosniac leadership turned to the Middle East and specifically Iran for assistance. Despite the UN arms embargo, arms equipment, and Mujahedeen trained fighters to use it, were successfully smuggled into Bosnia, and this became a common worry for the EU and the US. Thus the shifting of policy from neutral to joint partisan action against the Serb forces had not only to do with the unacceptable behavior of the Serb leadership in Pale and Belgrade, but also with the increasing concern among Europeans and Americans about the growing ties of Bosniacs to the Middle East, and with the reaction from the rest of the Muslim world. In a declassified document following a closed-door meeting between French and American officials, the French and US diplomats agreed that

> there would be far reaching problems if Bosnia were extinguished. Muslims worldwide will draw unacceptable conclusions. [not declassified] said he fears the possibility of a fundamentalist Bosnia in the long term, especially if the Muslims there perceive themselves as having been betrayed by the West.[4]

Early in 1994, the United States increased its diplomatic efforts in Bosnia with the attempt to create a working confederation between the Croats and the Bosniacs. "Croatia continued to pursue two separate and contradictory policies, their secret collusion with the Serbs and their formal alliance with the Muslims" (Silber and Little 1997, 308). The strengthening of the alliance and the creation of a workable Federation became a priority for Washington, as this was seen as the only hope of assisting the Bosnians. The Federation was achieved with threats of sanctions against Croatia in the case of non-compliance and with "a promise to help (and hasten) Croatia's economic, political and military integration into the West" (Silber and Little 1997, 322). The delivery of arms was part of the agreement. Despite the official UN arms embargo, the US gave unofficial approval for transfer of arms to BiH through Croatia. As stated by the former US Ambassador to Croatia Peter W. Galbraith, President Clinton decided that he would tell Croatian President Tudjman that there were "no instructions" on whether Croatia should allow BiH to receive arms through its territory. As noted by Galbraith, this was "diplomatic code for saying we did not object if Croatia facilitated a flow of arms to Bosnia" (Galbraith 2002, 142). The US plan also included the use of NATO for air attacks to roll back of some of the Serb gains. Although the Federation and the delivery of arms strengthened the position of the Bosniacs, it was not until NATO's air campaign that the situation on the ground changed significantly.

In the face of blatant evidence of atrocities and non-cooperation from the Bosnian Serbs, the Contact Group began to push for increasing use of NATO to bomb Serbian positions. In 1995, as a response to the unabated shelling of Sarajevo by the Bosnian Serbs, and with authority from the UN, NATO responded with a limited air campaign. In retaliation, on May 26, Bosnian Serbs began to take hundreds of UN personnel hostages, chaining them to potential NATO targets such as ammunition dumps and bridges. To the horror of European countries that had contributed troops, the UN hostages were prominently displayed by the international media, sparking an immediate public reaction for international retaliation, or a humiliating withdrawal of the troops. The hostage taking necessitated a rapid modification in European policy. Carl Bildt, who replaced Lord Owen as the EU chairman of ICFY, noted that "the humiliation of the UN forces in the hostage taking which followed in May [1995] made a strong response necessary" (Bildt 1999, 19).

The UN/NATO relationship in BiH has been described as an oil and water mix, as it consisted of parallel neutral and partisan policies. The switch from a mixed intervention to a united–partisan approach required a corresponding switch from the UN to NATO. Since the use of NATO threatened the UN troops, a more robust use of NATO precipitated the removal of the lightly armed UN troops. The physical presence of the UN troops not only failed to prevent atrocities, it also prevented the use of airstrikes. In Srebrenica, where almost 10,000 unarmed Bosniac men were massacred while under the protection of the UN, the Dutch stationed there not only were unable to prevent the massacre, but their kidnapping obstructed the potential of a NATO airstrike. The massacre in Srebrenica was the final straw in convincing key European policy makers to move towards a decisive partisan intervention. According to National Security Advisor Anthony Lake,

> The turning point was in 1995 after Srebrenica. European public opinion shifted, and our allies were not looking forward to another winter on the ground in Bosnia where the humanitarian mission would be struggling. The European mood shift allowed us to proceed with military actions that helped to produce the Dayton Accords.
>
> (Lake 2006)

The increasing use of NATO airpower, strongly recommended by newly arrived American envoy Richard Holbrooke, had a formidable effect on the balance between the warring groups. The decision to use NATO was accompanied by a diplomatic push to isolate and punish the Bosnian Serbs, and gradually eliminate them from the talks by using President Milosevic to reel them in. Holbrooke threatened Bosnian Serbs and the Serbian Republic with air strikes if they did not comply with the demands of the IC. Having the support of most major powers, including contact members France and Germany, US President Clinton attempted to convince the British Prime Minister John Major, and pushed for a bombing campaign on the grounds that "it is better to go out with a bang than with a whimper; otherwise we go out with our tail between our legs" (Chollet and Freeman 2005, 17). On August 25, NATO received the green light from the UN to begin intensive air strikes. With US and NATO as the ultimate force behind him, Holbrooke pressed for a rapid end to the conflict.

It was a united–partisan intervention that forcibly ended the conflict in Bosnia, by forcing the parties, first Serbia and subsequently the Bosnian Serbs, into cooperation. The external intervention dramatically altered the balance between the parties, strengthening the Bosniac and the Croat forces at the expense of the Bosnian Serbs fighters. For many, the united–partisan intervention came years too late. Former US Ambassador to Belgrade Warren Zimmermann resigned in protest at the refusal of the Bush administration to commit forces early, calling US inaction at the beginning of the conflict the biggest mistake of the entire Yugoslav crisis. According to Zimmerman, it "was our greatest mistake of the entire Yugoslav crisis. It made an unjust outcome inevitable and wasted the opportunity to save over a hundred thousand lives" (Zimmermann 1999, 216).

US strategic interests to intervene were heightened after seeing the potential of an extremist threat coming from the Middle East. As noted by General Sewall, American strategic interests were focused on "stabilizing the area … removing it from the influence of Muslim extremists who arrived from the Middle East" and leaving "the area as quickly as possible by rapidly arming and training a Bosnian army."[5] In return for US assistance in a training and equipping program, Bosnia severed its ties with Middle Eastern countries. As one US declassified document noted, "Bosnia terminated its military relationship with Iran at our insistence, and a vacuum now exists in military support to Federation Military Forces."[6] This vacuum was quickly filled by multimillion dollar pledges of military support from the US and European countries. The Americans ensured that their military pledges were visible, insisting that the military air lift would be well publicized. As noted in a declassified document, "[F]or maximum exposure, this airlift should be to Sarajevo during daylight hours, with international media present."[7]

The American administration pushed forward a policy that relied heavily on military air campaigns and the creation of military balance. The US emphasis on the creation of military balance reflected the perception that it was the strong military might of the Serbs and the relative weakness of the Bosniacs that resulted in the atrocities. Defense Secretary Perry promised Izetbegovic to increase the US effort to train and equip Bosnian forces:

> I told them that I believed and our government believed, that the imbalance of forces back in 1992 had been a contributing factor to the war starting in the first place….Therefore, when NATO forces left in a year, we did not want to leave an imbalance.[8]

Consequently, the largest aspect of the US efforts was in training and equipping a joint Croatian and Bosniac Army.

> Tony Lake, the President's National Security Advisor, pressed a new diplomatic approach dubbed "The Endgame Strategy." The goal was to end the war and to maintain a single, though divided, state in which the warring parties – the Croat and Muslim Bosnians and the Serbs – would be separated. The exit strategy rested on the establishment of a military balance of power among the warring factions to deter additional fighting and allow for the removal of US troops at the end of one year.[9]

A concept left over from the Cold War, the balance of power may have been effective policy for creating regional balance, but the creation of two separate armies in a single state was highly problematic. It took the Americans a couple of years to realize that having two armies in a single state was not conducive to nation building. "What happened into 1996 and really into 1997 was that we changed our goals from establishing a military balance of power on the ground to building a new Bosnia," explains Ivo Daalder. "And it becomes clear that this is going to take a long time. It also becomes clear that if we're ever going to resolve this issue the military, as the most capable instrument inside Bosnia, will probably have to do more" (Belloni and Deane 2005). Having two armies was only one aspect that made Dayton a successful peace agreement that ended the war, but not a helpful framework towards the creation of a workable state. Essentially, neither the Europeans nor the Americans were able to formulate a successful long-term strategy that dealt with identity group dynamics within the new state. Holbrooke's approach of "whatever it takes to force a deal" was successful in ending the conflict and imposing a solution but was less effective in visualizing long term resolution for the new BiH state, which continues to be troubled by internal divisions (Curran et al. 2004).

The shift from divided–neutral/partisan to a united–partisan intervention process

The shift from divided–neutral/partisan to a united–partisan intervention was a mixture of exogenous and endogenous factors. Exogenous factors included domestic public pressure, pressure from international media and NGOs, fear of internationalization of the conflict, fear of the growing ties between the Middle East and Sarajevo and lack of effectiveness of neutral intervention. The endogenous factors, namely the uncooperative, hostile and aggressive behavior of the Bosnian Serb leadership, as well as the crossing of red lines including the massacres of civilians in UN safe zones and the kidnappings of UN troops, convinced the Europeans of the necessity of a partisan intervention. The intervention was less about transformation and more about an effective and united use of force. The divided–neutral/partisan intervention prolonged the conflict, having little impact on the extremists. The divided–neutral/partisan intervention also created an oil and water mixture in which one type of process undermined the other. Although the Serb leadership crossed red lines that facilitated the justification of a partisan intervention, the decision was not entirely altruistic. For example, the use of NATO for a powerful partisan intervention was a strategic attempt by the US and Europe to bring a defunct organization out of the post-Cold War dustbin.

As discussed in Chapter 2, the expected behavior of the groups as a result of a neutral or a partisan intervention is partly related to the interpretation of the conflict. There is an academic as well as a practitioners' debate about the best approach to use when one party in a conflict is interpreted as behaving badly or "as a bully." One possibility envisages that the aggressive state or group will adopt a reciprocal response, whereas another possibility could be an inverse response. Prominent members of the American negotiation team, notably Holbrooke, believed that there would be an inverse response to hostile actions. In an inverse response, the aggressive state takes advantage of cooperative actions but will cooperate in response to hostile ones. According to the inverse theory, when faced with hostile actions by an external intervener, an aggressive actor will become more cooperative towards a neighbor/group but will become more hostile when faced with a cooperative outside power (Goldstein and Pevehouse 1997). Americans tended to adhere to this approach, which advocated a strong response against Serbian forces.

Unlike the American leadership, the key European policy advisors on Bosnia adhered to a reciprocal or a warring school of thought. In the warring-faction school of thought, the Serb forces would be more likely to respond to accommodation rather than to force. Thus, according to European policy advisors, it was expected that "lifting arms embargo or using air strikes would increase Serbian hostility towards the Bosnian government and probably towards the international community as well, leading to an upward spiral of violence in the region" (Goldstein and Pevehouse 1997, 518). In line with this argument, the best policy was one of neutrality, which generally prevailed among the Europeans until 1995. The opposing views on the potential repercussions of partisan intervention prevented a united intervention. Although Serbian hostility did increase subsequent to air strikes, it was this hostility that helped to shift the mood towards a united–partisan intervention.

It was only subsequent to a united–partisan intervention that external interveners, namely the US and EU and NATO, were able to act cohesively to forcibly end the conflict. The united–partisan military intervention came partly due to a fear of the creation of an unstable Muslim state linked to Iran in the center of Europe. Although the international partisan process was effective in ending the bloodshed and stopping the war, it did not foster many bridges across the dividing lines. Divisive international strategies, as designed and implemented at Dayton, worked to institutionalize fault lines, ensuring that the conflict between the groups continued though through a different means.

Intervention strategies – from partitioning to institutionalizing divisions between groups

Although the Dayton Agreement mediated by the US ended the bloodshed, it did not create a functioning institutional framework for an independent workable state. Indeed, from its resurrection in 1995 at Dayton, BiH can be said to be a failed state in the making. What had been sufficient to end the war was not sufficient to create a viable state and gradually resulted in an international protectorate (ICG 2003). BiH was a tragic case of radical ethnic engineering, where members of the IC, convinced that the causes of the conflict had primordial ethnic roots, had designed a soft partitioning model to appease the extremists. Guaranteed returns of minorities and reconciliation were supposed to return BiH into a multi-ethnic country. The institutions and the goals set at Dayton, however, were at their root contradictory. The Dayton Agreement offered a military balance between the groups and affirmative identity policies that institutionalized and solidified differences along ethnic lines.

The divisions drawn at Dayton partitioned BiH into separate ethnic entities with minimal integration. According to the agreement, on the one hand, the BiH is committed to "sovereignty, territorial integrity and political independence." On the other hand, BiH is comprised of "two distinct entities each of which has its own political structures, controls citizenship, issues passports, can establish special parallel relationships with neighboring states and has no integrated army or police force to secure its borders and territory" (Campbell 1998, 156). Although there has been some progress, particularly with regard to policing and the army, more than 20 years later, the central state institutions of BiH continue to be weak, dysfunctional and are unlikely to survive without external intervention or significant restructuring.

Presumptions about identities of the conflicting groups molded international interpretation of the conflict in BiH as an ethnic conflict and led towards what was presumed to be the required solution, from the beginning of the violence to the strategies designed at Dayton. The interpretation of the conflict as an ethnic war, which places one national group against the other, presumes a direct link between group identity and territory, and thus easily lends itself towards solutions of territorial partitioning. The numerous peace agreements, ceasefire arrangements, and international peace proposals all contained explicit or subtler attempts to divide BiH along ethnic lines. From the beginning of the violence in BiH, non-ethnic or non-nationalist resolutions were generally deemed to be unrealistic and were thus not attempted. This is despite the realities of the multi-ethnic nature of BiH before the war. The question for most external intervention-ists was not whether to partition the country or separate the conflicting groups but how to accomplish it, given the reality of the mixed population.

As early as 1992, the top EU and UN officials gravitated towards this trend. Principal EU negotiator Lord Carrington chaired the EC conference on Yugosla-via (ECCY), holding numerous talks between 1991 and 1992 on constitutional arrangements on Bosnia. Carrington focused on keeping Yugoslavia together, but proposed solutions that focused on local ethnic rule, advocating ethnic can-tonization. Even before the first outbreak of violence in Bosnia in February 1992, the ECCY, headed by Carrington, adopted the Statement of Principles, which, in subtle diplomatic jargon, promoted ethnic partitioning within BiH. Drafted by Lord Carrington and Portuguese ambassador Jorge Cutileiro, the Statement of Principles for the future New Constitutional Arrangement for Bosnia and Herzegovina was the first peace proposal dealing exclusively with BiH. The first section stated: "Bosnia and Herzegovina would be a state, com-posed of three constituent units, based on national principles and taking into account economic, geographic and other criteria." Despite the mixed nature of BiH, the recommendations made a clear link between territory and ethnic/reli-gious identity. Section E stated that

> a working group will be established in order to define the territory of the con-stituent units based on national principles and taking into account economic, geographical and other criteria. A map based on the national absolute or

relative majority in each municipality will be the basis of work in the working group, and will be subject only to amendments, justified by the above-mentioned criteria.

(Campbell 1998)

A working group made up from local and international actors was set up to draw the partition map. A 1991 census figure was to be the basis for the partition. Using the 1991 census map, which did not account for the mixed cities, or hundreds of thousand mixed marriages, the working group attempted the incredible task of carving up BiH. Even after this proposed ethnic division, "nearly 18 percent of the Muslim population, 50 percent of the Serb population and 60 percent of the Croat population would after partition reside outside the constituent units designed for them" (Campbell 1998, 129). This was the first of many partitioning options that was never to be implemented, but bequeathed extremists inspiration for the ethnic cleansing.

In October 1992, a BiH working group set up by the Steering Committee and co-chaired by Cyrus Vance and David Owen identified five options for the future of BiH. The options ranged from a central state, promoted by the Bosnian government, to ethnic partitioning. In the end, the Steering Committee chose to pursue the option of a decentralized state of three constituent peoples, with most governmental functions to be carried out by ethnic-majority provinces. Though not the most divisive model in term of ethnic separation, it once again promoted divisions along ethnic group lines. According to the agreement, there were to be nine provinces, three for each ethnic group, with Sarajevo under a special multiethnic arrangement. Although Vance and Owen were careful not to label each province as belonging to only one nation, this was how it was interpreted both internationally and locally.

EU mediator David Owen was partial to the ancient hatreds interpretation of the conflict, advocating deterministic proposals of ethnically carving up BiH. In his memoir, *Balkan Odyssey*, Owen justified the policy, describing "a tradition in the Balkans of a readiness to solve disputes by the taking up of arms and acceptance of the forceful or even negotiated movement of people as a consequence of war" (Owen 1997, 3). Clearly influenced by Rebecca's West's personal account of the Balkan history and by Ivo Andric, who fictionalized Bosnia as a "country of fear and loathing," Owen was convinced that the various ethnic groups in BiH did not have the capacity to live together in peace (Andric 1977; West 1941). It was Owen's view that partitioning was the best and only option. In hindsight, the chief EU negotiator Owen felt that the divisions along ethnic lines formulated at Dayton and in previous attempts to solve the conflict did not go far enough.

The unwarranted insistence on ruling out changes to what had been internal administrative boundaries within a sovereign state was a fatal flaw in the attempted peacemaking in Yugoslavia.... Of course the world has to be aware of the dangers of drawings state borders along ethnic lines; but the world also has to recognize the dangers of ignoring ethnic and national voices.

(Owen 1997, 343)

Although the Vance–Owen plan was rejected by the Serb Parliament and vanished as a viable option, its effects were devastating on the ground, as it was used by the extremists to further ethnic cleansing.

> When those maps were first introduced in the negotiation process in March 1992 in Lisbon, Serbian forces started an intensive campaign [to] "cleanse" the territory designated on the map as "theirs". They embarked upon yet another campaign of killing, raping, imprisoning, and expelling all non-Serbs. When those maps were again reintroduced in January 1993, during Vance–Owen negotiations in Geneva, incidents of the same type occurred in areas classified as supposedly Croatian.

(Campbell 1998, 144)

The massive ethnic cleansing and the resulting changes on the ground sparked by the war between the Bosnians and Croats led to discussion on a complete ethnic partition between the three ethnic groups. "The Union of the Three Republics Plan" or the "Owen–Stoltenberg Plan" was agreed on by Serb and Croat leadership and rejected by the Bosniacs. Proposed in September 1993 by EU/UN diplomats, it was a *de jure* partition of BiH. Its nine principles included dividing BiH into a confederation with three constituent people, a tripartite constitutional arrangement with a rotating presidency. It was welcomed by the extremists among the Bosnian Serbs, since the Bosniacs, according to a member of the Bosnian Serb delegation: "are going to be like walnuts in a Serbo-Croat nutcracker" (Silber and Little 1997, 303). Despite the dire situation on the ground, Bosnian President Izetbegovic rejected the plan, asking for international intervention or at least an end to the arms embargo that prevented the Bosnians from having arms. Despite US inaction, Izetbegovic hoped the Americans, who took a harder stance against Serbia, might assist the collapsed and devastated country. The American assistance, as noted in the previous section, did eventually come, but only after a five-year war that devastated the country and its population.

For the most part, the Dayton Peace Agreement, mediated by the Americans, was negotiated between nationalistic extremists who had fought hard to ethnically carve up Bosnia. Neither Serbian President Milosevic, who represented the Bosnian Serbs, nor Croatian President Tudjman, who represented the Bosnian Croats, at Dayton, believed in a functioning Bosnia. Their essential premise rested on the non-recognition of Bosniacs and the inability of Serbs, Croats and "Muslims" to coexist. President Tudjman and President Milosevic also had their own priorities – the return of Eastern Slavonia to Croatia, and the lifting of economic sanctions, respectively – which had nothing to do with a functioning Bosnia. As the nationalistic "ethno-guarantors" for the Bosnian Croats and

Serbs, both pushed for maximum separation and autonomy for their respective groups. Despite being the sole representative of the Bosniacs, the recent victims of attempted genocide, President Izetbegovic brought to Dayton diverse ethnic representatives from Bosnia and pushed forth a vision of an ethnically mixed central state. However, the voices of the moderate Bosnian delegation were not heard.

Regardless of intention, much of the Dayton Agreement was designed on the basis of a primordial and unchanging understanding of group identity. Although the final agreement included annexes on human rights and rights of refugees, the IC delegation at Dayton devoted most of its time to how to carve out the Bosnian territory among the different ethnic groups. Little to no attention was devoted to the functioning of the future state. As NATO refused to take on the role for the consolidation of a single army, negotiating one army for the future state was initially also not on the cards. Finally, much of the territory gained through ethnic cleansing with the use of paramilitaries was to be retained by the warring parties.

The Dayton Agreement was supposed to be built on pillars of political democratization and a functional multinational institutional framework (McMahon 2004). However, the institutional framework designed at Dayton carved BiH from within. The institutions were structured so that the two entities, the Federation and the Serb Republic, held the core of the powers including policing, military, education and the judiciary, while the role of the state was almost symbolic and thus ineffective. Accordingly, the state budget was smaller than that of the two entities, and even more than ten times smaller than some of the Cantons in the BiH Federation (Belloni and Deane 2005). At the top was a three-headed rotating Presidency. The three Presidents, each representing a separate ethnic group, were to be elected directly by their own ethnic group; the Bosniac and Croat representatives were elected within the Federation, while the Bosnian Serb was elected in the Serb Republic. The Presidency was designed to function on the basis of a consensus, with each having the right to block decisions by invoking "the vital interest" of his/her ethnic group, making the top leadership completely ineffective.

As noted by Patrice McMahon, the problem in Bosnia is not only linked to the implementation of international strategies but also to strategy design. Whereas the implementations "impede the Western mission in Bosnia, the problems of design are different because they undermine the very goals of the nation building endeavor" (McMahon 2004, 571). Thus, we return to the catch-22 described in the beginning of the chapter, where the desired outcome is impossible to attain because of the rules drawn up within the peace agreement. At times referred to as the "Frankenstein constitution," the Dayton Peace Agreement, imposed by the IC, created a complex political structure,

> composed of one state, two entities, three peoples, 4 million citizens, five layers of governance led by 14 prime ministers and governments, making Bosnia the state with the highest number of presidents, prime ministers and ministers in the whole world. Even a cursory overview of the institutions

created by the Bosnian constitution confirms the judgment that this is a Frankenstein constitution.

(Belloni and Deane 2005, 231)

It is unsurprising that a country with three presidents, 14 prime ministers and some 140 different ministries had trouble functioning as a state. One only has to consider the amount of funding required to run and coordinate between the ministries. What was more troubling is that majority of the ministries were tied to a specific ethnic group.

The concern with Dayton is not only the complex and overburdened institutional arrangement but the inherently contradictory nature of the agreement and its constitutions. The state constitution designed at Dayton recognized three "constituent peoples": Bosniac, Croat and Serb. However, the Federation Constitution recognized only Bosniacs and Croats as "constituent peoples" and the Serb Republic constitution referred to the "alienable right of the Serb people to self-determination." As noted by Belloni and Deane, "These clauses in the entity constitution create the basis for discrimination against the Bosnian Serbs in the Federation and Bosniaks and Bosnian Croats in the RS" (Belloni and Deane 2005). In essence, the constitutional arrangement translated into discrimination against the minorities within both the Federation and the RS. "In RS, Serbs enjoyed full citizenship, while Bosniaks and Croats were relegated to second-class status. Similarly Bosniaks and Croats were perceived as nations in "their" part of Bosnia, while Serbs were reduced to national minority status" (Guzina 2007, 224). None of the constitutions allowed for the basic individual right not to belong to a specific group or to attain membership of multiple groups. Despite some progress, minorities continue to face discrimination on many levels, including access to housing assistance, employment, health care and pensions. Identity politics were institutionalized in such a fashion that rights of groups overtook the rights of individuals. According to Guzina, "despite all of the constitutional references to the full recognition of human rights, a 'citizen' emerges in a residual category that is of less significance than the national group to which such a person belongs" (Guzina 2007, 226).

The Dayton Agreement imposed an equality of status strategy for managing the different groups. The state promoted an even-handed recognition of various ethno-religious groups. The Agreement allowed the three recognized groups to set up their own schools, curriculum and religious education. The agreement institutionalized a separation between the groups, giving little space for integration of individuals from non-majority groups. The Dayton Agreement institutionalized and formulized an ethnocracy. In effect, the institutional framework discriminates against non-national minorities in BiH. Designed to appease the most nationalistic element from each group, the ethnocratic institutional framework is the most exclusive form of accommodation. The exclusive framework affects minority returns and the general tolerance of other groups. This, of course, is particularly troubling for those of mixed backgrounds.

To make matters worse, ethnic cleansing did not end with the Dayton Agreement. Following signing of the peace agreement, and under the watchful eye of

NATO, UN, OSCE and other international organizations in BiH, more than 100,000 Serbs were ethnically cleansed in 1996. The cleansing was orchestrated by nationalist Serb politicians, who used threats and promises to remove ethnic Serbs from Sarajevo. As noted by Holbrooke, who was highly critical of the expulsion,

> Bosnian Serbs forced tens of thousands of Serbs who had lived in Sarajevo, many of them for centuries, to leave and burn their houses, thereby effect-ively segregating the city and snatching from their own defeat a partition of the city on ethnic grounds. Now, NATO forces stood by. The NATO com-mander and American admiral refused to take the fire trucks out of the bar-racks. He refused to do anything to stop the burning until the very last minute, when he did [it was] too little too late.... And I think there is no excuse for it.[10]

Holbrooke attributes the inaction to the initial narrow mandate of NATO. However, the problem goes deeper, as the international community was fully in charge with strong political directives and 60,000 soldiers on the ground and felt it unnecessary to prevent the expulsion of Serbs from the last places where the population was still mixed.

The design of the election rules and the actual running of elections was another troubling spot for the international community. At Dayton, there existed deep divisions over the future voting rights for all BiH citizens, including refugees displaced by the war. Milosevic insisted that voters must be physically present to be registered to vote, while the Bosnians wanted the voters registered where they lived in 1991. As a negotiated compromise, the US suggested that the voters themselves would be able to determine where their votes would be applied.[11] In the end, voters could choose between having their ballots counted where they used to live prior to the war, where they lived at the time of elections or where they planned to live in the future. This flexibility gave a free hand to extremists, who not only changed registrars but handed out rewards to those casting votes in strategic areas that could be taken over with a ballot rather than a gun. To make matters worse, at Dayton, the OSCE (Organization for Security and Cooperation in Europe) was given the role of running the elections. This was the first time the OSCE ever ran elections, and it was given the task not due to its expertise but because it was agreed by the Americans and Europeans that the organization would be strengthened as a result of the experience.

The end result was that the first elections following the war were disastrous and have had consequential impacts until today. First, the voter turnout was a little too good, far exceeding 100 percent of eligible voters (ICG 1996). Second, the election rules discriminated against politicians and political parties that did not belong to one ethnic group. Third, not enough time and negligible support was given to non-nationalist politicians, and the elections helped to entrench the nationalist politicians who were in charge during the war. Thus, the first election gave legitimacy to many wartime warlords and criminals who had profited from the war and retained the necessary connections and influence on the ground to garner votes. Support was thus channeled through existing government structures into the hands of nationalist politicians, and moderate politicians were not given an opportunity to develop a constituency. The long-term effect has been felt not only politically but also economically. As noted by McMahon, "the unintended result of the West rushed apolitical approach to political and economic development was that the moderated politicians were not given an opportunity to develop a constituency and nationalist politicians gained even more control over scarce jobs and housing" (McMahon 2004). OSCE never took the fall for the badly run elections and, when their own official spokesperson admitted problems and spoke about some of their irregularities, he was fired.[12] Still, the OSCE tried to learn from its experience and future elections it ran were an improvement over the first one.

Another area of disappointment has been with regards to minority returns. Guaranteed by Annex 7 of the Dayton Agreement, minority returns were supposed to be the means for restoring multi-ethnicity in BiH. So far, from more than a million returnees, less than half (467,000), returned to their original homes to live as minorities. Many minorities only returned officially to repossess their homes. Although around 90 percent of the people repossessed their former homes, most chose to sell or exchange them for homes where they would become part of the national majority. Mixed families were one of the least likely groups to return to BiH. This was first, because many mixed families may not have perceived the present divisive makeup in BiH as welcoming. Second, countries including Canada, and several European countries, granted mixed families from Bosnia legal status of permanent residency. The prioritization of mixed couples over non-mixed couples was made on humanitarian grounds, as UNHCR considered families from mixed ethnic groups or mixed marriages a category of people under risk of return.

The institutional framework became a hindrance to minority return, which in turn has been a major hurdle for a multinational BiH and the transformation of conflicting group identities. How much of this can be blamed on endogenous versus exogenous factors is up for discussion. However, regardless of intention and the billions of dollars invested, the IC has contributed little to group transformation. The so called "Bonn powers," such as the power to remove troublesome political leaders from office, were given to the main international implementing agency, the Office of the High Representative (OHR), to help bypass or eliminate nationalist and uncooperative policies. Ever since, OHR has operated in a quandary over whether to use the powers to impose necessary policies or actions, which may also result in a lack of local ownership and responsibility. Common identity symbols, such as a country's anthem, a common flag, one currency, a single license plate, have been helpful in having symbols of a state and freedom of movement within a state, but have all been imposed due to vetoes by group representatives. Fundamental structural and institutional changes, however, have been hindered by the Dayton Agreement.

Still, much of the population, though for the most part divided ethnically, does not see alternatives to a common state. Although partitioning is still an option advocated by certain nationalist leaders, the population is anxious about such an option, fearing it could result in another round of violence. The 2007 UNDP Survey conducted by Oxford Research International found that the majorities within each of BiH's communities favor reform of the state "based on building a common identity of Bosnia and Herzegovina" (ORI 2007). According to the survey, only a minority within each community favors options based on exclusive identities and the de facto break up of the country.

There is some local political demand for constitutional change leading to a more functioning state. The need for institutional change has been raised by some politicians and resisted by others. In 2000, Haris Silajdzic, while serving as a co-chair of BiH's Council of Ministers, published a "memorandum on change." This memorandum argued for the reconstruction of Dayton and the need to eliminate nationally exclusive political options and stressed that it is "essential to urgently and radically reconstruct those elements which are non-integrative, ineffective and even partly counterproductive" (ICG 2003).

Despite the recent war and the institutionally divisive framework that continues to divide BiH, the majority of the population do not define themselves by their exclusive identities. The majority of the Bosnian population or about 75 percent of Serbs, Croats and Bosniacs, identify themselves as a member of their own group and as citizen of BiH. Only 14 percent of the population of BiH identify themselves exclusively as part of an ethno-religious group. This number is the highest among Serbs, where about 38 percent of the population identifies itself exclusively by its ethnic group. In the case of the Bosniacs, less than 1 percent identifies itself exclusively with their ethno-religious group, while about 4 percent of the Croat Bosnian population identifies themselves primarily by their exclusive identities. Dual or multiple group identities, however, do not tend to pose a threat to national cohesion. It is only when identities are exclusive that minorities are more likely to favor separatism and might constitute a threat to state cohesion (ORI 2007, 19).

Funding and membership of the EU has become the most significant carrot in the process of becoming a more effective state. Only sovereign and self-sustaining states can become members of the EU and the majority of the population in BiH wishes to join the EU. Since the focus of most of the population has been on employment, economic development and general well-being, external investment is a large priority. However, without significant transformation of the institutions designed as part of the Dayton Agreement, the country is likely to continue to be ineffective and divided. Groups homogenized within the new constitutions offered little space for mixed, multiple or overlapping identities. Most of the local and international programs targeted a specific group, and very little effort has been put on bridging the deep divides. Thus, group transformation from the hostile mode during the war has not been significant.

With no deep reconciliation or common institutions, including common education, media, the judiciary and the police, the hostile relationship between the three groups simply moved to a less violent sphere, without any significant transformation. As noted by the International Crisis Group report, "The trouble was that the starting point (partition) was so uncompromising, the tools (the Bonn Powers) so blunt, the helpers (the international community) so fractious, the locals (the three constituent peoples) so divided, and the destination so obscure" (ICG 2003, 41). The institutional framework entrenched ethnic separation and hampered transformation. As described by David Campbell, "the process that culminated in the Dayton Agreement, which supposedly disavows partition in favor of unity, in actuality fostered partition albeit in the name of 'multi ethnicity'" (Campbell 1998, 116). Regardless of intention, the accommodative group strategies drawn up in the Dayton Peace Agreement have failed to contribute to the building of bridges between the conflicting groups.

Conclusion

A key missing element that was required to end the war swiftly was united international intervention. At the beginning of the conflict, the IC was divided on not only whether to intervene but also how and who was to be blamed for the conflict. The key European interveners took a neutral stance, buying in to the argument of ancient ethnic hatreds. On the other hand, the US leadership tended to take a more partisan approach, placing the bulk of the blame on Serbia, and was the first to jump towards advocating (though not participating in) a partisan intervention. Different interpretations of the conflict created an ineffective strategy in which peace agreements were never implemented and Americans blamed Europeans for lack of action, and Europeans blamed Americans for unhelpful and unconstructive meddling. The neutral/partisan–divided intervention had little positive impact on the parties and their behavior. It took a united–partisan intervention to pressure President Milosevic into compliance and rein in the Bosnian Serbs. It also took a united intervention process to pressure Croats and Bosniacs into a solid military and political alliance.

Although the united–partisan intervention forcibly ended the violent aspects of the conflict, international strategies institutionalized a divisive framework that contributed to freezing the hostile relations between the groups. International identity strategies as imposed on the parties at Dayton were constructed on the basis of separation rather than integration. Identity interpretations resulted in assumptions that the three warring groups needed to be separate, which led to a framework that enhanced divisions and formulated group rights on the basis of exclusion. The nexus between identity and territory was ingrained into the Dayton Agreement and divisions along ethnic lines were consolidated. The Dayton Agreement allowed for soft partitioning along ethnic lines and created several constitutions that contradicted each other and ingrained group divisions. Somehow, the pre-war Bosnia, with a high degree of coexistence and the highest rate of mixed marriages in the region was forgotten.

The implementation of the Dayton Agreement highlights the importance of the creation of flexible institutional arrangements that promote rather than hinder identity transformation. It is only natural that, in the midst of a violent conflict, groups having no trust in the others will push to create separate institutions.

However, in the case of Bosnia, there were moderate voices including among top politicians, but their voices were muzzled in favor of the extremists who promoted ethnic separation. This was intensified by the nexus between land and group identity promoted by prominent international interventionists and local extreme nationalists. Both the IC and the extreme nationalists operated under the assumptions that groups were unable to live together and therefore the best solution revolved along ethnic territorial separation. Ethnic divisions were ingrained into the institutions, which were not only dysfunctional and ineffective but also exclusive, solidifying differences between groups. Thus, a key lesson from Bosnia is that institutions, particularly when created or imposed during a conflict, should be flexible, promoting rather than hindering the potential of transformation of group relationships. It is tragically ironic that, despite positive intentions, the international strategies resulted in a hardening of divisions and that the Dayton Agreement, which was imposed on the parties by the IC, has in effect become one of the largest barriers towards positive group transformation.

Notes

1 International Tribunal for the Former Yugoslavia, the Prosecutor of the Tribunal against Zeljko Raznjatovic. www.un.org/icty/indictment/english/ark-ii970930e.htm
2 United Nations Security Council, Special Forces S/1994/674/Add.2 (Vol. I) December 28, 1994.
3 David Binder, "Conversations/Herbert S. Okun; What Comes After Containment? It May Be Son of Containment," *New York Times*, July 11, 1993.
4 General Sewall visit to Paris US document, PTQ9406, E142, Declassified August 2005, p. 6 http://intelfiles.egoplex.com/bosnia-train-equip/.
5 General Sewall visit to Paris August 1996, Unclassified US document, PTQ9406, E142, Declassified August 2005, http://intelfiles.egoplex.com/bosnia-train-equip/.
6 Declassified Document, PTQ7584, E110, July 1996, p. 2 PTQ7584, E110.
7 Declassified Document, PTQ7584, E110, July 1996, p. 3 PTQ7584, E110.
8 Ibid., p. 233.
9 Mokhiber and Rick Young, "Nation Building in Bosnia" Frontline Documentary Give War a Chance, www.pbs.org/wgbh/pages/frontline/shows/military/etc/peace.html.
10 Interview with Elizabeth Farnsworth, Online Focus, PBS. May 19, 1998. www.pbs.org/newshour/bb/bosnia/jan-june98/holbrooke_5–19.html.
11 Unclassified Document, PTQ7584, E110, July 1996, PTQ7584, E110.
12 The author was an election monitor for the first three elections, including the first one in 1996, and personally witnessed many irregularities.

References

Andric, Ivo. 1977. *Bridge over Drina*. Chicago: University of Chicago Press.
Banac, Ivo. 1993. "Bosnian Muslims: From Religious Community to Socialist Nationhood and Postcommunist Statehood, 1918–1992." In *The Muslims of Bosnia-Herzegovina, their Historic Development from the Middle Ages to the Dissolution of Yugoslavia*, ed. Mark Pinson. Cambridge MA: Harvard University Press.
Belloni, Roberto and Shelley Deane. 2005. From Belfast to Bosnia: Piecemeal Peacemaking and the Role of Institutional Learning. *Civil Wars* 7 (3): 219–243.

Bennett, Christopher. 2012. *Bosnian Paralyzed Peace*. New York: Columbia University Press.

Bildt, Carl. 1999. *Peace Journey; the Struggle for Peace in Bosnia*. London: Weidenfeld and Nicolson.

Campbell, David. 1998. *National Deconstruction: Violence, Identity, and Justice in Bosnia*. Minneapolis MI: University of Minnesota Press.

Census. 1991. *Ethnic Composition of Bosnia-Herzegovina Population, by Municipalities and Settlements*. Sarajevo: Zavod za statistiku Bosne i Hercegovine.

Chollet, Derek and Bennett Freeman. 2005. *The Secret History of Dayton, US Diplomacy and the Bosnia Peace Process 1995*. Washington: National Security Archive. www. gwu.edu/~nsarchiv/NSAEBB/NSAEBB171/index.htm%3E.

Cigar, Norman. 2000. *Genocide in Bosnia: the Policy of "Ethnic Cleansing."* College Station TX: Texas A & M University Press.

Coles, Kimberley. 2007. "Ambivalent Builders: Europeanization, the Production of Difference, and Internationals in Bosnia-Herzegovina." In *The New Bosnian Bosaic: Identities, Memories and Moral Claims in a Post-War Society*, eds. Xavier Bougarel, Elissa Helms and Ger Dujizing. Hampshire, UK: Ashgate Publishing Limited.

Curran, Daniel, James Sebernius and Michael Watkins. 2004. Case Analysis: Two Paths to Peace, Contrasting George Mitchell in Northern Ireland with Richard Holbrooke in Bosnia. *Negotiation Journal* 20 (4): 513–537.

Fine, John V. A. 1993. "Medieval and Ottoman Roots of Modern Bosnian Society." In *The Muslims of Bosnia-Herzegovina*, ed. Mark Pinson. Cambridge MA: Harvard University Press.

Galbraith, Peter W. 2002. "Turning Points: Key Decisions in Making Peace in Bosnia-Herzegovina and Croatia." In *Islam and Bosnia, Conflict Resolution and Foreign Policy in Multi Ethnic States*, ed. Maya Shatzmiller. Montreal: McGill Queen's University Press.

Gibbs, David N. 2009. *First Do No Harm: Humanitarian Intervention and the Destruction of Yugoslavia*. Nashville TN: Vanderbilt University Press.

Goldstein, Joshua S. and Jon C. Pevehouse. 1997. Reciprocity, Bullying and International Cooperation: Time-series Analysis of the Bosnian Conflict. *The American Political Science Review* 91 (3): 515–559.

Guzina, Dejan. 2007. Dilemmas of Nation-building and Citizenship in Dayton Bosnia. *National Identities* 9 (3): 217–234.

Holbrooke, Richard. 1998. *To End a War*. New York: Random House.

ICG. 2003. *Bosnia's Nationalist Governments: Paddy Ashdown and the Paradoxes of State Building*. International Crisis Group Balkans Report. 146.

ICG, International Crisis Group. 1996. *ICG Bosnia Report 16*.

Juncos, Ana E. 2005. The EU's Post-Conflict Intervention in Bosnia and Herzegovina: (re) Integrating the Bakans and/or (re)Inventing the EU? *Southeast European Politics* VI (2): 88–108.

Kauffman, Chaim D. 1996. Possible and Impossible Solutions to Ethnic Conflict. *International Security* 20 (4): 136–175.

Lake, Anthony. 2006. Between War and Peace, How to Manage Threats to Global Security. *Harvard International Review* 25 (Winter): 177–196.

LeBor, Adam. 2004. *Milosevic, A Bibliography*. New Haven CT: Yale University Press.

Little, Alan and Laura Silber. 1996. *The Death of Yugoslavia*. Penguin Books.

Malcolm, Noel. 1994. *A Short History of Bosnia*. London: Macmillan.

McMahon, Patrice C. 2004. Rebuilding Bosnia: A model to Emulate or to Avoid? *Political Science Quarterly* 119 (4): 569–593.

Mueller, John. 2000. The Banality of Ethnic War. *International Security* 25 (1): 42–70.

ORI. 2007. *Bosnia and Herzegovina. Executive Summary of Main Findings and Key Policy Recommendations.* Oxford Research International for UNDP.

Owen, David. 1997. *Balkan Odyssey.* New York: Mariner Books.

Rieff, David. 1995. *Slaughterhouse, Bosnia and the Failure of the West.* New York: Simon & Schuster.

Silber, Laura and Allan Little. 1997. *Yugoslavia: Death of a Nation.* London: Penguin Books.

Stewart, Rory and Gerald Knaus. 2011. *Can Intervention Work?*: New York: W. W. Norton and Company.

UNSC. 1994. *Special Forces: Final Report of the United Nations Commission of Experts.* United Nations Security Council S/1994/647/Add2.

Watch, Helsinki. 1993. *War Crimes In Bosnia.* New York: Helsinki Watch.

West, Rebecca. 1941. *Black Lamb and Gray Falcon: A Journey through Yugoslavia.* Edinburgh: Canongate.

Woodward, Susan L. 1995. *The Balkan Tragedy: Chaos and Dissolution After the Cold War.* Washington DC: Brookings Institution Press.

Zimmermann, Warren. 1999. *Origins of a Catastrophe: Yugoslavia and Its Destroyers.* New York: Three Rivers Press.

5 Northern Ireland

The beginning of the end of the "Troubles"

Among the case studies examined in the research, the 1990s intervention in Northern Ireland was the most united in its process and most effective in its strategies contributing to group transformation. During the mid to late 1990s, British, Irish and American intervention processes took an increasingly united–neutral approach that had a transformative impact on the conflict and on the identities of the conflicting groups. The resulting Good Friday Agreement (henceforth GFA) set up local and regional institutions that promoted overlapping identities through different layers of representations. Great Britain, the Republic of Ireland, the EU and the United States have all contributed significantly towards making violent conflict in Northern Ireland today simply unacceptable. Although, for the time being, the political dynamics within Northern Ireland remain a challenge, Northern Ireland and its context have changed and the remaining hardliners have had little choice but to gradually adapt to the new reality.

Many of these transformations resulted from the shifting of international and regional process and strategies. Intertwined within the conflict, Great Britain and the Republic of Ireland engaged both as internal and external players.[1] As such, they assumed crucial roles in transforming their positions and, subsequently, the conflict itself. Until the 1990s, the British and Irish intervention process remained partisan and divided, as the two powerful "ethno-guarantors" played a fundamental role in supporting their respective sides. Since the beginning of the troubles, Britain and Ireland made some small principled diplomatic strides towards a united stance; however, these did not bear much fruit. Various attempts at arrangements for internal and consociational power sharing collapsed in favor of the default British rule.

The resulting GFA undertook more liberal and flexible strategies to deal with group identities. Focusing on rights for all groups and local consociational power sharing, the agreement took into account the future identity transformations of people living in Northern Ireland. The agreement also encouraged supra- and multi-layered identities through flexible, multiple representation. These included Northern Ireland political representation linked to Britain, the Republic of Ireland and an accommodative framework within Northern Ireland. Although the internal framework for Northern Ireland remained consociational and, at times, froze relations between the groups, the GFA offered a mixture of affirmative and transformative policies encouraging overlapping identities. The GFA's flexibility with regards to identity issues created an open door towards identity transformation and became arguably one of the contributing factors that made Northern Ireland the most successful of the cases analyzed in this book.

Although Northern Ireland has not become completely free from violence and group transformations have only begun, the level of violence has dropped substantially and transformations have become evident. The 2007 power-sharing agreement between Sinn Fein and the Democratic Unionist Party would have been unthinkable and unworkable without the GFA. Britain and the Republic of Ireland have sustained a constructive and active role in bridging differences, contributing to the transformation rather than to the escalation of the conflict. The US has remained engaged, when necessary playing a mediating role between London and Dublin. After providing a brief historical background of the Northern Ireland conflict, this chapter will examine the shifting of external process and strategies that led to the beginning of transformations in Northern Ireland.

Background to the Northern Ireland conflict

Northern Ireland was born in a state of violence, division and dually constructed antagonistic narratives. The history of the conflict and its interpretations is dependent on the narrative. A Nationalist Irish view describes the conflict as the 800-year "brutal English oppression that has brought nothing but trouble to Ireland" (Dixon 2008). In an opposing narrative, hardline Unionists have broadly described their actions as "using constitutional means to defend themselves against violent Irish Nationalists" (Dixon 2008). Northern Ireland came to be as a result of the Irish War of Independence. In 1916, the Irish parliament declared independence and began a campaign to oust British rule, resulting in the War of Independence. In 1920, the British Parliament partitioned Ireland into the North and the South. In the South, the partitioning sparked a civil war, eventually resulting in the establishment of the Republic of Ireland. In the North, the British established rule from London, a "home rule" that in the eyes of many discriminated against the Catholic population and eventually sparked the violent "troubles." Hardline Unionists, or those who favored integration with the British union, exploited the threat from the IRA to justify discrimination and violence against the Nationalists. Nationalists, or those who traditionally supported a united Ireland, used the political and economic discrimination against the Catholic population to justify revolt and Republican violence.

Depending on the focus of analysis and its interpretation, the conflict in Northern Ireland has been portrayed academically as a sectarian conflict stemming from ethnic and religious divides, an economic/political dispute linked to unjust economic and political practices, or a territorial dispute between Britain and the Republic of Ireland (Clayton 1998; McGarry and O'Leary 1995). Most commonly, the conflict has been constructed as a sectarian or an ethnic conflict that marked the divide between the Protestant (British) and the Catholic (Irish) populations (Bruce 1986; Stringer and Robinson 1991). The majority of the sectarian interpretations have understood identity to be salient and permanent, and regarded religion as the ultimate dividing line between the groups. The interpretation of the root causes of the conflict has been directly related to the type of external processes and strategies. This background draws attention to the differing narratives and interpretations of the conflict as constructed and disputed by the diverse leaderships and among academia.

Although often categorized as a sectarian struggle, the conflict in Northern Ireland can better be understood as a dispute over two contested national identities: unionism versus nationalism (McGarry 2001; McGarry and O'Leary 1995). The Unionists (mostly Protestants) prefer Northern Ireland to remain in Britain while the Nationalists and the Republicans (mainly Catholics) wish Northern Ireland to be linked to the Republic of Ireland. As noted by numerous surveys, important differences also exist within and between "British" unionism and "Irish" Nationalism. Among those who see themselves as British, a notable minority do not describe themselves as Unionists. Not all Catholics identify themselves as Nationalists and claim territorial identity with the rest of Ireland (Hayes and McAllister 1999). Also, not all Protestants perceive themselves as British or adopt a Unionist label. A sectarian or religious struggle depiction also does not give space to the shifting of meaning or ethnic salience.

Despite popular myths reproduced on public murals and public displays during the marching season, identity group divisions have never been completely clear cut historically. The 1798 attempt to oust the British from Ireland was not only supported by some Presbyterians but was actually dominated by the Presbyterian United Irishmen (Clayton 1998). In the early twentieth century, sectarianism referred to disputes between the Church of Ireland and the Irish Presbyterian Church. This is not to say that the Irish and the British have not been involved in historical sectarian violence which has been the making of modern myths and has permeated the public mentality. However, the circumstances were far from static and the relations between and among groups were constantly in flux. For instance, the conditions for the Irish Catholics had changed significantly from the seventeenth century, when penal laws forbade them from carrying weapons, to the eighteenth century, when they were well armed and disproportionally involved in running the British Empire (McVeigh and Ralston 2007, 6).

Early British discrimination, economic exploitation and dire circumstances for the Catholic population including the great famine, however, all added to past grievances and became a rallying point for the Nationalist cause. In the seventeenth and early eighteenth centuries, Irish Catholics had been prohibited by penal laws from owning land, voting, holding political office and obtaining an education (Hickey 2007). Absentee landlord policies contributed to the Irish potato famine (1845 to 1852) when approximately a million people died and another million emigrated to North America. As noted by historians, the great famine was one of the most traumatic experiences endured by the Irish (Larkin

1998). Myths surrounding the famine, including accusations of attempted genocide, have been the subject of grievance and mobilization. As noted by Larkin,

> At home and abroad, generations of Irishmen have predicated a good many
> of their attitudes and actions on the assumption that, during the period of the
> Great Famine, England plotted and very nearly succeeded in the destruction
> of the Irish people.
>
> (Larkin 1998, 63)

Although the charges of genocide, forced emigration and attempts to destroy
Irish culture have been proven false by modern historians since the 1950s, they
have been prominent in the shaping of Irish identity and played a significant role
in justifying the modern conflict in North Ireland (Larkin 1998).

The focus on past events and their interpretations have become part of the
battle ground during the recent conflict. Historical atrocities committed by the
"other," such as the 1641 Massacre of Protestants at Portadown, the Potato
Famine of 1845, or the Easter Rising of 1916, became the subject of mass-
produced dramatic images. Public commemorations, such as marches through
opposing neighborhoods, have been used to inflame passions. The marches or
parading was considered to be an assertion of a group's control over a particular
area and thus often led to violence. Modern leadership evoked the revival of past
myths and promoted a vision of a separate future, constructing new narratives.
Arthur Griffith, the founder of Sinn Fein, maintained that the English government deliberately used "the pretext of the failure of the potato crop to reduce the
Celtic population by famine and exile" (Larkin 1998, 62). The bitterness over
the famine was also fierce among the Irish exiles in North America and became
a rallying point of anti-British sentiment. The myth evoked by the famine "maintained that British rule was not only immoral in its origins, but irresponsible as
well as impractical in its effects" (Larkin 1998, 63).

Ethnic and religious rifts have frequently been outlined in academic literature
as the foremost cause of the conflict (Clayton 1998). A proponent of the religious fault line, Steve Bruce noted that "religious division is the cause of the
conflict: Catholicism and Protestantism are essentially oppositional in nature and
if native and settler had shared the same religion, marriage would have eroded
the ethnic boundaries" (Clayton 1998, 41). Although some of the hardline
leaders, such as Ian Paisley, the former leader of the Democratic Unionist Party,
are fervently religious, differences in religion are not the cause of the violence.
McGarry and O'Leary demonstrate that cultural and religious differences that
commonly define the content of the ethnic divide are not linked to communal
violence. There is greater violence in the cities where people are more secular,
than in the villages where they tend to be more religious (McGarry and O'Leary
1995). Violence has for the most part not been directed against religious icons
such as priests and clergy. There has also been significant inter-church
cooperation during the height of the violence. Finally, the lack of correlation
between religion and violence is also noted by surveys, in which the respondents

living in Northern Ireland attribute the causes of the conflict to political disputes rather than cultural or religious differences (Hayes and McAllister 1999). Although clashes have been exacerbated by different cultural and religious preferences, the cultural and religious divide is not the cause of the conflict. The focus on a religious and ethnic divide has often come at the expense of the economic and colonial explanations that offer a deeper insight into the conflict.

The importance of the colonial dimension of the conflict in Northern Ireland has been highlighted by several academics. Among them, David Miller noted the colonial aspect to be a fundamental part of the conflict "ignored by majority of academics writing on Northern Ireland" (Miller 1998, 36). Nationalists and Republicans have frequently depicted Northern Ireland as a colony that has never been a candidate for integration into the British nation (McGarry and O'Leary 1995). As noted by McGarry and O'Leary, the Unionists rejected this interpretation, "depicting Northern Ireland as a victim of irredentism and external aggression" (McGarry and O'Leary 1995, 314). The colonial interpretation has steered the international community towards a more sympathetic ear to the Nationalist cause. According to Adrian Guelke, much of the international community accepted the colonialist narrative, which is why traditionally Nationalists enjoyed greater international backing (Guelke 1996). With the exception of financial support from some Irish Nationalists living in the US, this backing has been more in principle than in practice.

Economic divisions, some of which cut across religious lines, have been evident. Indeed, it is difficult to fully comprehend the conflict in Northern Ireland without examining the policies of economic discrimination leading up to the present. The policies of colonization differed in Northern Ireland from other parts of the Island where colonizers were integrated into the life of the Irish population. As Mari Fitzduff explained,

> it had been a deliberate tactic of the 17th and 18th plantation owners in the Northern part of the Island to ensure the communities developed independently from each other in order to maintain the dominance of the unionist planters over the indigenous Irish.
>
> (Fitzduff 2001, 256)

Segregationists and extreme groups operating within their own societies have contributed to solidifying group identities. Extreme Unionist and Republican groups played a powerful role in mobilizing and radicalizing the population. The Orange Order was born in 1795 following a violent confrontation between the "Protestant" Peep O' Day Boys and the "Catholic" Defenders. Although its membership did not go beyond 100,000 men, this secretive order played a central role in politics, organizing marches, and promoting a distinctive segregated British identity on the Island (McAuley and Tonge 2007, 36). The currently leading Ulster Unionist Party developed out of a meeting of the Orange Order in 1905, and it has continued to give UUP support. Between 1921 and 1972, all six Northern Ireland Prime Ministers were leading members both in the Unionist

Party and in the Orange Order (McAuley and Tonge 2007). Although the power and the prestige of the Orange Order have declined, it continues to play a role in pushing a hard-line sectarian agenda. Many prominent Unionist politicians, such as David Trimble, prominent Northern Ireland politician and former leader of the Ulster Unionist Party, maintain their membership of the Orange Order.

The Irish Republican Army (IRA), a self-declared Irish Army, became the focal point for the radical Republican cause. Between 1919 and 1921, the IRA fought a guerilla war against British soldiers and offered protection to the Catholic population, facing reprisals from violent Unionists. In a compromise solution that satisfied no one, the British Parliament passed the "Government of the Ireland Act" that partitioned Ireland into North and South. Irish Nationalists and the IRA, however, did not accept the legitimacy of the partition. In the South, the partitioning sparked a civil war. After years of violence, the 26 counties of the South became the Republic of Ireland. Home rule was established by the British in the six counties of the North with Protestant majorities, and was likewise rejected by the Irish Nationalists.

Political and economic discrimination against the Irish population in Northern Ireland between 1921 and 1969 has been the subject of much debate and is perceived by many as one of the contributing factors to grievance and violence. Discrimination in housing, often due to the prejudices of local representatives against the Catholic population, was a significant area of grievance (Whyte 1983). The Irish in Northern Ireland also pointed to biased voting systems, unrepresentative policing and discrimination in education and the workplace (McAuley and Tonge 2007). The discrimination was apparent in the cultural sphere as well. The Irish language was banned from radio and television in Northern Ireland until 1981, and the use of Irish street signs was forbidden until 1992. Top Northern Ireland politicians did not improve the situation. Sir James Craig, the first Prime Minister (1921–40) in Northern Ireland, made little attempt to reach out to Catholics and proudly professed to have constructed a "Protestant parliament for a Protestant people" (McGarry 2001, 113).

The violent protests known as the "Troubles" began in the 1960s in parallel with other civil rights movements that attempted to address situations of inequality and exclusion. The IRA was invigorated during the Troubles. Previously, the Communist stance adopted by the IRA during the 1950s had dampened its local popularity. A new leadership disposed of the old Communist leaders and the IRA's backing of the civil rights protesters dramatically increased its popularity and legitimacy. "The IRA garnered legitimacy as the army of the "people," representing the martial prowess of the Irish nation for a substantial section of the Ulster Catholic community" (Mulholland 2002, 72). However, the focus on grievances dissipated as the Troubles began a cycle of violence.

Internationally, the Troubles shed light on the discrimination felt by the Nationalist community in Northern Ireland and drew the involvement of Irish Americans. In a 1980 census, around 40 million Americans, or 18 percent, claimed some Irish heritage. Although only a small proportion supported the

Republican cause, Irish Nationalists have always looked to America for support of their cause. The Troubles prompted the formation of a number of American expatriate organizations, including Irish Northern Aid (or NORAID), the Irish National Caucus (INC) and the Friends of Ireland (Guelke 1996). NORAID was closely tied to the Provisional IRA and collected considerable sums for the Republican cause. In a 1982 famous defense case of Irish Americans charged with smuggling weapons to the Provisional IRA, the accused claimed that arms shipments to the Provisional IRA had been sanctioned by the Central Intelligence Agency "because of fears that the Provisional IRA might otherwise turn to the Soviet Union for support" (Guelke 1996, 524). All charges were subsequently dropped.

From 1969 to 2010, more than 3,500 people were killed, the majority of whom were civilians (Cain 2011). Violence in Northern Ireland was perpetuated by three groups: the Irish Republican/Nationalist paramilitary organizations (primarily the Provisional Irish Republican Army); Protestant/Loyalist paramilitary organizations; and the British security (White 1993b). The Republican paramilitaries were responsible for the greatest number of deaths, followed by the Loyalist Paramilitaries and the British security forces. Catholic areas were treated as the strongholds of the IRA, and, in an attempt to root out extremists, British forces exerted brutal repression. The levels of violence dropped significantly in 1994 from the heights of the 1970s, with a brief resurgence in 1998.

The cycle of violence, combined with economic and cultural discrimination, hardened the divisions within the society. An analysis of the census results of 1971, 1981 and 1991 suggests that the violent conflict was accompanied by deepening physical segregation of the society (Hayward 2006). Connected to the violence were also shifts of in-group identification. In 1968, before the period of sustained violence, 39 percent of the Protestant respondents categorized themselves as British, 32 percent saw themselves as having an Ulster identity and 20 percent described themselves as Irish. A decade later, two-thirds of Protestants saw themselves as British, one-fifth chose the Ulster identity, and only 8 percent chose to categorize themselves as Irish (Muldoon et al. 2007, 90). Although the differences among Irish national populations were far less pronounced, these shifted as well.

The deepened polarization and segregation among the population contributed to alienation from the dominant political culture in Northern Ireland. Research into communities in Northern Ireland undertaken in 1966 by Robin Jenkins and John MacRay found that the higher the level of polarization, the less the two sides engaged in contact with each other or participated in a democratic process.

> For example, the more polarization there was in any particular town the greater was the prejudice held by both groups, the more likely it was that the Catholic population would abstain from voting and the fewer would be the number of contacts between the two communities.
>
> (Elliot and Hickie 1971, 80)

The shifts in polarization and hostility in Northern Ireland were influenced by external elements, particularly from Britain, Ireland and the US. This external role has often been overlooked when analyzing the dynamic nature of the Northern Ireland conflict. Until the mid-1980s, most external players, with the exception of Ireland, considered the conflict in Northern Ireland as an internal British dispute. Britain and the Republic of Ireland both laid territorial claims on Northern Ireland, providing moral, political and military support to their respective patriotic representatives of ethno-national groups. Northern Ireland Unionist and national leadership considered Britain and the Republic of Ireland as their respective powerful allies, representing their own distinct interests. It was the relations between the two "ethno-guarantors", the British and Irish governments, and the Nationalist/Unionist leadership that played a significant role in both exacerbating and eventually resolving the conflict.

Intervention process: from divided–partisan to united–neutral intervention

The journey towards a united–neutral interventionist process in Northern Ireland was long and arduous. Great Britain, the Republic of Ireland, the EU and the US played a pivotal role in the Northern Ireland conflict. Whether adding fuel to the fire, or attempting reconciliation, Great Britain and the Republic of Ireland assumed the roles of ethno-guarantors with entrenched ties to the groups in conflict. As has been discussed in earlier chapters, the impact of the interveners is dependent on the type of external strategies and process. Whether the intervention process is united–neutral, united–partisan, divided–partisan or a mixed divided–neutral/partisan, impacts on the conflict and the dynamics between the conflicting groups. As discussed in Chapter 2, a divided intervention and, in particular, divided–partisan intervention in support of opposing sides tends to escalate the conflict and has a hardening effect on the identities of the groups in conflict. On the other hand, united intervention may contribute towards a transformative effect on the groups in conflict. The subsequent section will examine and evaluate the shifting role of external interventionist process, mainly the increasingly united–neutral intervention process from London, Dublin and Washington and its impact on the conflicting groups in Northern Ireland. What were the main factors that contributed to this shift?

A shift in the type of process may be attributed to endogenous or exogenous factors. Exogenous factors could be related to interpretations of the conflict, relationships between the intervener and the target group, domestic considerations, and the behavior of friends and foes of the intervener. Endogenous factors could be related to the behavior of the groups in conflict or expected impact or reciprocity of the type of intervention. In Northern Ireland, what were the most crucial factors behind the shift from a divided–partisan to a united–neutral external intervention? What kind of impact did the shift in the type of intervention have on the groups in conflict?

Britain and its allies considered the Northern Ireland conflict as an internal conflict, which required some type of internal political, economic and military solution. A critical change took place in British positions when London began to acknowledge the link between the internal and the external causes of the conflict (Beggan 1999). Rather than seeking only local solutions, stemming from the 1985 Anglo-Irish Agreement, Britain sought to reach a compromise with Ireland. European integration played a role in the increased cooperation. Opening the door towards constructive external involvement, particularly that of Ireland and then later the United States, was a first step which helped to foster a united external position. Internalization of the Northern Ireland conflict had a tremendous impact on the conflict and on the leadership of the groups.

In principle, British strategies since the start of the Troubles highlighted the creation of more equitable internal economic and political power-sharing arrangements between the opposing groups. In practice, Britain considered Northern Ireland a security issue and spent most of its efforts attempting to suppress the violence, focusing on a military solution to the problem. In addition, politically, London was tied to Unionism and tended to cave in to Unionist demands. Until the 1990s, other potential external interventionists, the Americans and the Europeans, did not wish to meddle in what was perceived as an internal British affair. Thus, Britain as the sole intervener was free to pursue its own process to end the violence. In practice, British intervention was decidedly partisan, which had a detrimental effect on the conflict and the conflicting groups. Indeed, for the most part, British practices until the mid-1980s were counter-productive and served only to harden divisions between the opposing communities. Although the Republic of Ireland was interested in internationalizing the conflict, until the 1990s, its engagement was limited to supporting the Nationalist cause, through financial and principled backing. The policy pursued by the Republic of Ireland was likewise partisan and had an affirmative, rather than a transformative, effect on the identities of the groups in conflict. The shift from partisan to neutral intervention from London and Dublin was a gradual change that had a significant impact on the identities of the conflicting parties.

Analysts have disputed change versus continuity in British policies in Northern Ireland. Some authors, such as Paul Dixon, have argued that, since 1969, British policy in Northern Ireland has been characterized by continuity. According to Dixon, successive governments, whether Labour or the Conservatives, were forced to pursue a bipartisan position in order to manage the Northern Ireland conflict (Dixon 2001). Other authors, such as Padraig O'Malley, argued that there has been no British strategy towards Northern Ireland just "ambiguity, inconsistency and crisis management," as Westminster strove to reconcile the divergent claims of both the Nationalists and the Unionists (O'Malley 1983). Brendan O'Leary argued that British strategies have undergone painfully slow yet significant learning that led to major shifts in its policies. For instance, the policies pursued by the Health government in 1973–4, which led to the failed Sunningdale Agreement, were later reversed by Margaret Thatcher (1975–9) and revived in the 1990s (McGarry and O'Leary 1995).

The divergent views are relying on different elements of British policies, focusing on principles, practice or perceptions. Dixon's analysis is mainly dependent on analysis of principles, which since the 1970s have indeed been marked by continuity and an official principled stance of neutrality (Dixon 2001). There were several principles behind British policies from 1972 to 1998. First, there was the recognition that Britain had to remain active in Northern Ireland until a stable political settlement was reached. Second was a principle of neutrality that outlined that Britain had no political or economic interests in Northern Ireland. Third, the main emphasis was on local solutions that stressed that the best resolution would ensue from some type of power-sharing arrangements within Northern Ireland. Lastly, there was a general agreement that peace would require a dialogue with the Republicans even if done in secret (Tuck 2007). Although, in principle, British policies have remained publicly constant since 1972, when one examines those policies from the point of view of practice, one discovers that these have undergone fundamental changes. First, until the election of Tony Blair, all of the British governments were deeply dependent on votes from the Ulster parties. Thus, in practice, London was unlikely to take steps that would challenge the Unionist cause. Second, the actions of Britain's key implementing agents, in particular the army and the secret service, have been anything but neutral.

The army and the secret service were the main tools used by Westminster to deal with what was perceived in London as primarily a security issue. In 1969, the British army was officially deployed to support political and economic reforms. Although sent in as peacekeepers, the role of British soldiers and of the secret service became remarkably partisan as they took strong steps to eradicate extremism, primarily among the Catholic community. From 1971 to 1976, more than 250,000 house searches were conducted. For the most part, these targeted the Catholic community and, indeed, by the 1980s, every Catholic household in Northern Ireland had been on average searched twice (Tuck 2007). The numbers of incarcerations were significant. There was also a lax policy on the use of torture in prisons and the army's killing of wrongful targets was abysmal. Between 1969 and 1989, the security forces killed 136 intended targets and 178 unintended or wrongful targets (Tuck 2007, 173). Scholarly research has noted the existence of "conflict lock-ins," where actions taken as part of a government's counter insurgency campaign were directly linked to an increase in the level of violence (Tuck 2007). Thus, in practice, the actions of the British army and secret service were irremediably perceived as biased and intertwined in the conflict and became a powerful mobilizing symbol for the Republicans.

The reality on the ground affected the average person in Northern Ireland far more than the more neutrally framed principled policies designed in London. The harsh security tactics enacted by the British Army and the secret police served to harden identities and increase grievances among the Catholic population. In a poll conducted in 1990, 48 percent of the Catholic population listed "the British Army and their use of violence" as a very significant cause of the troubles (Irwin 2001). Many working-class Catholics joined the IRA after experiencing violence in their neighborhoods at the hands of the British Security forces (White 1993a).

London, unsuccessfully, also attempted to play the role of a mediator. In the 1970s, Britain engaged Unionist and Nationalist political parties in a dialogue to find a political solution to the conflict. The emphasis was on the creation of a workable political power-sharing arrangement within Northern Ireland. The 1973 Sunningdale Agreement was one of the first attempts to construct a consociational power-sharing agreement for the Northern Ireland conflicting parties. It contained provisions for a minority veto, legislative coalitions and proportional representation of minority groups. In a significant concession, Britain also invited the Republic of Ireland to play a minor role in a newly created all-Ireland institution, the Council of Ireland (Jesse and Williams 2006).

Although the Council was to have only an advisory function limited to tourism, conservation and aspects of animal health, it ignited huge protests from the hard-line Unionists. The day after the agreement was announced, loyalist paramilitaries formed the Ulster Army Council, an umbrella organization of paramilitary groups that coordinated joint paramilitary activities. Due to fierce opposition and a strike organized by hard-line Unionists, the agreement collapsed after five months. The Irish Government placed the largest portion of the blame on the British government, arguing that "it showed a lack of commitment to the settlement and caved into the pressure too soon" (Hayward 2006, 261). The failure of the agreement stemmed from several factors, such as the limited political inclusion, since only three parties were present in the negotiation talks and those excluded were able to derail the process. Other factors included the lack of fundamental public support for the agreement and the absence of significant change in the partisan intervention of Ireland or Britain.

The next attempt at a settlement was Ireland's 1983 establishment of the New Ireland Forum. At the behest of the Government of the Republic of Ireland, the New Ireland Forum sought to push for all-party negotiations to seek a regional solution to the conflict. The Forum reflected a slight shift in Irish policies towards a less partisan approach. Within the Forum, the Irish Government for the first time recognized the identity and the interests of the Unionists (Jesse and Williams 2006). The discussions came up with three options for the future of Northern Ireland: a unitary united Ireland, a federal united Ireland and a joint British–Irish authority over Northern Ireland. The government of Margaret Thatcher and the Unionist parties rejected all three options.

Although the proposals that came out of the Forum were dismissed by Britain, they became the basis for new talks and eventually led to the signing of the 1985 Anglo-Irish Agreement. At the time, it was the US President Ronald Regan who placed diplomatic pressure on the Prime Minister Margaret Thatcher to sign the agreement (Clancy 2007). As part of the Agreement, London and Dublin committed themselves to resolving their own differences. This was a significant shift towards a united British and Irish intervention and was a first turning point in the conflict. The Republic of Ireland was allotted a more active role in engagement towards the resolution of the Northern Ireland conflict. The Anglo-Irish Agreement established a joint Ministerial conference of British and Irish Ministers to resolve political, security and legal matters through a power sharing arrangement in Northern Ireland.

The Anglo-Irish Agreement was also not well received by the hard-line Unionists, who viewed it as a betrayal by London. Although the loudest objections came from hard-line Unionists, none of the major Northern Ireland political parties, including Sinn Fein, supported the agreement since it was perceived as imposed. In a famous public speech to tens of thousands of loyalists protesting against the agreement, Ian Paisley, founding leader of the hard-line currently ruling Democratic Unionist Party, said that the Unionists would "never, never, never" accept the Irish Republic involvement in Northern Ireland (Paisley 1986). The Anglo-Irish Agreement, as the Sunningdale Agreement, collapsed due to the British Government's caving in to protests coming from the hard-line Unionists. Although the Agreement failed, it established a greater unity between Britain and Ireland that laid the foundations for further talks. The Anglo-Irish Agreement also demonstrated that there were alternatives to direct rule and partitioning.

The end of the Cold War changed the regional reality and opened up new opportunities and obligations for British overtures. As noted by Adrian Guelke, "The end of the Cold War made it possible both for the British government to declare that it had no selfish strategic or economic interest in Northern Ireland and for this to be accepted by the Republican movement" (Guelke 2012). In 1989, the new Northern Ireland Secretary of State Peter Brook took a sharp turn towards a less partisan intervention. Reflecting that the British state was not neutral, Brook pushed for overtures towards the Nationalists and the Republic of Ireland (Campbell 2008, 36). Brook believed in dialogue with the Republicans and making public overtures to Ireland over former British policies. The day Mary Robinson was elected to the Presidency, Brook, encouraged by John Hume, made a public announcement that "the British government has no selfish strategic or economic interest in Northern Ireland" (Campbell 2008, 37).

The parallel gradual removal of British support for hard-line Unionists was fundamental for the transformation of Nationalism and of Unionism. Hard-line Unionist leaders grew increasingly suspicious of what they perceived as the shifting of policies in favor of Nationalists coming from London. Many Unionists, including Ian Paisley, presumed that London would continue to protect their interests. As argued in previous chapters, the way in which conflicting groups perceive the policies of their respective "guarantors" influences their actions and potential transformation. A withdrawal of this vital protection had a dramatic impact on the conflict and on the identities of the groups. The acknowledgement among the top Unionists of a change in Britain's role as the guarantor led to significant alteration in their own strategies. The leading Nationalists (The Social Democratic and Labour Party) and the Republicans (Sinn Fein) also noted that British policy towards Northern Ireland had undergone some shifts since the 1980s.

Ireland also played a significant role in the transformation of the Nationalists. In 1992, the newly elected Taoiseach of Ireland Albert Reynolds moved Fianna Fail and his new Irish Government closer towards accommodation with Britain over Northern Ireland. He entered into two parallel dialogues: first with Britain, and second with the prominent Nationalist Northern Ireland politicians John Hume, from the Social Democratic and Labour Party (SDLP) and Gerry Adams from Sinn Fein. Reynolds, Humes and Adams attempted to establish a common Nationalist position that could be used as a base for all-party talks (Mitchell 2001). The common view was that, since 30 years of violence had not achieved the goal of a United Ireland, it was time to open the door to a political approach (Chastelain 1999). The Republic of Ireland pushed for Sinn Fein to be allowed a seat at the negotiating table in return for the IRA's ceasefire and willingness to compromise on the demand for unification with Ireland. The Republic of Ireland also began to soften its stance on Articles 2 and 3 of its constitution, which called for the unification of the Island of Ireland. The pressure from Reynolds appeared to have had an impact on the Nationalists.

Significant change took place in British positions in 1993 when Britain softened its stance on self-determination and having Northern Ireland as its exclusive domain. The Downing Street Declaration (DSD) stated that any future agreement had to be based on the entitlement of people in both parts of the island to "exercise the right of self-determination on the basis of consent freely and concurrently given, North and South, to bring about a united Ireland if that is their wish". The common goal of the Irish and British Governments was also the inclusion of all those who had a stake in the conflict, including parties linked to paramilitary organizations (Chastelain 1999). The DSD thus opened the door for official British discussions with Sinn Fein.

The DSD was well received by the Nationalist and the Republican leadership. As commented by Gerry Adams: "[i]t was clear to me that the Downing Street Declaration marked a stage in the slow and painful process of England's disengagement from her first and last colony, Ireland" (Adams 2003, 165). The IRA's ceasefire of August 1994 was seen by many as a response to the DSD. The Unionist leadership was split in its response. Ian Paisley called the DSD a "sellout" to Dublin. However, more moderate Ulster Unionists were prepared to consider the document. Ulster Unionist Party leader James Molyneaux insisted the DSD was merely a statement of principles and it "posed no threat to the Union" because any change required the support of the majority of people in Northern Ireland (BBC 1993).

The United States became directly engaged in the Northern Irish conflict only in the 1990s, following the election of President Bill Clinton. In 1983, there had been a call from the US Senate to appoint a special envoy to Northern Ireland. This did not materialize, however, because of the special relationship between President Ronald Regan and Prime Minister Margaret Thatcher, and Regan's reluctance to become involved in British matters in ways that could antagonize Thatcher (Beggan 1999). For Clinton, engagement in Northern Ireland offered a win–win situation, since it would be popular domestically and lacked the complications of military engagement in highly volatile conflicts such as Bosnia-Herzegovina or Somalia (Clancy 2007). US intervention, however, was still not accepted in London. Indeed, Prime Minister John Major was wary of President Clinton coming to power and had leaked some sensitive information, hoping to keep Clinton out of office (Beggan 1999). Although the US began its engagement following Clinton's election, a significant shift of attitude in Westminster with regard to American involvement did not take place until the election of Prime Minister Tony Blair.

Nationalists within Northern Ireland and the leadership in the Republic of Ireland welcomed deeper US engagement. The head of the Sinn Fein party Gerry Adams was one of the advocates of American mediation in the conflict. "I stressed the role of the US in helping to resolve the differences that might emerge. We needed someone outside the frame, friendly with all sides, and with the ability to exercise influence and persuasion" (Adams 2003, 199). In January 1994, despite deep objections from Britain, the US government gave Gerry Adams a visa for a visit to the US. Although the visit was unofficial, the British Government began an intense private and public battle to keep Adams out of the US. According to Adams, "the British government's hysterical handling of the issue had ensured that the trip was a huge media story" (Adams 2003, 161). Due to British laws that forbid individuals linked to or supporting violent organizations to be heard in the British media, all public talks in the US with Adams, including Larry King live, needed to be dubbed. The dubbing of Adams, often done poorly, was subject to much parody and helped only to heighten the publicity for his visit. Following the Adams visit, the *Daily Telegraph* described the relations between Britain and the US as "the worst rift since Suez" (*Daily Telegraph*, 1994). Adam's highly publicized visit to the US helped to secure Sinn Fein as a representative included in the peace talks. However, this did not happen until the election of Tony Blair, as John Major remained unconvinced. As noted by Dixon, former PM Margaret Thatcher and John Major "failed to recognize the importance of bringing in the Republican movement from the cold" (Dixon 2001, 341).

In 1995, the British and Irish Governments formulated a neighborhood agreement entitled the Framework for the Future, which outlined a new relationship between Northern Ireland, the Republic of Ireland and Great Britain. The Framework specified the creation of new cross-border institutions, launching both North–South and East–West inter-governmental bodies. It also proposed an elaborate system to protect minority interests as well as a referendum on any constitutional change for Northern Ireland. In effect, Framework for the Future attempted to build bridges between the groups and make space for the construction of new common and multi-level identities for North Ireland. As Neal Jesse noted:

> The document concentrated on revising the interests and the identity of the Unionists away from the in-group out-group divisions of Protestants versus Catholics towards an identity and interest that complemented and overlapped with those of the Irish Catholics and the Republicans of Ireland.
>
> (Jesse and Williams 2006, 98)

Once again, the Framework was not well received among the more hard-line Unionists. Ian Paisley branded the Framework document as a "nefarious conspiracy" and claimed that the British and Irish Governments were "planning the eventual betrayal and dismantling of the Union" (Cash 1996, 211). The suggestion of a referendum in both Ireland and Northern Ireland was seen by the hardline Unionists as a ploy by the British Government to separate the hard-line political leadership from its community.

> It appears that the government believes it can create a divide between the greater number of people in Northern Ireland and the Unionist leadership and hopes to use the referendum to deliver Northern Ireland's affairs into the hands of all Ireland political institutions.
>
> (Cash 1996, 210)

Along the same lines, Peter Robinson, also a member of the Democratic Unionist Party, spoke of the betrayal of Unionists by Britain.

> For a quarter of a century, they (unionists in Northern Ireland) have refused to bow to terrorism and many paid for it with their life's blood. They have been bombed and shot at, bullied and blackmailed, yet even in the darkest hour, they held on to their cherished membership of the British family. Being British for them was no nominal condition. Their citizenship was under attack but that danger only caused them to cling more tightly to their Britishness. A dagger wielded by the hand of a friend is the cruelest cut of all.... For the Unionist community of Northern Ireland, this document confirms their worst fears – that they are no longer wanted and that their government no longer has any selfish, strategic, or economic interests in them.
>
> (Cash 1996, 212)

John Taylor of the Ulster Unionist Party took a more moderate view, promoting the transformation of Unionism. He spoke about the need to promote Unionism in a manner that would appeal and gain support both in Northern Ireland, Britain, Ireland, the US and the EU. "The onus is upon the Unionists to convince the SDLP and the Dublin Government of our willingness to co-operate and to normalize relations based on democratic will and the resolve of the people in the two parts of the island," said Taylor (Cash 1996, 216). Although the shifts in policies in Britain were viewed with disdain by the hardliners, the change of tide was noted and had transformational impact on some of the group leaders, acknowledging the importance of the need to transform Unionism.

The Framework also opened the door to the increased engagement of the Irish Republic in the resolution of the Northern Ireland conflict. Following its rapid economic growth beginning in the 1990s, the Republic of Ireland became known as the Celtic Tiger, undergoing major transformations. The prospect of economic growth subsequent to a peace agreement was used to give incentives to Northern Ireland political leaders as well as to the public. Unionist leadership could no longer point to Irish economic backwardness as a disincentive for increasing ties with the Republic of Ireland. Economic betterment has often been used as one of the incentives for parties to shift their policies towards peace. Northern Ireland's business community pushed for deeper cooperation and stressed the importance of a peace agreement. As noted by Guy Ben-Porat, "the linkage established between peace and economic growth or prosperity allows more involvement (and influence) of business in peace process" (Ben-Porat 2008, 9).

Deeper integration within the EU and regional economic cooperation were two constructive factors in building bridges between group identities. Northern Ireland became a top recipient of regional aid, which played a role in boosting the economy. Northern Ireland's more moderate politicians, including John Hume, put an emphasis on a European common identity strategy. Hume noted that a "European Union model might be applied so that the state identity is not the terminal identity – the highest allegiance" (Grove 2001, 383).

The Framework also helped to accelerate American involvement and all-party talks chaired by US Senator George Mitchell. London acquiesced to the use of international mediation with a focus on the thorny issue of disarmament. As outlined by former US Senator George Mitchell, Britain was influenced by three factors: "they wanted to accommodate the Irish Government, they did not want to offend or embarrass President Clinton, and they were reassured by my [Mitchells] performance as a special advisor to the President" (Mitchell 2001, 26). In addition, Britain was encouraged by the IRA ceasefire, but demanded decommissioning prior to the talks.

George Mitchell played a key role in overcoming one of the largest hurdles to the actualization of the peace talks. The proposed all-party talks were stalled on a chicken or egg dilemma: decommissioning prior to talks or talks towards decommissioning. Neither the Unionists, Nationalists nor Britain were willing to back down from their opposing positions. Mitchell, along with the two other members of the international body, Harry Holkeri, the former Prime Minister of Finland and John De Chastelain, Canada's Chief of Defense Staff, were requested by the British and Irish Governments to work on decommissioning. A key recommendation of the international panel was to conduct decommissioning in parallel with discussions, a compromise that was eventually used to start up the talks. Other recommendations made by the body included having all parties join the talks and holding elections that would determine who would participate in the negotiations (Crocker et al. 1999, 444).

Facilitating the discussions, Senator Mitchell was adamant that all parties, even those with affiliations to paramilitary groups, should be included in the talks. He instigated the "Mitchell principles of non-violence and democracy": every party that participated in talks had to agree to the "use of democratic and exclusively peaceful means of resolving political issues" (Mitchell 2001). Although the talks were to begin in 1994, the debate on the decommissioning stalled the process for two years. The talks only began in 1996, two weeks after the IRA grew tired of waiting and canceled its ceasefire. Thus, the talks began initially without Sinn Fein, which was only included after the IRA agreed to another ceasefire in 1997, subsequent to the election of Prime Minister Tony Blair.

The election of Tony Blair led to the first official meeting between a British Prime Minister and leaders of Irish Republicanism. As Adams pointed out: "for the first time in my lifetime we had a British Prime Minister listening directly to Irish Republicans and hearing our concerns and our hopes" (Adams 2003). Blair put pressure on Sinn Fein and the IRA to renew its call for a ceasefire in an effort to be included in the peace talks. "The settlement train is leaving. I want you on the train. But it is leaving anyway and I will not allow it to wait for you" (Mitchell 2001, 101). On July 20, two months after the election of Tony Blair, the IRA announced its second ceasefire. In his memoirs, Tony Blair noted that his robust emphasis on ending the conflict had to do with the changing global reality:

> I thought it was no longer in anyone's interest to tolerate conflict, not in Northern Ireland, but more importantly not outside it. I thought the whole thing had become ridiculously old-fashioned and out of touch with the times in which the island of Ireland lived.
>
> (Blair 2011, 158)

The pressure on the Republicans to transform came from their constituency, the general public as well as externally. As Adams became accepted as a legitimate political actor by the international community, his domestic constituency broadened and he became representative of a broader public (Grove 2001). As his constituency widened, Adams took on a more moderate tone both for domestic and international audiences. "In 1996 and 1997, his more inclusive strategies coincided with his need to convince the Clinton administration that he was keeping up his end of the deal by trying to get his (potential) domestic audience behind a permanent peace agreement" (Grove 2001, 385).

The majority of the public in Northern Ireland was supportive of peace talks and reaching a political agreement. Public opinion polls were used to initiate the peace process and place pressure on politicians to remain committed to negotiation until a final agreement was reached. Polls offered suggestions for a compromise that would be acceptable to all parties. The first poll in 1996 found that power sharing within North–South institutions but without joint British–Irish authority was a viable compromise for the majority of the public (Irwin 2002, 12). The second poll, conducted in March 1997, found that 94 percent of those interviewed "supported the principle of a negotiated settlement for the political future of Northern Ireland" (Irwin 2002, 14). A third poll strategically asked whether the constituency of each political party favored continuing with the talks. "In today's circumstances do you want the political party you support to stay in the talks?" From those polled, 92 percent said yes, ranging from 100 percent of the Sinn Fein voters to 76 percent of the DUP voters (Irwin 2002, 16). The public thus sent a clear message to the politicians and Northern Ireland's political representatives to stay in the talks until a solution was reached.

The consensus talks encompassed eight political parties (including the Social Democratic and Labour Party, Northern Ireland Women's Coalition, the Ulster Unionist Party, and the Alliance Party), and two governments. Northern Ireland Women's coalition, established only six weeks before it went to the polls, was one of the few parties that managed to bridge the ethno-religious divide. According to Mitchell, the largest push towards common positions came from the British and Irish Governments (Mitchell 2001). The two Governments negotiated a united position on changes in the Irish and British Constitutions, on prisoners, policing, criminal justice and on a new British–Irish Council. In fact, much of the discussions and the agreements took place away from the all-party talks, with the Governments keeping certain members of the discussions in the loop.

> As to their [Blair and Ahern] negotiations in London, I hoped that they would come up with an acceptable agreement. Since Blair was keeping Trimble advised and Ahern was doing the same for Hume and Adams, [this] was a reasonable expectation.
>
> (Mitchell 2001)

With the deadline set for Good Friday, the two heads of Government negotiated in person with the parties as part of the final push towards an all-inclusive agreement. As outlined by Mitchell,

> Throughout the day on Thursday, April 9, and into the night, the parties moved closer to agreement. Blair and Ahern played a central role in these negotiations. They obviously had developed a warm personal relationship; that made progress possible. They didn't just supervise the negotiations; they conducted them. Word by word, sentence by sentence, paragraph by paragraph, the compromise came together.
>
> (Mitchell 2001, 175)

The agreement was signed by all parties and endorsed in a referendum held in Northern Ireland and the Republic of Ireland.

The GFA has had its share of critics and challenges but has transformed the conflict from violence on the city streets to the newly designed, if at times dysfunctional, political institutions. A key difference from previous power-sharing agreements, such as the Sunningdale Agreement, came from two sources: changes in the British and Irish approach to resolving the conflict, and the engagement of the US in the process. By 1998, London and Dublin had ironed out their own differences and utilized their influence to push for a workable arrangement. As part of the GFA, the Republic of Ireland dropped Articles 2 and 3 of its Constitution that contained its territorial claim on Northern Ireland. Likewise, the British Government agreed to respect any free decision of the majority of the people in Northern Ireland and Republic of Ireland as to its future relationship with Britain. The British shift towards neutral policies was appreciated by the Nationalist and Republican leadership and opened the door for a ceasefire and all-inclusive talks. Although some of the hard-line Unionists perceived new British policies as a betrayal, the GFA led to a split between the moderate and hard-line Unionist policies and ultimately to the beginning of a transformation of Unionism. Under a more moderate influence from Dublin and incentives from the US, Nationalism and Republicanism also transformed, giving space to a political solution to the conflict.

Many interlinked factors contributed to the shift of the mediators from a divided–partisan to a united–neutral intervention process. Some of the shift had to do with exogenous factors, such as the changing domestic considerations of London and Dublin, the changing international and regional context, and the internationalization of the conflict. Endogenous factors such as public support for a peace process and the willingness of extremists to contemplate an alternative non-violent route also contributed to the shift. However, a very crucial element that needs to be highlighted was the direct impact of the exogenous shift on the groups in conflict. Changing the exogenous context that ended partisan support for the respective groups placed pressure on the groups to transform. Mitchell's inclusive mediation process helped to bring more moderates to the mediation table and forced the extremists to choose a path between inclusion and disarmament or exclusion and violence. Had the British and Irish positions not changed and remained partisan, continuing to support their respective brethren, a peace agreement would have been unlikely.

Group identity strategies in Northern Ireland: making consociationalism work

Though not without problems, group identity strategies mediated by the interveners were ones of accommodation with some creativity, flexibility and the potential of group identity transformation. Unlike the BiH case, the consociational arrangement in Northern Ireland was created with some flexibility. The British, Irish and American strategies that culminated in the GFA were not only meant to produce a functioning internal power-sharing arrangement but also to mediate a regional agreement with deep connections to neighboring states. The text and the institutions of the GFA promoted cross categories and overlapping identities. In addition to the internal Northern Ireland power-sharing institution, the GFA set up a North–South Ministerial Council that dealt with the relationship between the Governments of Northern Ireland and the Republic of Ireland. The GFA also set up the British–Irish Council and the British–Irish Intergovernmental Conference that guarantees the Government of Northern Ireland a say in areas of bilateral co-operation not devolved to the Northern Ireland Assembly or the North–South Ministerial Council. The final level of representation is the Northern Ireland representation to the European Union.

The largest disagreement during the mediation revolved around the future status of the North–South Council and the source of its authority. Although London and Dublin had reached an agreement, the proposal was not acceptable to the Unionists. Hard-line Unionists were tied to the Northern Irish Assembly (NIA) in that they thought they would exert control over any North–South political bodies, and hoped that those be placed under the control of the NIA. The Nationalists, on the other hand, wanted a strong north–south assembly independent of the Assembly in Northern Ireland. As described by Mitchell, the Unionists feared that the Nationalists would make the north–south institutions function and then sabotage the Assembly. On the other hand, the Nationalists feared that the Unionists would make the Northern Ireland Assembly function and then undermine the north–south institutions (Mitchell 2001). A compromise on the NIA and the North–South body was sealed by what Blair referred to as "a mutual destruction" provision. To ease the concerns of both sides, the GFA made the institutions "mutually inter-dependent" and stipulated that "one cannot successfully function without the other" (Mitchell 2001, 176). Although the mutual destructive clause overcame a major hurdle in the mediation, it later became a source of grievance.

Unlike the Dayton Agreement, the GFA did not link each conflicting group with a specific territory and left open the options for the people of Northern Ireland to choose institutions and governing entities with which they could form identity linkages. The choice also included the ability to select a British or an Irish passport. The text of the Agreement outlined that

> it is the birthright of all the people of Northern Ireland to identify them-selves and be accepted as Irish or British, or both, as they may so choose, and accordingly [the two Governments] confirm that their right to hold both British and Irish citizenship is accepted by both Governments and would not be affected by any future change in the status of Northern Ireland.

According to Neal G. Jesse and Kristen P. Williams, "the end result is that both Northern Ireland Communities should feel more secure, thereby reducing the ethnic security dilemma because policy does not rest in a single political arena (e.g., The British House of Commons or the Northern Ireland Assembly" (Jesse and Williams 2006, 107).

Although this was a more liberal and flexible group identity strategy, its all-embracing shift into the political arena has not been easy. The elections of hard-line parties, decommissioning, policing and the consociational power-sharing arrangement have been great challenges for a fully functioning Northern Ireland democracy. On the progressive front, violence has dropped dramatically and is generally unacceptable for all groups. Almost 20 years after the signing of the GFA, the question is not only about ending the violence but to what extent the group identity strategies in the GFA and the subsequent agreements promoted or inhibited transformation of groups.

As noted in Chapter 3, consociational arrangements are designed to establish balanced power-sharing internal institutional arrangements for conflicting groups. Although designed to appease the conflicting groups, many of the prob-lems of the GFA stem from its consociational framework. Key sections of the GFA were based on consociational principles, which outline groups in a solid and unchanging framework. For example, since proportional representation is used to facilitate power sharing between groups, the 108 members of the new Northern Ireland Assembly are required to register a designation of group iden-tity – Nationalist, Unionist or other. Although there is the option of "other," the framings of groups in a fixed unchanging and oppositional manner will unlikely contribute to transformation of the conflicting groups. As noted by Jenkins, a consociational solution for Northern Ireland "won't nurture the gradual development of non-sectarian civil society in Northern Ireland. It won't encourage people – whether they identify themselves as Catholics, Protestants or something else – to engage in non-sectarian politics.... It won't foster new modalities of local group identification" (Jenkins 2006, 19).

Still, the consociational agreement in Northern Ireland is far more flexible and unique than the BiH model, since it blends traditional consociational principles with innovative proportional and multi-layered representation. McGarry and O'Leary argued that in Northern Ireland "what makes consociations feasible and work is joint consent across the significant communities, with the emphasis on jointness" (McGarry and O'Leary 2004, 15). McGarry and O'Leary point out that Northern Ireland is a pioneer in using a d'Hondt portfolio allocation process for fair power sharing between contentious groups. The d'Hondt method is a mathematical formula regarding allocation of party seats, favoring large parties and coalitions over small parties. The authors note that the d'Hondt power-sharing allocation strategy has the

> advantage of halting protracted negotiations over ministerial portfolio allocations; it provides strong incentives for parties to stay within an executive even if they have disagreements – because if they don't stay, their entitlements will go to other parties, including parties from different national or ethnic blocs.
>
> (McGarry and O'Leary 2006, 61)

The arrangement, however, has worked against the small moderate parties.

The consociational strategies have been made functional with the now constructive role of Britain and Ireland. Since the 1970s, consociationalism has been suggested by Britain as the essential political solution to the Northern Ireland conflict. Consociational principles were already evident in the failed 1973 Sunningdale Agreement promoted by Britain. The most significant difference between the Sunningdale Agreement and the GFA was the role of Britain and Ireland. Unlike the GFA, Sunningdale focused on relations between groups in Northern Ireland, ignoring the external dimension. For Britain until the 1990s, although space was to be given for political and economic accommodation, certain red lines were not to be crossed, such as the role of the Republic of Ireland, which was to be limited. As noted by the then Secretary of State: "priority had to be given to ending the violence and any measures that contributed to that end would have to be kept" (Document 1973). On the other hand, the GFA substantially widened the role of the Republic of Ireland and changed the role of Britain, in particular ending the use of the British forces.

A significant lapse in the assessment of success and the challenges of consociational arrangements is the lack of examination of external influence. Theoretically, the consociational debates have been inward focused, concentrating on the extent to which parties can manage their differences within an institutionally representative internal political system. As noted by McGarry, traditional consociational research has a tendency to treat political systems as closed entities, ignoring exogenous factors that have dramatically influenced the conflict in Northern Ireland (McGarry 2001). Most internal conflicts, however, including that in Northern Ireland, tend to be fuelled or assisted by external and/or regional players. What has been neglected from the debate is the significant role played by external actors in the promotion and support of consociational settlements.

External players, in this case the "ethno-guarantors," tend to play a substantial role in influencing the potential success of any political power-sharing arrangement. As argued by John McGarry,

> an important reason why unionists refused to share power with nationalists was not because they were committed normatively to the Westminster model of government but because, as British nationalists, they preferred the default of direct rule from Westminster to the risk of power sharing with Irish Nationalists.
>
> (McGarry 2001, 16)

Hard-line Unionist political leaders have always considered direct rule to be not too different from their goal of an integrated United Kingdom. The Republican and Nationalist leadership also did not concentrate their efforts on attempting to construct a just internal arrangement within Northern Ireland, but rather focused on attempts to separate from Britain and join the Republic of Ireland. Until the 1990s, the Republic of Ireland publicly and constitutionally supported this effort.

Prior to the election of PM Tony Blair, many hard-line Unionists, including Ian Paisley, believed that Britain would continue to cave in to their demands. Paisley was one of Blair's harshest critics. In a fiery speech, Paisley said

> The British Government has again surrendered to the murderers and terrorists of the IRA. The only reason that the Orangemen of Portadown cannot be permitted to march back from their church to their homes is the utter cowardice of the Blair administration.
>
> (Paisley 2004)

Tony Blair noted that relationship building and empathy played a key role in group transformations.

> Many of the hundreds of hours I spent in discussion with the parties were not simply about specific blockages or details of the negotiation, but rather about absorbing and trying to comprehend why they felt as they did and communicating that feeling to the other side. In this way, they became my friends, because I then had inside me something of the passions they felt inside them. In addition, as the process wound its way, the parties got to know each other and started to look upon each other as human beings with a different perspective, not as enemies mired in evil and incapable of good.
>
> (Blair 2013)

By the mid to late 1990s, European institutions were also performing a more constructive role in the Northern Ireland conflict and presented an alternative framework to the nation state. As discussed in the previous chapter, in 1992 Europeans were divided and unprepared to deal with a national crisis such as those in BiH or Northern Ireland. By 1998, European institutions had reached a deeper maturity and were able to become involved in the Northern Ireland conflict in a more cooperative, united and effective manner. European integration had offered to national leadership another layer of potential identity affiliation. McCall draws a link between post-modernity, the influence of the EU and the transformation of identities. As noted by McCall, the development of the EU represented a substantive challenge to the concept of the nation state (McCall 1999). EU initiatives also encouraged cross border cooperation, helping to ferment rather than block connections between the communities across state lines. The Government of the United Kingdom and the Government of the Republic of Ireland conducted many of the initiatives jointly. The initiatives influenced the political processes affecting Ulster Unionists and Northern Irish Nationalist communal identities alike (McCall 1999).

Decommissioning and creating an unbiased police force was another challenge subsequent to the signing of the GFA. The removal of support from the US and Irish Americans towards a violent Nationalist cause was fundamental for the transformation of Republicans and the decommissioning process of the IRA. Although President George W. Bush's administration was at first uninterested in Northern Ireland, the links between the `IRA and international terrorist groups brought Washington back into engagement. In August 2001, three former IRA prisoners were caught with false passports in Columbia and accused of helping to train the FARC (Revolutionary Armed Forces of Columbia) guerillas. The Bush administration did not take the news lightly and sent a clear message to Sinn Fein and the IRA that terrorism was not to be tolerated. The demand was even more serious, subsequent to the attacks on New York and the Pentagon. Following September 11, 2001, US special enjoy to Northern Ireland Richard Haass told Gerry Adams that links to any terrorism will be met with zero tolerance and that immediately the Republicans would be prevented from any fundraising in the USA (Clancy 2007). The lack of support from Irish Americans for assisting the IRA subsequent to September 11 contributed to the start of decommissioning in October 2001 (Ruddock 2001).

Much of American strategy in the Northern Ireland conflict rested on finding a compromise between London and Dublin. Since the engagement of the Clinton Administration, America assisted in playing a balancing power act between the political groups and the two Governments. As one State Department official from Clinton's administration noted:

> On one level, it is a question of trying to accommodate both Catholic and Protestant communities. On another level ... it's [as] much the relationship between Dublin and London. You could say, looking at it over the long

haul, that our role is to help strengthen the weight of Dublin over the pre-dominant weight of London. We never say this of course, but that is implicit in everything.

(Clancy 2007, 158)

Since the signing of the GFA, Northern Ireland has been largely self-governed, although not without problems. The Northern Ireland Assembly has been suspended on a couple of occasions in favor of direct rule from London. The longest suspension took place from 2003 until 2006, subsequent to the "Stormontgate Affair." The scandal began with a police raid on Sinn Fein at Stormont and accusations of a Republican spy ring. The subsequent court case collapsed, as one of the key Republicans charged, Denis Donaldson, admitted to working as a British agent. In a public statement, Donaldson declared that the "so-called Stormontgate affair" was "a scam and a fiction invented by (police) Special Branch" (BBC 2005). Although no one was formally charged, it took years for the dust to settle and for the general trust in the police to be rebuilt. It also took years to reactivate the trust in the power-sharing political process.

In 2006, Tony Blair initiated new all-party discussions to restart the negotiation process and restore the devolved institutions into operation. Britain used tough pressure tactics to ensure that the process would succeed, noting that, if deadlines were not met, the British government would disband the Assembly and impose a joint British–Irish direct rule over Northern Ireland. As a consequence, all Northern Irish politicians would lose their positions and income. The resulting St Andrews Agreement, signed in 2007, outlined further devolution of power to Northern Ireland and the restoration of power-sharing institutions. The US once again played a small, yet vital, role in ensuring the success of the St Andrews Agreement. Sinn Fein members, including Gerry Adams, had been denied US visas for funding drives to the US and funding was a serious problem for the Republicans. In an effort to have a more functioning Northern Ireland police, US officials told Sinn Fein that they would once again allow fundraising in the US if Sinn Fein cooperated with the restructuring of the police. The ban on Sinn Fein fundraising in the US was lifted shortly after the agreement was signed.

Subsequent to joint pressures from Britain and the Republic of Ireland, in 2007, Ian Paisley formed the first joint government in Northern Ireland with Sinn Fein's Martin McGuinness as Deputy First Minister. Critics noted that the DUP and Sinn Fein were essentially "bribed to run a coalition as absurd as a joining of Likud and Hamas, or white supremacists and Islamists in England" (West 2010). The relations, however, were better than anyone had expected. Indeed, the duo was often referred by the media as the "chuckle brothers," since the two kept laughing at each other jokes. The Nationalistic coalition between the dominant parties, however, came at the expense of more moderate parties.

Aspects of the consociational arrangement have hindered cooperation between the groups at the domestic political level and, in particular, limited the role of more moderate smaller parties. Centripetalism, a strategy situated between consociationalism and multiculturalism, has been suggested as an alternative institutional framework to encourage a more profound transformation between conflicting groups in Northern Ireland. As noted in Chapter 3, centripetalism uses a political and electoral system to promote cooperation between different groups by encouraging political representatives to look for support from outside of their own group (Briey 2005). The Alliance Party of Northern Ireland (APNI), a nonsectarian liberal political party, has been one of the proponents of the use of a centripetalist system. The APNI represents the so-called "third coalition," or those who have refused to be categorized as Orange or Green, giving space for the potential transformation of group identities. Enthusiastic about European integration, APNI is critical of consociational power-sharing arrangements, noting that it tends to deepen the sectarian divide. APNI put forward a proposal for a coalition of a minimum 65 to 70 percent in the Northern Ireland Assembly. This means that any governing coalition would have to draw support from across community divisions (McCall 1999).

As noted by McCall,

> The APNI provides a natural conduit for the representation of such identities. As a result, urban, middle class Catholics could satisfactorily retain an Irish cultural dimension to their identity in such an arrangement, while at the same time, conceivably identify economically with a structural link to Britain. Similarly, though perhaps more fantastically, potential hybrid identities in the Protestant farming community could conceivably maintain a sense of cultural Britishness, defined in terms of Ulster Protestantism, while seeing their economic interests in the EU best served by representation in an Irish regional or border region context.
>
> (McCall 1999, 186)

However, thus far, the centrist parties that have supported the end to sectarian politics have not done well in the polls and the road to transformation is far ahead. Some of the physical barriers still remain. Under pressure from the Northern Ireland Office and Downing Street, the current First and Deputy First Ministers set 2023 as their target date for bringing down all of Belfast's "peace" walls.

Still, external process and strategies, which were introduced and implemented during the peace process in Northern Ireland, contributed to the beginning of a transformation of group identities in the conflict. Transformation takes time and is dependent on numerous domestic factors such as equality, justice and the attainment of basic human needs. As noted by Jennifer Todd, "Inequality and injustice do not constitute ethnic difference. They can push it through the essentialization threshold, making it at once personally salient and oppositional" (Todd et al. 2006, 30). The more flexible and liberal consociational group strategies have contributed to transformation, though Northern Ireland continues to be dependent on constructive exogenous factors.

Conclusion

The shift from divided–partisan to a united–neutral external intervention was related to several crucial factors, most importantly the changing of the context and internationalization of the conflict. London and Dublin both played a crucial role in ending ethno-guarantors' support for their respective groups. Washington played a key role in bridging the gaps and controlling fundraising in the US. A united–neutral intervention process, dependent on cooperation from domestic elements, proved sufficient to end the conflict. Northern Ireland has been fortunate to have had a united international process that has encouraged transformation. The consociational arrangement, though far less divisive then the institutional strategies imposed in BiH, has had mixed results.

In the 1990s, international interveners in the Northern Ireland conflict did not share the common presumption that deeply divided groups in a violent conflict cannot coexist. Although partitioning was left as a possibility if all affected voted in favor, the prevailing solutions on the mediation table leaned towards a more integrative and flexible aspects of accommodation. The GFA focused on recognition of group rights and accommodation of groups within a consociational power arrangement. The institutional framework proposed and implemented by the GFA was multi-layered and flexible, catering to different layers of identities. The strategies for the most part did not freeze the divisions along conflicting group lines, opening the door for gradual transformations in the future. In other words it did not fall into the trap of promoting consociational arrangements that would encourage segregation or "Lebanization" of relationships between groups in conflict. The presumptions about the nature of group identity and the potential of transformation were some of the reasons behind the strategy of different provisions.

Despite the challenges, the GFA set up unique and flexible multi-layered institutions that encourage overlapping of identities through different levels of representation. Although the transformation has been slow, the GFA and the subsequent St Andrews Agreement shifted the Northern Ireland groups from violent confrontation into the political arena. The constructive engagement of London, Dublin and Washington has ensured that hard-line Unionists and Republicans have had little option but to pursue a peaceful track. For the most part, external intervention took an innovative approach to the question of identity, promoting group transformation and contributing to the building of bridges between groups.

Note

1 The distinction between internal and external players is fuzzy in many conflicts since, once a country intervenes, it becomes an internal player in the conflict. In the case of Northern Ireland, the external/internal distinction is non-existent since Northern Ireland is officially a part of Britain, was partitioned from Ireland and both countries until recently considered Northern Ireland as part of their own territory.

References

Adams, Gerry. 2003. *Hope and History: Making Peace in Ireland*. Dublin: Brandon.

BBC. 1993. "Downing Street Declaration." *BBC News*.

BBC. 2005. "Sinn Fein Man Admits he was an Agent. *BBC News* (December 25).

Beggan, Dominic Rathnam Indurthy. 1999. The Conflict in Northern Ireland and the Clinton Administration Role. *International Journal of World Peace* 16 (4): 3–25.

Ben-Porat, Guy. 2008. *The Failure of the Middle East Peace Process?* Jerusalem: Van Leer Jerusalem Institute.

Blair, Tony. 2011. *A Journey, My Political Life*. Toronto: Vintage Canada.

Blair, Tony. 2013. "Tony Blair: Pain, Passion and Empathy – What I've Learned about Peacemaking." *Guardian*, 24 October.

Briey, Laurent de 2005. "Centripetalism in Consociational Democracy: The Multiple Pro-portional Vote." Université Catholique de Louvain.

Bruce, Steve. 1986. *God Save Ulster: the Religion and Politics of Paisleyism*. Oxford: Clarendon Press.

Cain. 2011. "Northern Ireland Violence." In, ed. CAIN – Conflict Archive on the Internet.

Campbell, Beatrix. 2008. *Agreement! The State, Conflict and Change in Northern Ireland*. London: Lawrence & Wishart.

Cash, Daniel John. 1996. *Identity, Ideology and Conflict, the Structuration of Politics in Northern Ireland*. Cambridge: Cambridge University Press.

Chastelain, John, De. 1999. "The Good Friday Ageement in Northern Ireland." In *Herding Cats: Multiparty Mediation in a Complex World*, eds Chester A. Crocker, Fen Osler Hampson, and Pamela Aall. Washington DC: United States Institute of Peace Press.

Crocker, Chester A., Fen Osler Hampson, and Pamela Aall. 1999. *Herding Cats: Multi-party Mediation in a Complex World*. Washington DC: United States Institute of Peace Press.

Clancy, Mary Alice C. 2007. The United States and post-Agreement Northern Ireland, 2001–6. *Irish Studies in International Affairs* 18: 155–173.

Clayton, Pamela. 1998. "Religion, Ethnicity and Colonialism as Explanations of the Northern Ireland Conflct." In *Rethinking Northern Ireland*, ed. David Miller. New York: Addison Wesley Longman.

Daily Telegraph, The. 1994. Article in edition of 2 February, cited in Robert A. Strong. 2005. *Decisions and Dilemmas: Case Studies in Presidential Foreign Policy Making*. London: Routledge.

Dixon, Paul. 2001. British Policy towards Northern Ireland, 1969–2000: Continuity tacti-cal adjustment and coexistence. *British Journal of Politics and International Relations* 3 (3): 340–368.

Dixon, Paul. 2008. *Northern Ireland, The Politics of War and Peace*. Hampshire: Pal-grave Macmillan.

Document, Declassified. 1973. *Note of Talks bettween the Secretary of State, The Alli-ance party, The Social Democratic and Labour Party and the Ulster Unionist Party at Stormont Castle on October 5, 1973*.

Elliot, R. S. P. and John Hickie. 1971. *Ulster, A Case Study in Conflict Theory*. London: Longman.

Fitzduff, Mary. 2001. The Challenge to History, Justice, Coexistence and Reconciliation Work in Northern Ireland. In *Reconciliation, Justice and Coexistence*, ed. Mohammed Abu-Nimer. Lanham, MD: Lexington Books.

Grove, Andrea 2001. The Intra-National Struggle to Define "Us": External Involvement as a Two-Way street. *International Studies Quarterly* 45: 357–388.

Guelke, Adrian. 1996. The United States, Irish Americans and the Northern Ireland Peace Process. *International Affairs* 72 (3): 521–36.

Guelke, Adrian. 2012. "Perspective," *BBC, Eye Witness, Perspective*. www.bbc.co.uk/northernireland/learning/eyewitness/changing/perspectives/index.shtml.

Hayes, Bernadette C. and Ian McAllister. 1999. "Ethnonationalism, Public Opinion and the Good Friday Agreement." In *After the Good Friday Agreement: Analysing Political Change in Northern Ireland*, ed. Joseph and Jennifer Todd Ruane. Dublin: University College Dublin Press.

Hayward, Katy. 2006. Reiterating National Identities: European Union Conception of Conflict Resolution in Northern Ireland. *Cooperation and Conflict* 41 (3): 261–284.

Hickey, Raymond. 2007. *Irish English: History and Present Day Forms*. Cambridge: Cambridge University Press.

Irwin, Colin. 2001. How Public Opinion Polls were Used in Support of the Northern Ireland Peace Process. *The Global Review of Ethnopolitics* 1 (1): 62–73.

Irwin, Colin. 2002. *The People's Peace Process in Northern Ireland*. London: Palgrave Macmillan.

Jenkins, Richard. 2006. When Politics and Social Theory Converge: Group Identification and Group Rights in Northern Ireland. *Nationalism and Ethnic Politics* 12: 389–410.

Jesse, Neal G. and Kristen P. Williams. 2006. *Identity and Institutions: Conflict Resolution in Divided Societies*. Albany NY: State University of New York Press.

Larkin, Emmet. 1998. Myths, Revisionism and the Writings of Irish History. *New Hybernia Review* 2 (2): 57–71.

McAuley, James W. and Jonathan Tonge. 2007. For God and the Crown, Contemporary Political and Social Attitudes among Orange Members in Northern Ireland. *Political Psychology* 28 (1): 33–52.

McCall, Cathal. 1999. *Identity in Northern Ireland: Communities, Politics and Change*. New York: St. Martin's Press.

McGarry, John. 2001. "Northern Ireland, Civic Nationalism and the Good Friday Agreement." In *Northern Ireland and the Divided World: Post Agreement Northern Ireland in Comparative Perspective*, ed. John McGarry. Oxford: Oxford University Press.

McGarry, John and Brendan O'Leary. 1995. *Explaining Northern Ireland: Broken Images*. Oxford: Blackwell Publishers.

McGarry, John and Brendan O'Leary. 2004. *Nortnern Ireland Conflict: Consociational Engagement*. Oxford: Oxford University Press.

McGarry, John and Brendan O'Leary. 2006. Consociational Theory, Northern Ireland's Conflict, and its Agreement. Part 1: What Consociationalists can learn from Northern Ireland. *Government and Opposition* 41 (1): 43–63.

McVeigh, Robbie and Bill Rolston. 2007. From Good Friday to Good Relations: Sectarianism, Racism and the Northern Irish State. *Race and Class* 48 (4): 1–23.

Miller, David. 1998. "Colonialism and Academic Representations of the Troubles." In *Rethinking Northern Ireland*, ed. David Miller. New York: Addison Wesley Longman.

Mitchell, George 2001. *Making Peace*. Berkeley, CA: University of California Press.

Muldoon, Orla, Karen Trew, Nathalie Rougier, Jennifer Todd and Katrina McLaughlin. 2007. Religious and National Identity after the Belfast Good Friday Agreement. *Political Psychology* 28 (1): 89–103.

Mulholland, Marc. 2002. *Northern Ireland, A Very Short Introduction*. Oxford: Oxford University Press.

O'Malley, Padraig. 1983. *Uncivil Wars*. Belfast: Blackstaff.

Paisley, Ian. 1986. "Ulster Says No." In *Protest Rally*. Belfast: Cain Web Service.

Paisley, Ian 2004. "Speech by Ian Paisley, then Leader of the DUP, to the Independent Orange Demonstration, 12 July 2004." In: Cain Web Service.

Ruddock, Alan. 2001. "How America held the IRA over a Barrel," *Observer*. 31 October.

Stringer, P. and G. Robinson (eds). 1991. *Social Attitudes in Northern Ireland*. Belfast: Blackstaff Press.

Todd, Jennifer and Theresa O'Keefe, Nathalie Rougier, and Lorenzo Canas Bottos. 2006. Fluid or Frozen? Choice and change in ethno-national identification in contemporary Northern Ireland. *Nationalism and Ethnic Politics* 12 (3/4): 323–346.

Tuck, Christopher 2007. Northern Ireland and the British Approach to Counter Insurgency. *Defense and Security Analysis* 23 (2): 165–183.

West, Ed. 2010. "Can Northern Ireland Work? History Suggests Not." *Telegraph*.

White, Robert W. 1993a. On Measuring Political Violence: Northern Ireland, 1967 to 1980. *American Sociological Review* 58 (4): 575–585.

White, Robert W. 1993b. *Provisional Irish Republicans: Oral and Interpretive History*. Westport, CT: Greenwood Publishing Group.

Whyte, John. 1983. "How Much Discrimination was there under the Unionist Regime – 1921–1968." In *Contemporary Irish Studies*, ed. Tom and James O'Connell Gallangher. Manchester: Manchester University Press.

6 Intervention in Israel-Palestine

The troubled road to partitioning

In November 2014 my 11-year-old son Amir came to his public school in Jerusalem to find the grade one class burned down and the words "There is no coexistence with Cancer" and "Death to Arabs" written in Hebrew over the walls of the school. The bilingual Arab–Hebrew public school is one of the few bastions of coexistence in Jerusalem where parents send their kids to receive a bilingual and more tolerant education. Although the attack shocked the kids in the school, it came as no surprise to Jerusalem residents, who had become accustomed to monthly and at times weekly attacks against civilians, stabbings by Palestinian or Israeli youths, demonstrations, arrests, house demolishing and the removal of citizenship from Palestinian families linked to terrorist attacks. The recent escalation of violence followed the devastating Gaza war, which angered and alienated Palestinians including those living within Israel, shaking the already fragile coexistence between various groups living in the country.

As the recent surge of violence spirals, the question remains whether the international community is contributing to the escalation or the transformation of the ongoing conflict. Although the blame for the Israeli–Palestinian conflict is generally attributed to one of the groups in the conflict or to unsolvable relations between Israelis and Palestinians, some of the external intervention, regardless of intention, has tended to fuel rather than contribute to the resolution of the conflict. Due to the length and the perceived strategic importance of the Israeli–Palestinian conflict, external intervention has been plentiful, but far from ideal. Indeed, external process in the Israeli–Palestinian conflict has suffered for the most part from divided international process and non-constructive group identity strategies. From the beginning of the conflict, the international intervention process has been divided, with different countries supporting opposing parties. As was discussed in Chapter 2, divided–partisan intervention tends to harden group divisions and fuel a conflict and this has been grossly evident in the Palestinian–Israeli case. Peace agreements have been discussed and not signed or signed and not implemented.

Spanning more than 60 years of engagement, the majority of external interveners in the Israeli–Palestinian conflict have been politically, militarily, economically and diplomatically supporting different groups in the conflict. American policy makers have traditionally supported Israel, while the USSR (later Russia) and regional actors have for the most part supported the Palestinians. Key European powers, depending on the governments, wavered between supporting Palestinians and supporting Israel but, until recently, had a relatively negligible role and political influence. A minor shift from a divided–partisan to a more united external intervention has begun to take place in the past few years. The creation of the Quartet, the Arab Peace Initiative and greater engagement of the EU have all contributed to a more united intervention. However, as will be discussed in this chapter, this shift has been more along the lines of establishing common principles than in practice.

Key international group strategies have also been unconstructive, contributing to building walls rather than bridges between the groups in conflict. Conflicting group identities have been impacted by external strategies stemming from the interpretation of the "intractable" nature of the Israeli–Palestinian conflict. The focus on partitioning has reflected an accepted external interpretation of an unsolvable conflict between two ethno-religious groups fighting over a single territory. This is based on an interpretation of two solid, one-dimensional ethnic group identities that are cohesive, unchanging, and presumed to be lacking in the capacity to coexist. Thus, the emphasis has been on separation, dividing territory and changing borders in line with ethno-religious groups, contributing to building walls rather than bridges between the groups.

Although the length and nature of the Israeli–Palestinian conflict has indeed created deep divisions between opposing groups, the conflict is far more complex. Dividing lines but also coexistence may be found in many spheres. It is questionable whether the nexus between presumed homogeneous group identity and territory should also be readily accepted. For one, it does not reflect the present reality, since more than one million Palestinians (referred to by Israel as Israeli Arabs) live on the territory of Israel and over 300,000 Israelis live within Palestinian territory inside the West Bank. In effect, as evident in the surge of violence in Jerusalem, a two-state solution, which creates two exclusive, ethno-religious states, would be unlikely to resolve the Israeli–Palestinian conflict. Indeed, if the "solution" also included ethnic cleansing and border adjustments along ethno-religious lines, it may very well serve to heighten divisions and intensify the conflict, as was the case in Bosnia and Herzegovina.

This chapter will examine the external intervention process and conflict resolution identity strategies in the Palestinian–Israeli conflict. Following a brief historical overview, the chapter will reflect on external process and identity strategies during Oslo, Camp David 2000 and the more recent post-Annapolis process. The chapter will analyze the impact of the type of external process on the groups in conflict. Second, it will examine the recent principled shift towards more united international intervention. Lastly, it will analyze the impact of external strategies focused on partitioning along ethnic and religious lines. As in the other case studies, the question posed is whether the international community is contributing to a transformation or a solidification of the divisions between the conflicting groups.

The Israeli–Palestinian conflict is one of the longest and most written about conflicts. This chapter cannot summarize the whole conflict but will rather focus on more recent key external interventions in the conflict. Subsequent to a brief background, the focus will be on external intervention during Oslo, Camp David II, and the more recent external attempts to bring peace up until the present time. Recent key events will be highlighted to shed light on the international process and identity strategies and their impact on groups in conflict.

Historical background

Perpetuated by nationalists and extremists over the many years of conflict, the Israeli–Palestinian conflict contains one of the deepest divisions between ethno-religious groups. The divisions have been real as well as construed by those fearing annihilation, conversion, assimilation and domination. Ethnic and religious separation had been the foundation of policies promoted by much of the Jewish leadership fleeing from European persecution and hoping to create a safe Jewish homeland. Although arguably not the case before the massive European Jewish settlement in the 1930s and 1940s, one can say that since the large influx, Palestinians and Jews living on the territory of Palestine have been in a state of perpetual conflict, which has led to little space for the development of coexistence or non-conflicting group identities. The separation, segregation and uprooting of Palestinians not only destroyed the lives of the native Palestinians but also deepened the lack of trust and clashed with the potential for coexistence.

Zionism emerged from the desire of Jews to create a homeland in Palestine and became a political and humanitarian necessity as a consequence of the persecution of Jews in Europe and Russia. The settlement of Palestine by European Jews was conceived and presented as something that could potentially benefit the barren land and the Arab natives. The Father of Zionism Theodor Herzel wrote in 1899 that Zionism would not pose a threat of displacement for the Arab inhabitants of Palestine but "rather the arrival of the industrious, talented, well-funded Jews would materially benefit them" (Morris 2001, 21). However, as vividly illustrated by the Zionist slogan: "land without people for a people without land," which brought tens of thousands migrating Jews into Palestine, the policy treated the local, mostly Palestinian, inhabitants as invisible. Unsurprisingly, the massive migration was perceived as very threatening by the native population, which feared displacement.

The displacement of the Palestinian population using economic and other incentives was indeed promoted from the beginning of the Jewish settlement. The Jewish National Fund was established to acquire property from the Arabs and give or sell it to the Jews. Funds were allocated for the purchase of lands that became the key to settlement as large lands were bought, displacing the economically disadvantaged Palestinian tenants (Morris 2001). Absent or profiteering Arab landowners readily sold properties for a good price, not concerned with the fate of the dispossessed tenants (Segev 2000). The fear of territorial displacement and dispossession was the key motivation in Palestinian antagonism towards the arriving Jews (Khalidi 1997). Many of the local Palestinian elite became tarnished politically, since on the one hand they were publicly outraged by the sale of land, while, on the other, privately directly profiteering from the sales (Segev 2000).

The establishment of a "Jewish" homeland in Palestine was not achievable without the support and help of major powers. The Zionist movement turned to Britain as the protector of Jewish self-determination. Britain readily agreed, first, in order to gain favor with American and Russian Jews in an effort to persuade their countries to join in World War I and, second, to counter French claims to Palestine (Morris 2001). The 1917 Balfour declaration gave official support to the establishment of a Jewish homeland in Palestine. Subsequently, in 1922, the League of Nations included it in the mandate it gave to British rule over Palestine. As noted by Tom Segev, the 30 year British rule of Palestine achieved little, but the arriving desperate and industrious Jews managed to carve out a state (Segev 2000).

The Peel commission was sent by Britain to propose changes to the British Mandate following the outbreak of violence, notably the 1936–39 Arab revolt in Palestine. Headed by Lord William Peel, it was sent to investigate the cause of the violence and judge Arab and Jewish grievances. The commission found the conflict to be "irrepressible" and "insoluble" and recommended partitioning the land between Jews and Arabs (Morris 2001). The commission also recommended an exchange of populations between the future states numbering in hundreds of thousands of Palestinians. According to the commission, the exchange of populations would be carried out by an agreement with compensation but "if the Arabs objected, the transfer should be implemented by the British 'in the last resort' by compulsion" (Morris 2001, 138).

Partitioning was perceived as the simplest of the options, since for the most part it did not involve untangling linked communities. The Yishuv, or the Jewish settlers who arrived in the late thirties, built separate communities, which had no intention of mixing with the local Arab population. Language, religion, culture, economics, violence and racism all served to divide the Arab and Jewish populations. The Haganah protected the Yishuv's settlements while the Irgun and Etzel, more radical groups, attacked Arab settlements (Laqueur 2003). Lack of trust in other communities deepened Jewish inclinations to remain isolated and independent from other groups. For the Palestinians, the partitioning option was unacceptable. The Arab leadership in Palestine perceived no justice in being displaced from land they saw as theirs. As exclaimed by local Arab leader Abd al Hadi, "We will fight. We will struggle against the partition of the country and against Jewish immigration. There is no compromise" (Morris 2001, 138).

Although the Jewish leadership was willing to accept partitioning, it was not perceived as a permanent solution for peace but rather as an opportunity for strengthening the Zionist hold on Palestine. Hence, the Jewish leadership was eager to accept a state regardless of the size, with the intention of expansion. According to David Ben Gurion, a primary founder and first Prime Minister of Israel, a Jewish state in part of [Palestine] is not an end, but a beginning.... Our possession is important not only for itself ... through this we increase our power, and every increase in power facilitates getting hold of the country in its entirety. Establishing a [small] state ... will serve as a very potent lever in our historical efforts to redeem the whole country.

(Morris 2001, 138)

The importance of the establishment of a Jewish state was perceived and sold as an existential necessity. Ben Gurion noted that "Jews could not rely on the benevolence of nations but had to forge their own national destiny" (Gurion 1945, 173).

European and American guilt over their own anti-Semitism and failure to prevent Jewish genocide during World War II helped to promote partitioning and generate a partisan intervention at the expense of the Palestinians. Although the British came to view the Zionist homeland idea as a mistake, they were unable or unwilling to reverse it. Following the Holocaust, the British found themselves incapable of stopping the waves of settlement and unwilling to "have a war with Jews in order to give Palestine to the Arabs" (Segev 2000). International and particularly European racism, anti-Semitism and most profoundly the Nazi rule made the creation of Israel be seen as a necessity. The murder of close to 6 million unarmed Jewish men, women and children in extermination camps across Europe was reflective of one of humanity's worst moments in history. Even today, few Jewish families are not directly affected by the loss, which wiped out two-thirds of European Jews, including a million children. Consequently, standing up against the uprooting of hundreds of thousands of native Palestinians was not considered an urgent international priority in the 1940s. The Palestinians attempted to stop the Jewish settlement and their displacement with official protest, terrorism and violence. The motivation of the survivors who fled the Holocaust helped to create a small but powerful army. It was an army that the international community was unwilling to fight, and Arab countries were unmotivated and too disorganized to defeat (Morris 2001).

Unable to control the violence, the British threw the hot potato into the hands of the UN, which also opted for territorial partitioning. The UN partition plan of 1947 formulated the establishment of a Jewish State in about 55 percent of Mandatory Palestine, and an Arab state in about 44.9 percent, with Jerusalem under international control (UN Res 181 1947). The "Jewish state" included more than half a million Arabs, making the population almost equal to the number of Jews living within the proposed boundaries. Although the UN plan enacted minority rights, it did not outline any enforcement mechanisms. Britain refused to enforce the partition plan, creating a power vacuum following the end of the British Mandate. The subsequent declaration of Israeli independence sparked further violence and a regional war that opened up opportunities for a solution to Israel's demographic problem. The newly established army managed to defeat a combined invasion by Egypt and Syria, together with forces from Iraq. 1948 infamously became a year of celebration for the Jews, having established their own state, and a Nakba or national tragedy for the Palestinians, with the loss of their struggle, Arab defeat by the Jewish army and subsequent massive displacement.

Since, within the new "Jewish state," the population of Arabs almost equaled the population of Jews, some of the more nationalistic Jewish leadership felt that expulsions were both necessary and, under the cover of war, quite possible. Within the span of a few months "more than 350 villages would vanish, [Palestinian] urban life would all but evaporate – war and exodus reducing Jaffa's population from 70,000–80,000 Palestinians to a remnant of 3,000–4,000 – and 500,000 to one million Palestinians would become refugees" (Kimmerling and Migdal 1993, 127). As noted by Kimmerling and Migdal, "the experience of exile – of a tragedy perceived as both personal and national would overshadow all else for this generation" (Kimmerling and Migdal 1993, 128). As noted by Sari Nusseibeh, the surprised and outgunned Palestinians did not stand much of a chance.

> There were hundreds of villages and cities to defend, and nearly no one to do so. Even more fatally they had no clear understanding of what the fighting was all about. In earlier rebellions against the Turks, territory was never the bone of contention. The Turks didn't take over a village in order to drive out its people and replace them with settlers. With the Zionists, the struggle was for every inch of soil.
>
> (Nusseibeh 2007, 45)

The subsequent dispersion of refugees and the experience of exile would become a defining element of group identity for the Palestinians. The IC condemned the expulsions of Palestinians and demanded a full return of all those displaced, and Palestine became a humanitarian issue, with the UN launching the largest and longest refugee aid project to Palestinians scattered throughout the Middle East.

Palestinians, however, were not the only refugees as the consequence of the Israeli–Palestinian and Israeli–Arab conflict. Beginning in 1948, between 800,000 and 1,000,000 Mizrahi and Sephardic Jews either fled from their homes or were expelled from Middle East and North African countries, namely Iraq, Iran, Morocco and Egypt (Shulewitz 2000). Most were forced to flee quickly, leaving behind belongings and property. In some cases, centuries of coexistence came to an abrupt end. Although much attention has been given to the plight of the Palestinians, many of whom retain refugee status, the Jewish refugees and their entitlements to reclaim their lost or stolen property have essentially been ignored. Part of the reason is that, unlike the Palestinians who were unable to become absorbed into wherever they settled in the Middle East, the Jews were readily and well absorbed into the state of Israel.

The Six-Day War in the 1960s only served to escalate the regional conflict. In 1967, subsequent to escalation of border disputes between Egypt and Israel and Syria and Israel, Egyptian closure of the Snapir and Tiran Straits to Israeli shipping and the massing of Egyptian troops along Israel border prompted a surprise Israeli air attack. Israel's well-planned and orchestrated attack destroyed virtually all of the Egyptian Air Force and, in the subsequent days, Israeli forces had taken control of the Gaza Strip and the Sinai Peninsula from Egypt, the West Bank and East Jerusalem from Jordan, and the Golan Heights from Syria. Israel's complete military victory during the Six-Day War was not only a humiliating defeat of the neighboring states of Egypt, Jordan and Syria, it resulted in further grief for the Palestinians. Although the Sinai Peninsula was returned, the West Bank, Gaza and the Golan Heights remain occupied territory and are the main source of the current disputes. For Israel, taking over the heavily populated territory of the West Bank and Gaza brought in new populations "who were clearly not part of any conceivable notion of a nation and thus the cause of concern" (Migdal 2004).

Following the Six-Day War, the UN Security Council unanimously adopted Resolution 242, which emphasized implementation of the "land for peace" formula and withdrawal of Israeli armed forces from occupied territories in return for peace with the Arab states. The UN resolution paved the way for the proposal of a two-state solution to the conflict. The current two-state solution is based on a formula, according to which Israel would relinquish the territory it had occupied during the Six-Day war, and Gaza, the West Bank and parts of Jerusalem would become included within the new borders of a future Palestinian state.

The occupation of the West Bank, Gaza and East Jerusalem radically altered regional politics up to today. With the second humiliating Arab defeat by Israel, the Palestinians felt they had to turn to their own resources rather than hope for assistance from their Arab neighbors. As noted by Kimmerling and Migdal,

> With the 1967 defeat, Palestinians felt the pan-Arab foundations of their hopes disintegrated. In the war's wake, many turned to the feday [Palestinian infiltrating guerilla] – especially represented by Fatah and its record of direct, violent action against Israel – as their only chance for salvation.
>
> (Kimmerling, 222)

Led by Yasser Arafat, the Fatah became the most organized group within the nationalist Palestinian Liberation Organization (PLO) and the leader of violent resistance. Arafat launched terrorist attacks against Israel, operating from Lebanon and Tunisia.

The 1967 conflict became a source of disagreements between the major international actors, as the US became a stronger ally of Israel, while Russia took sides with the Arab states. As noted by Harold Saunders of the US National Security Council,

> For twenty years Israel has sought a special relationship – even a private security guarantee – with us. We have steadfastly refused in order to preserve our other interests in the Middle East. We argued that our policy

worked to Israel's best interest too. Now we are committed to side with Israel and, in opening the Straits of Tiran, even to wage war on the Arabs. In short, we have chosen sides – not with the constructive Arabs and Israel but with Israel alone against all the Arabs.

(Saunders 1967)

Although divisions among external interveners over Israel-Palestine always existed, the Cold War deepened the external political split into pro-Israel versus pro-Palestinian camps. During the Cold War, Americans viewed Israel as an essential barrier to Soviet inroads in the Middle East. On the other hand, Palestinians were regarded by the Americans as the tools of the Soviets (Christison 2004). Palestinian leadership during the height of the Cold War fitted nicely within the USSR camp and adapted ideological framing and language to garnish support. Although officially the Soviets stood against the use of terror, in practice they helped to arm and train the PLO (Golan 1986). Beyond clandestine military aid, in 1974 PM Leonid Breznev provided an official invitation to Yasser Arafat and, in 1978, gave USSR's official recognition of the PLO as the sole legitimate representative of the Palestinian people.

Despite US protests and Arafat's terrorist activities, Arafat was able to gain international recognition. Yasser Arafat's 1974 famous "freedom fighter gun and olive branch" speech played a key role in the UN's recognition of the PLO as a legitimate representative of the Palestinian people, so that it received observer status within the UN. In 1988, when Arafat was once again invited to speak at the UN, Americans who were the host to the event denied him a visa. The UN response was to move (at exorbitant costs) the entire General Assembly from New York to Switzerland. Not wishing to be left out, the US then trumped the UN with the announcement of its official recognition of the PLO and their own bilateral diplomatic initiative (Bennis 1997).

The end of the Cold War and disintegration of the USSR changed the dynamics of the region, making the Americans the primary interveners in the conflict. The new reality had a dramatic impact on the PLO. As noted by Andoni,

> Indeed, it was the US primacy and the increasing weakness of the Soviet Union, which had done nothing to challenge the US conduct of the Gulf crisis ... [that] confirmed what was already clear, [that] the PLO strategy based on the Cold War and Moscow's role as a counterweight to the US was irrevocably shattered.

(Andoni 1991, 3)

With the collapse of Soviet Union, the PLO was left without superpower support, changing the dynamics and the power relations and opening some doors towards a peace process. However, the divided international intervention process did not end. The following discussion will begin to explore the external intervention process in the Israeli–Palestinian conflict, beginning with Oslo.

The divided international intervention process in the Palestinian–Israeli conflict

In recently disclosed 2009 secret discussions between US Senator George Mitchell and Saeb Erekat, the Palestinian top negotiator, Erakat begged Mitchell not to prevent Palestinians from going to international bodies to address their concerns.

> They [Israel] won't refrain from doing the illegal things that they do. If they refrain OK but they won't. This is my only weapon. We have actions by settlers, attacks, provocations, Al Aqsa, home demolitions, families thrown out of their homes. Either we retaliate in a civilized manner or through violence. Which one should we choose?
>
> (Papers(4899) 2009)

asked Erakat. Michell responded that going to international bodies such as the UN would amount to negotiating in bad faith. "I would agree with Israel if you were negotiating and bringing actions against them it would be in bad faith" said Mitchell, requesting that the Palestinians refrained from approaching international bodies (Papers (4899) 2009). Regardless of intention, the repercussions of the type of external intervention, in this case the US preventing Palestinians from pursuing a legal means of protest, have the effect of weakening the moderate Palestinian leadership and a long-term impact on the conflicting groups.

Divisions between the main interveners – the US, UN, Middle Eastern states and the EU – have defined the international intervention process in the Israeli–Palestinian conflict. Unlike in BiH and Northern Ireland, where the external players eventually agreed on the type of intervention process and moved towards united–partisan and united–neutral intervention respectively, reaching a consensus on the type of intervention in the Israeli–Palestinian case has been arduous. The formations of the Quartet, the Arab Peace Initiative and deeper engagement of the EU have all contributed towards a greater attempt at a more united intervention; however, the shift has been more towards principles than practice. Although a consensus has been reached on the necessity of a two-state solution, the IC has thus far found it impossible to navigate a united process to get there. Differing interests and interpretations of the conflict have meant that key external players have been intervening in a partisan fashion, supporting opposing sides. The Americans, who have been the most active interveners, have remained partial to Israel, shielding the Israeli government from international condemnation. On the other hand, Russia, the majority of the UN General Assembly and regional players have tended to support the Palestinians. The EU, having until recently been left out of the peace process, has struggled to manage a single united policy, but has been progressively making slow strides towards tougher sanctions against Israel.

Perceptions of external intervention in the Israeli–Palestinian case have reflected the polarization of the different narratives. Both Israelis and Palestinians tend to perceive most external interventions as partisan against them. This inclination is illustrated in the media, in which Palestinians and Israelis viewing an identical news report both believe the report is biased against them (Goldstein and Pevehouse 1997). This sentiment is linked to Israelis and Palestinians both perceiving themselves as victims in the conflict. Thus the perception that the IC is biased against their group is common among Palestinians and Israelis. For example, in a December 2009 survey, 69 percent of Palestinians said Obama's policy was biased in favor of Israel.[1] Among the Israelis, only 12 percent thought his policies were more supportive of Israel while 40 percent believed they were more biased towards the Palestinians.[2]

The perception of victimhood among Israelis is perpetuated by what some have called a siege mentality common among the Israeli public. As described by Daniel Bar-Tal and Dikla Antebi, siege mentality is a belief by group members that "the rest of the world has highly negative behavioral intentions towards them" (Bar-Tal and Antebi 1992, 49). Bar-Tal and Antebi note that the siege mentality has several effects, including that the threatened group develops a negative attitude towards the other groups and the rest of the world and, in view of a perceived threat, uses all means to protect itself (Bar-Tal and Antebi, 1992). Although particularly strong among the Israelis due to their regional isolation and the history of persecution and the Holocaust, a siege mentality is common among many groups in the midst of violent conflict and has been used to justify sentiments of victimhood and rationalize aggressive policies and violence.

The debate on the type of intervention has resulted in a divided intervention that, I would argue, has been a hindrance to a resolution. As noted in Chapter 2, partisan and neutral interventions can be differentiated on the basis of principles, practice and perceptions. Many of the recent key principles concerning international intervention in the Israeli–Palestinian conflict may be construed as neutral, arising from a more inclusive and united formal process. For instance, the Quartet Roadmap for Peace, and the Arab Peace Initiative, launched in parallel in 2002, were an attempt towards a more united intervention. The Quartet roadmap outlined phased steps towards a two state solution, while the Arab Peace Initiative offered normalizing relations between the Arab region and Israel, in exchange for a withdrawal from the Occupied Territories and a "just settlement" of the Palestinian refugee crisis. Most of the official statements from US and European administrations as well as from many Arab countries reflected a principled consensus on strategies calling for a two-state solution, comprehensive peace settlement, complete settlement freeze and an end to terrorism. However, in practice, when it came to monitoring or implementation of the various agreements, or placing blame for lack of progress, different external players supported their own brethren's interests and their inability or unwillingness to implement aspects of the agreements.

The subsequent section will analyze the external process and its success or failures during Oslo, Camp David II, and more recent international attempts to mediate an end to the conflict. To what extent was the international process united or divided, and what effect did it have on the peace process and groups in the conflict? What factors accounted for a shift between neutral and partisan intervention? Numerous academic accounts have described the Norwegian non-partisan role in the 1991 unofficial discussions that led to the signing of the Oslo Agreements (Rabinovich 2004; Waage 2004). The talks gradually became official and acceptable to other key international players including the US. The following section will revisit the Oslo process to examine its nature and consequences. Did the external processes include elements that promoted a positive shift in group identities or did the international intervention process harden group identities?

The Oslo Accords arose out of unofficial or track two secret discussions among Israeli and Palestinian academics and middle-range politicians, orchestrated by the Norwegians in the early nineties. Arguably the largest step forward in the peace efforts between the Israelis and Palestinians, the Oslo process offered a small window into the potential of a neutral external intervention in the Israeli–Palestinian conflict. Unofficial diplomatic intervention by Norway has generally been credited with bringing the Palestinians and Israelis closer to reconciliation, with the initial – symbolic – step of mutual recognition. The Norwegian secret channel was nestled between the unsuccessful American efforts at Madrid, which commenced in December 1991, and the failed 2000 US-led Camp David summit. There are two things that can be highlighted from the Oslo process: first, the role of Norway versus the Americans; and, second, the engagement of the PLO, pulled in by Norway, which until then had been shunned by the Americans and the Israelis.

The Norwegian channel provided an alternative to the American-led process that, during the 1990s, was essentially the only game in town and was perceived by the Palestinians as biased towards the Israelis. Subsequent to US victory in the Gulf War and the disintegration of the Soviet Union, Americans became the unchallenged power in the Middle East. Strategically aligned with Israel, the US mediators were accused by the Palestinians of adapting positions from the Israeli delegations and imposing them on the Palestinians. In one American proposal, which was to have a combined Israeli–Palestinian position, Arafat claimed "that 65 percent of the points in the US synthesis had been taken from an Israeli paper, 28 percent from an earlier American paper, and only 7 percent from the Palestinian delegation's paper" (Sanders 1999). As noted by Arafat in 1993, "the PLO was having to negotiate against not one but two delegations, the Americans with Israeli accents and the Israelis with American accents" (Sanders 1999, 5).

The Norwegians had good ties with both the Israeli and the Palestinian leadership and, being a minor power with no major interest in the region, were perceived as being potentially far more neutral. The PLO was keen to stall the American-led mediation effort, from which it was left out, in order to be included in the Norwegian channel. Reportedly, "Palestinian strategy was to block progress in Washington in order to prompt [Israeli PM Yitzhak] Rabin to deal directly with Arafat" (Makovsky 1995, 30). The Norwegian mediation team used their good relations to allow the secret channel to help build dialogue and trust between parties that had previously not spoken to each other. These were the first meetings between Israeli officials and the PLO since they had been banned by Israel and the US. Due to the official ban on Israeli contacts with the PLO, the talks were held in secret, but were gradually accepted by the Israeli government. As was noted by Norwegian historian Hilde Henriksen Waage, for the Israeli government "it became clear that there would not be any progress as long as the PLO remained excluded" (Waage 2005, 7). As discerned by Waage, the PLO had "nothing to lose and everything to gain," and the Norwegian setting would bring the marginalized PLO back to the center stage and "give Arafat complete and direct control over the Palestinian side in the negotiations" (Waage 2005, 8).

Wary of American dominance in the peace effort, Norway presented Oslo as a supplementary rather than a competing peace track to assist in resolving the impasse in the American-led negotiations (Makovsky 1995, 27). The Accords were officially signed on September 13, 1993 in Washington and outlined principles of Palestinian self-rule, leaving final status issues for later discussions. The three key elements of the Oslo agreements were a phased Palestinian self-rule, renunciation of violence and mutual recognition. In the statement of principles, the PLO recognized "the right of the state of Israel to exist in peace and security" and committed itself to the Middle East Peace Process. In return, Rabin offered an official recognition of the PLO as the representatives of the Palestinian people and a negotiating partner. The Accords were based on an incremental strategy, allowing for future Palestinian elections, the establishment of the Palestinian Authority, cooperation on security and economics, and a timetable for reaching final status talks. With no accountability, and no improvement in the daily lives of Palestinians and Israelis, it did not take long before the process began to unravel.

Although Oslo represented a step forward in dialogue and progress towards an agreement between Palestinians and Israelis, Oslo did not improve the lives of most Palestinians or Israelis. Rather, it achieved recognition of the PLO, or the handing to the PLO of the reins over Palestinians in the West Bank and Gaza. The PLO, and most notably Arafat, earned this honor with populist nationalism and terrorism. In 1988 Arafat, as the chairman of the Palestinian Liberation Organization, and with the support of the Palestinian National Council, declared Palestinian independence and assumed the title of President of Palestine. During the 1980s, Arafat had received significant financial assistance from Iraq, Libya, and Saudi Arabia, assistance that he used to fund the first intifada from Tunis where he was based until 1993. Oslo recognized the PLO as a representative of the Palestinian people and allowed Arafat to return to the West Bank, and, in return, the PLO officially renounced violence. However, Arafat lacked full control over all the disgruntled groups and the violence continued.

The Oslo accords and recognition of the PLO as the sole representative body of the Palestinians did not please much of the Palestinian leadership within the West Bank, Gaza or in the Diaspora. As noted by some local Palestinian representatives, as a consequence of attaining its international recognition, the PLO became far less demanding in its postulations for rights for Palestinians and its monopoly on power led to corruption. At the moment of the signing of Oslo, prominent local Palestinian leaders such as Hanan Ashrawi noted the irony.

> It's clear that the ones who initiated this agreement have not lived under occupation. You postponed the settlement issue and Jerusalem without even getting guarantees that Israel would not continue to create facts on the ground that would preempt and prejudice the final outcome.
>
> (Swisher 2004, 137)

The Oslo period was also plagued by an increase in Israeli settlements and violence from Palestinian extremist groups, notably Hamas and Islamic Jihad. Palestinian extremist groups, notably Hamas, were funded and militarily equipped by neighboring players including Hezbollah and Iran. Hamas and Islamic Jihad rejected Oslo, from which they were excluded, and worked together to derail the process. In a series of suicide bombings and attacks, Hamas and Islamic Jihad targeted Israeli civilians in crowded restaurants, buses and malls. The terrorism worked to frighten the population and tarnished the popularity of the peace talks. Although prohibited in the Oslo accords and condemned widely, to make matters worse, the establishment of Israeli settlements in the Occupied Palestinian Territories continued, indeed increased, as did the violence surrounding the settlements. As noted by Shaul Arieli, a third of the Israelis living in the West Bank and Gaza strip moved to the settlements prior to the signing of the Oslo Accords (25 years), another third during the Oslo Accords period (8 Years) and another third between 2001 and 2009, following the official freezing of the settlements (Arieli 2010, 349). The Foundation for Middle East Peace noted that the settler population increase in the West Bank between 1994 and 2000 was 54 percent, compared to a 16.4 percent population increase within Israel (Foundation 2011). The settlements run up against the Fourth Geneva Convention, which states that "the Occupying Power shall not deport or transfer parts of its own civilian population into the territory it occupies" (Convention 1949). Moreover, the increase of the Israeli settlements during the peace talks worked to bolster Palestinian extremists and weaken the moderates who supported the peace process.

The Oslo process, however, brought more funding into the conflict and opened the door for increased engagement of the EU. At a donors' conference in October 1993, following the signing of the agreement, the EU collectively pledged over $500 million for economic recovery and development needs in the Palestinian Territories, making the EU the leading donor to the Palestinians (Peters 2010a). In 1995, the EU also increased its economic trade relations with Israel, signing the EU–Israel Association Agreement. However, despite playing a more significant economic role in supporting Palestinians and widening its economic ties with Israel, the EU continued to have marginal political leverage over the parties, in particular the Israelis, or enough strength to counter US influence (Peters 2010a). The funding was also not properly monitored, resulting in much corruption and public disillusionment with the PLO.

With little accountability, monitoring agreement or consensus on how to approach non-compliance, the IC stood by and watched the peace process disintegrate. Interventions were largely symbolic with little impact. Following a 1994 incident when an Israeli settler killed 29 Palestinian worshipers inside the ancient Al-Ibrahimi Mosque (Abraham Tomb) in Hebron, Norwegian and Italian observers were sent to Hebron. However, the tiny monitoring mission had little impact. Referred to as the "ice cream soldiers" because of the white color of their uniform and their limited mandate, which forced them to "melt" at the first sign of trouble, the soldiers had small impact even within Hebron (Bennis 1997). The limited mandate gave them reporting power, but, with no authority to intervene, they became merely witnesses to the ongoing violence.

The regional politics, however, were bolstered by the peace talks and heightened external economic investment. In 1994, the US played a prominent role in helping to secure a historic peace treaty between Jordan and Israel. As noted by Zittrain Eisenberg, Amman's worsening economy required a massive foreign intervention and, in exchange for signing a peace agreement with Israel, Washington offered generous assistance including US forgiveness of Jordan's $700 million foreign debt (Eisenberg 2003). The treaty made Jordan the second Arab country after Egypt to sign a peace agreement with Israel. Egypt also played a positive role in the negotiations and supported the final agreement. As noted by Israeli President Shimon Peres, who was the then Israeli Foreign Minister, "President Mubarak, whose effort to advance the peace process has not received sufficient recognition, showed great willingness to assist both sides" (Peres 1993, 22).

The 1994 peace agreement had initially given a sense hope to a regional transformation. However, outside of Jordan and Egypt, the peace process did not have much regional support. Iran conducted a terrorist campaign designed to undermine the process, funding the militant group Hezbollah (Rabinovich 2004). Hezbollah launched rockets into Northern Israel, which incited Israel to dispatch large-scale military operations into Lebanon. The Israeli population was already dissatisfied with Oslo, since it did not lead to a decrease in violence against Israeli civilians. Indeed, the period between 1993 and 1995 was marked by ten suicide bombings, injuring hundreds and claiming the lives of 77 Israeli civilians. In 1996 the US launched a global campaign against terrorism in Sharm al Sheikh, aimed at isolating Iran and Syria and boosting the popularity of Peres (Rabinovich 2004, 76). However, the initiative had little impact as the Israeli public turned away from the peace process.

The election of PM Benjamin Netanyahu in June 1996 was partly a response to the suicide bombings and public disillusionment with the peace process. Focusing on security, Netanyahu imposed economic restrictions and slowed down Oslo. The election of Netanyahu further worsened relations between Israel and the EU. As noted by Joel Peters,

> For European leaders, Netanyahu's policies were at best unhelpful and at worse catastrophic. In turn, Netanyahu dismissed Europe's projection of

normative power and its stress on cooperative security practices as naive
and reflective of its lack of capacity and weakness as a global security actor.

(Peters 2010a, 516)

Continued US support of Israel strengthened Israel's resolve to abandon the
peace process and continue the settlement build up.

Although the IC, in particular the EU and the UN, objected to settlements,
and the US voiced mild concerns, Washington took measures to protect Israel
against international condemnation. On May 1995, the UN Council voted on a
resolution condemning Israel's seizure of the Palestinian territory, but the US
vetoed the resolution. On March 7 and 22, 1997, the Security Council once
again challenged Israeli settlement policy as leading to violent clashes. The US
cast its veto on both occasions. The resolutions had overwhelming international consensus against the building of Israeli settlements on Palestinian
occupied territory. For example, in March 1997, the General Assembly voted
130 to 2 calling on Israel to abandon Har Homa, a new Israeli settlement built
in Jerusalem. Only Israel and the United States voted against, and Israel went
ahead with the construction. The building was met with violent protests and
the Palestinian cabinet issued a statement saying it was not useful to hold talks
with Israel as long as the policy of expansion of settlements and violating the
agreement is continuing.

Without an effective external broker, the two sides blamed each other for the
violence and the lack of progress in the implementation of the Oslo accords.
Under Article 15 of the Oslo Accords, Israel initially agreed to binding arbitration of the dispute if and when negotiation should fail. The arbitration panel
would have consisted of Israel, the Palestinians and the Madrid conference co-
sponsors, Russia and the United States (Makovsky 1995). However, the final
wording of the Agreement only called on the parties to establish an arbitration
process that never took place. Extremists on both sides managed to derail the
process that was designed as incremental implementation based on the growth of
trust. Hamas and Jihad conducted deadly attacks against Israeli civilians, and, in
1995, a Jewish extremist assassinated Israeli Prime Minister Yitzhak Rabin.
With the continuing of Palestinian violence, Israel saw no benefit in implementing Oslo. Although agreements were signed, with no trust and no external
attempt to monitor, guarantee, or assist in implementation of the agreements, the
process collapsed.

Oslo's gradual, incremental approach only worked to heighten mistrust
between the conflicting groups. The incremental approach went hand in hand
with a transformational method of mediation that worked well for the Norwegian
attempts at mediating the conflict. As noted by Hilde Henriksen Waage, "At the
outset, only minor issues are put on the negotiating table. Once some sort of
compromise has been reached on these, the parties move on to the more difficult
problems. This idea underlay the Oslo process" (Waage 2007, 162). However,
once Norway handed its gains to the Americans, Norway's role as well as the
positive incremental process came to an abrupt halt.

The gains, such as mutual recognition and bringing in the PLO, did not amount to much without group transformation. Although bringing in Arafat and the PLO was useful for an agreement, treating Arafat and the PLO as the de-facto representative of the Palestinian state had dire consequences felt to this day. Oslo created one party, which was led by the Palestinian authority, making it responsible for parts of the West Bank and Gaza but without a proper state apparatus, no national consensus, and no control over use of force. Both sides took advantage of the agreement to create facts on the ground. For Arafat, Oslo allowed Fatah to tighten its political hold over the Palestinian territories and opened up wide opportunities for corruption. The Israeli government created their own facts on the ground by increasing settlements. The UN's condemnation of Israeli settlements was overridden by American vetoes, reflecting the American continuing need to protect Israeli interests and weaken international tools.

Thus, although Oslo could be seen as an attempt at a united–neutral process, it failed for a number of reasons. First, international support was minimal and not united, local public support was marginal, and Palestinian and Israeli extremists were successful at derailing the process. Second, the interim step-by-step process in which the majority of the steps were implemented, worked only to deepen the mistrust when the steps were not implemented and the process lacked monitoring and accountability. Israeli, Palestinian and American participants in the center of the process all echoed this point. As noted by Alon Pinkas, the former Israeli political advisor to President Shimon Peres, "the longer the process was stretched, the more exposed and vulnerable it became to its detractors. Every delay or disagreement was magnified to vindicate the opposition" (Pinkas 2013). Erekat blamed the failure on the lengthy peace process with no accountability. As noted by Saeb Erekat, "Oslo failed because there was no accountability, because some parts of the international community took it as an end in itself" (Miller 2013). Former Clinton administrator Aaron David Miller noted that

> The key flaw of the Oslo process lay in the philosophical conceit that the most intractable differences could simply be deferred to the end of the process while the implementation of interim agreements would build the mutual trust and confidence to be able to tackle the tougher issues.
>
> (Miller 2013)

Although Norway began a constructive process, in the absence of international unity, accountability and a means of arbitration of disputes, Oslo failed to end the violence, occupation, or settlements or to improve the lives of Palestinians or Israelis. Neither the Israeli nor the Palestinian public saw gains from the peace process. In a final attempt for all-out resolution of the conflict, the US trumped the failing Oslo process with behind-closed-doors intense US-led final status mediation at Camp David. However, despite the mutual recognition achieved by Norway, the Oslo process in which neither party lived up to its promises had worsened trust between the parties, creating a poor backdrop to the mediation. The US, with its continuing and unconditional support of Israel, was also not perceived as an honest broker.

American mediation efforts at Camp David II, though well intended, can best be described as a textbook case for what international mediators should not do as process managers. By basic norms and practices, mediators should not let one side hijack the process, should not be manipulated by one of the sides, should not agree to have one side dictate the terms of the agreement and should not renege on their own promises. However, all of these were done at Camp David. On the other hand, mediators should attempt to set up a fair process, foster trust, encourage mutual gain rather than bargaining, and foster good communication between the conflicting parties. Sadly, none of these were evidently done at Camp David.

The reasons behind this well-recorded process failure were twofold: the US partisan position towards Israel; and the American overconfidence that PM Ehud Barak would deliver and was ready to make a historic compromise. According to chief US mediator Denis Ross,

> The [US] President was basically reluctant to say no to Barak.... I mean Barak was the guy who was taking the big leaps! Barak was the guy who was going to confront a terrible reality at home when he did this! Barak was the guy who had enormous courage to do it!
>
> (Swisher 2004, 260)

Regardless of intention, the US was unable to curb its support for Israel sufficiently to be an effective mediator between the two sides.

Overconfidence in Israeli leadership had led the US to essentially surrender summit controls to the Israeli team. According to Dennis Ross, Barak had his own completely arbitrary process strategy, in which nothing would happen the first two days, and the key point of decision should come on day five of the summit (Ross 2004). Barak was willing to have the US list Israeli and Palestinian issues, provided that he would have the chance to modify the parameters before they were presented to the Palestinians (Ross 2004). President Clinton, apparently to the frustration of Dennis Ross, acceded to Barak's demands.

> When the President briefed us on the meeting, he made it clear he had acceded to Barak's wish on how to handle the parameter exercise. He did not want to "jam him" at the start of the summit. Naturally, this meant that we had to redo the approach for the President's meeting with Arafat. Already we were altering our strategy for the summit. We were not bounding the discussions and crystallizing them; as a result we were not taking control of the summit at the outset.
>
> (Ross 2004, 656)

In the end, the American delegation not only gave sneak previews of official US drafts and ideas to the Israeli delegation but subsequently altered them and presented Israeli positions as if they were American proposals. According to a member of the US negotiation team Robert Malley "the US ended up (often unwittingly) presenting Israeli negotiating positions and couching them as rock bottom red lines beyond which Israel could not go" (Malley and Aqha 2001, 16). The proposals promoted by the Americans were those submitted by the Israeli team and tended to favor the Israeli side. For the Palestinian delegation, this intensified the sense of distrust about the fairness of the process. As noted by Swisher, "For the Palestinians, there was no conceivable way the Americans could have listed these principles as 'estimations based on the discussions with the parties,' unless the only parties they really listened to were the Israelis" (Swisher 2004, 268).

The fact that many members of the American negotiation team were Jewish Americans and the team attempted to use a divide and conquer method against the Palestinians did not help matters. Barak's personal strategy was to use the summit to place pressure on Arafat. When the frustrated Dennis Ross asked Barak why we were here, considering the lack of progress, Barak replied that "the pressure cooker had to work first on Arafat; then things would happen" (Ross 2004, 667). The US mediators' methods and process helped to confirm Arafat's worst fears that the summit was one great US–Israeli conspiracy (Swisher 2004). The Palestinian team became increasingly suspicious, perceiving everything presented by Americans as disguised Israeli proposals (Qurie 2008).

Backing down to Barak's pressure that nothing should be written down, to prevent the Palestinians from pocketing of concessions, the lack of written agreements meant miscommunication and misunderstandings. With no direct negotiations, nothing written down and Americans acting as go-between, the Palestinian and Israeli delegations experienced numerous misunderstandings, which reflected a children's broken telephone game. Although Arafat was blamed for the failure of Camp David, by any mediator's yardstick, the process was very mismanaged. Subsequent attempts at agreements, such as the one in Taba where direct negotiations took place in a more conducive atmosphere, came too late, since elections had removed both American and Israeli leadership from power. US President Bill Clinton's term ended shortly after Camp David and Israeli PM Ehud Barak was voted out of office.

The failure of the Camp David summit had dire long-term consequences. Israeli and Palestinian public disillusionment with the peace process, coupled with political incitement, led to an intifada and spiral of violence and shelved the possibility of a negotiated settlement. It also tarnished the Americans as the potential mediators, at a time when only the Americans were seen as capable of mediating an agreement. Unlike the case of BiH, where the US used its powerful leverage against the dominant and uncooperative party and had the capacity to impose an agreement, in the case of Israel-Palestine, this was considered impossible. The US did not use its leverage on the Israelis and was unsuccessful in imposing a solution on the Palestinians. Indeed, American mediation and support for the Israelis played a role in discrediting external intervention and undermining prospects for peace.

Regardless of intention, Oslo as well as the US-driven process at Camp David failed as an effective external process and served to tarnish future mediation.

The arduous road towards a united intervention process

Following the failure at Camp David and the subsequent escalation of violence, there was a US attempt towards a more inclusive and united international intervention in the conflict. While the US, headed by President George W. Bush, became less active directly in attempts to solve the conflict, the EU took the opportunity to become more actively involved. In 2002, the United States decided to formally expand external mediators in the Israeli–Palestinian conflict and called for the establishment of the Middle East Quartet. The Quartet, composed of the United States, the European Union, the Russian Federation and the Office of the Secretary General of the United Nations, was established to coordinate external peace efforts in the Middle East based on a two-state solution. The Quartet's road map, launched in 2003, was a performance-based, three-phase plan intended to conclude in a final agreement and a Palestinian state. Until this point, the Americans had generally snubbed the participation of EU, UN and Russia in Middle East negotiations.

The establishment of the Quartet and an attempt at united international intervention policies had more to do with September 11, Iraq and the war on terror than shifts in positions or events related to the Israeli–Palestinian conflict. President Bush began his term in office strongly allied to Israel but was forced to take a more cooperative stance alongside his European and Arab counterparts on the Israeli–Palestinian conflict. Former Middle East envoy Dennis Ross summed up the reasoning behind the new strategy:

> with the tactical need to gain support for or at least acquiescence in its Iraq policy, the administration agreed to work with the European Union (EU), the United Nations, and Russia in drafting a roadmap that might reflect the President's vision. While the United States would not let these other countries determine its response to Iraq, it would let them help shape the conduct of US diplomacy between Israelis and Palestinians, an unprecedented step in the US approach to Arab–Israeli issues.
>
> (Ross 2004, 788)

As noted by Laura Zitrain Eisenberg, Washington aimed to do just enough to satisfy its European and Arab allies, whose support it needed for Iraq and Afghanistan (Eisenberg 2010).

Although itself divided on how to intervene, the EU pushed for a need for a common strategy on the conflict and an end to an exclusive US-led partisan mediation process. The EU made a link between the Israeli–Palestinian peace process, September 11, and the rise of terrorism in Europe, emphasizing the need for regional peace to ensure regional security and stability. As noted by Joel Peters, "for the first time, the EU created a link between the collapse of the

Israeli–Palestinian peace process and its own direct security interests and, in particular, its efforts to combat terrorism and al-Qaeda ..." (Peters 2010a, 520). In its 2002 meeting, which included a Declaration on the Middle East, the Council of Ministers noted that the Middle East has reached a "dramatic turning point" at which "further escalation will render the situation uncontrollable" and called for an end to the Israeli occupation and the establishment of a sovereign Palestinian State (Council of Ministers 2002). The Council of Ministers outlined an urgent need for involvement by the Quartet and the "establishment of a democratic, viable, peaceful and sovereign State of Palestine, on the basis of the 1967 borders, if necessary with minor adjustments agreed by the parties" (Council of Ministers 2002, 35).

Sidelined by the Quartet, the Arab states in 2002 signed their own parallel peace initiative which included a full Israeli withdrawal from the territories occupied since 1967, a just solution to the Palestinian refugee problem, and the establishment of an independent Palestinian state. In return, the 22 Arab countries would consider the Arab–Israeli conflict ended and normalize their relations with Israel. The Arab initiative signaled a potential step towards a united intervention, since its propositions echoed those of the US, EU and the Quartet. However, in the immediate aftermath of September 11, the Americans were suspicious of a unified Arab position and did not accept an Arab-led framework of international legitimacy for its war against terrorism and rogue states (Awan 2007). Washington disregarded the Arab Peace Initiative until it was revived in 2007 and taken more seriously following the election of President Barak Obama.

Though the intervention process was united on principles, this was not always reflected in practice. Although the US created the Quartet and was its key member, Washington's continual support for Israel trumped and undermined its functioning. When the Quartet's performance-based road map was ignored by Israel and derailed by PM Sharon's disengagement plan, which called for a unilateral withdrawal from Gaza, the US supported Israel's actions. US President George Bush wrote a supporting letter regarding Israel's unilateral disengagement noting that "[t]he United States is strongly committed to Israel's security and well-being as a Jewish State" (Bush 2009). Despite ending the direct occupation of Gaza, Israel's unilateral disengagement meant a loss of an opportunity, altering Palestinian political dynamics with long-term dire consequences.

The presumably unintended consequence of the unilateral disengagement, made possible with American support, succeeded in strengthening Palestinian extremists and weakening the moderates. First, the Israeli pullout from Gaza was perceived as a victory for Hamas, boosting its popularity. Second, there was little attempt to hand over power in Gaza to the Abbas leadership, which eventually resulted in a Hamas takeover in Gaza and complete political separation between Gaza and the West Bank. To make matters worse, the evacuated areas bordering Israel were subsequently used to launch further attacks against civilians in adjacent Israeli cities including Ashkelon and Be'er Sheba, thus escalating the conflict and giving justification to fierce Israeli retaliation.

The withdrawal not only added fuel to extremists it also resulted in some regrettable lessons for Palestinians and Israelis, detrimental to the peace process. For many Palestinians, particularly those favoring Hamas, the lesson learned was: make the occupation costly in terms of Israeli lives and Israel will withdraw from the Occupied Territories. The lesson learned for many Israelis was: give land back to the Palestinians and it will be used for strengthening terrorism and launching further attacks against Israel. The Quartet, which was overseeing the handover, took the fall for the failure. As was noted by Levy, "The Quartet failed to seize the post-Arafat moment, failed to support Abbas after his election to the presidency, lent a hand to Israeli unilateralism, and gave no opening for engagement to the new Hamas government" (Levy and Shtender-Auerbach 2006).

The inability of the Quartet to be more pro-active was largely due to its own internal divisions. As noted by Costanza Musu, the

> US itself, despite being a member of the Quartet, has had a mixed attitude towards it, almost fuelling the suspicions that it had contributed to its creation in order to respond to external pressures (mainly from the European allies) while at the same time aiming to maintain an undisputed role as the sole mediator accepted by both parties.
>
> (Musu 2006, 13)

James Wolfensohn, the first Special Envoy of the Quartet, identified several issues requiring special attention: border crossings; connecting Gaza with the West Bank, air and sea ports; and transferring housing and the agricultural infrastructure (greenhouses) in the settlements (Peters 2010b). He was placed in charge of Israel's disengagement but eventually resigned in frustration, complaining that his mandate was too weak and his work undermined by the American administration.

The 2006 elections of a Hamas majority in Gaza deepened the existing divisions within the Quartet. According to Wolfensohn, there was no international consensus on how to operate under the new Hamas leadership in Gaza. The US and some EU countries listed Hamas as a "terrorist organization" while Russia considered the organization "a legitimate actor in Palestinian politics, not a 'terrorist' entity to be boycotted" (Pradhan 2008, 322). Russian President Putin proposed talking to the Islamic organization without any preconditions and officially invited a Hamas delegation to Russia. On the other hand, the US and EU coordinated a move to withdraw aid money from Gaza on the grounds that, until Hamas renounced violence, honored past peace agreements and recognized Israel, funding would be frozen.

Wolfenson noted his disappointment with American and European policy for completely cutting all aid to the Hamas-led Palestinian government. In a radio discussion with Condoleezza Rice, Wolfenson emphasized "it would surprise me if one could win by getting all the [Gaza] kids out of school or starving the Palestinians … I think that's losing gambit" (Kelemen 2006). The harsh policies resulted in an economic collapse in Gaza, a dysfunctional local government, and contributed to the complete takeover of Gaza by Hamas. Wolfenson placed the largest blame on the Americans. "I have no doubts that I may have made tactical, strategic mistakes, but the basic problem was that I didn't have the authority. The Quartet had the authority, and within the Quartet it was the Americans who had the authority." Wolfenson noted:

> There was never a desire on the part of the Americans to give up control of the negotiations, and I would doubt that in the eyes of [Deputy National Security Advisor] Elliot Abrams and the State Department team, I was ever anything but a nuisance.
>
> (Shahar 2007)

Although Wolfenson spent months negotiating an agreement between Israelis and Palestinians on border crossings, freedom of movement and checkpoints, seaports and airports, any gains went ignored. According to Wolfenson, Secretary of State Condoleezza Rice and Deputy National Security Advisor Abrams clarified to him that his mandate was limited and intervention in peace negotiations was not within his purview. As noted by Wolfenson,

> I had to fight my way into the November [2005] meeting when Secretary Rice announced the six-point plan. I was there with Javier Solana when it was announced, and what I didn't realize was that that was the death penalty, because after that the Israelis and the Americans took apart that agreement one by one, and I knew less and less what was happening. And my team of 18 people was fired. So I was left with no office and no people, and even though they asked me to stay on, it was pretty clear to me that the only thing to do was to get out.
>
> (Shahar 2007)

Although in principle the Quartet had shifted the multinational intervention towards a united–neutral intervention, in practice, intervention remained partisan and divided as Washington, regardless of intention, undermined a united external process.

The 2008 election of US President Barak Obama initially brought rays of hope for a more united and cooperative international approach towards resolution of the Israeli–Palestinian conflict. The Obama administration outlined adjustments from previous US administrations, including better cooperation and coordination among external interveners. However, the Gaza war that ended two days before President Obama was inaugurated and the subsequent Goldstone Report that investigated the war, once again divided the international community. Launched on December 27, 2008, in response to rocket fire from Gaza, Operation Cast Lead was a coordinated massive Israeli airstrike killing hundreds of people in Gaza within the first four minutes. Up to 1,400 people, mainly civilians, were estimated to have been killed in the 22 days of the war (Amnesty 2009). The attack was a response to the increasing number of Qassam rockets launched from Gaza targeting southern Israeli towns and killing or maiming dozens of Israeli civilians.

The Gaza attack once again divided the IC into countries that condemned the attack and those, mainly the US, that justified Israeli actions. The subsequent UN inquiry headed by Richard Goldstone accused Israeli Defense forces of war crimes, crimes against humanity and serious violations of international law, recommending further investigation and bringing those responsible to justice (Mission 2009). The UN Human Rights Council endorsed the report and the UN General Assembly urged Israel and Palestine to conduct an independent investigation into the alleged war crimes in Gaza. The EU Parliament also endorsed the Goldstone report, noting that EU member states should demand that the report's recommendations be carried out and that there should be accountability for all violations.

On the other hand, US Congress voted the Goldstone report to be "irredeemably biased" against Israel and called on President Obama to maintain his opposition to the report. The bill, passed by majority in Congress, "supports the Administration's efforts to combat anti-Israel bias at the United Nations and considers the UN report as 'unbalanced, one-sided and basically unacceptable'." The Congress called upon the President to "strongly and unequivocally oppose an endorsement of the report, including through vetoing any United Nations Security Council resolution that endorses its contents" (Congress 2009). The Congress also "reaffirms its support for the democratic Jewish State of Israel, for Israel's security and right to self-defense, and, specifically, for Israel's right to defend its citizens from violent militant groups and their state sponsors" (Congress 2009). President Obama called the report "flawed" and asked both parties to investigate the allegations. In response to the criticism, Goldstone noted that the report would have looked different had the Israeli government cooperated with the investigation.

In the end, Washington persuaded the Palestinian leadership to shelve their complaints to the UN and international legal forums, contributing to the plummeting credibility of the moderate leadership. The US diplomatic plan, known as a "non paper," presented by George Mitchell's team noted that "the PA will help promote a positive atmosphere conducive to negotiations; in particular during negotiations it will refrain from pursuing or supporting any initiative directly or indirectly in international legal forums that would undermine that atmosphere" (Swisher 2011, 67). The Palestinian public responded in uproar and disillusionment. Protests were held across the West Bank and Gaza, once again weakening the moderate leadership and strengthening the extremists. International and national human rights groups heavily criticized the decision. UN Special Rapporteur on Human Rights in the Occupied Territories Richard Falk noted with astonishment

> The Palestinians have betrayed their own people. This was a moment when finally the international community endorsed the allegations of war crimes and it would have been an opportunity to vindicate the struggle for the

Palestinian people for their rights under international law and for the Palestinian representatives in the UN themselves to seem to undermine this report is an astonishing development.

(Meloni and Tognoni 2012, 131)

The response to the 2009 Gaza war highlighted the ongoing divisions within the international community. Although there has been growing international consensus on principles to resolve the conflict, in practice the divisions have remained. The conflict over Palestinian versus Israeli legitimacy and accountability to international law has been fought within international bodies. For the Europeans, the plight of the Palestinians and unyielding behavior of Israeli governments has become an internal security issue. As noted by Joel Peters,

> Europe is increasingly looking at the conflict as constituting a direct threat to Europe's global, regional and, above all, its domestic security concerns. The daily images of the suffering and humiliation inflicted on the Palestinian population by Israeli policies are perceived as threatening the stability of many European capitals.
>
> (Peters 2010a, 526)

Although the EU has played an increasingly important role in the Israeli–Palestinian conflict, its influence on Israeli policies has been negligent (Pardo and Peters 2009).

The 2014 Gaza war that resulted in the death of 2,220 Palestinians including 1,492 civilians was the deadliest escalation in hostilities since the beginning of the Israeli Occupation in 1967 (OCHA 2015). In addition, almost 500,000 people were internally displaced and, because of the high level of destruction, a fifth have been unable to return to their pre-war homes. This is beyond the damage and destruction to schools, hospitals and infrastructure. The 2014 Gaza war also resulted in accusations of war crimes. Palestinians officially joined the International Criminal Court in hopes of prosecuting Israel for alleged war crimes and crimes against humanity during the Gaza war. It remains to be seen whether the Court will be able to investigate the war crimes, given the lack of support and cooperation from not only Israel but the US. Despite the widely covered conflict and atrocities committed against civilians, the lack of consensus among the international community has meant that little progress has been made.

In the past few years, with the establishment of the Quartet, the Arab Peace Initiative, and the election of US president Barak Obama, external policies have in principle shifted from divided to more united intervention and brought some rays of hope to the Middle East. There has been greater external agreement on the principles of the solutions as outlined by the Quartet and the Arab Peace Initiative. In practice, however, Europeans have had little political influence and Americans have continued to behave in a unilateral and partisan fashion, supporting Israel diplomatically, militarily and economically. Regardless of intention, the American intervention has contributed to strengthening hardliners and weakening the Palestinian moderate leadership. The divided intervention has had little positive transformative impact on either of the conflicting groups.

External identity strategies and their impact on the Israeli–Palestinian conflict

The type of group strategies or proposed solutions to the Palestinian–Israeli conflict has engaged the international community for decades. Internal Palestinian and Israeli discussions regarding group identity strategies in the Israeli–Palestinian conflict have ranged from coexistence and integration, to partitioning and expulsions. Decades of violence, occupation, segregation and political incitement have created a culture of anger, fear and distrust. Creative institutional options discussed have included the two-state solution, one-state solution, confederation and federation. The majority of official international solutions have focused on a two-state solution or partitioning along ethno-religious lines. Many members of the international community have accepted ethno-religious partitioning and segregation as the only possibility for the conflicting groups for the foreseeable future. The policies of division have risen out of general local and international belief in the inability of Palestinians and Israelis to coexist.

From the initial external intervention, international strategies in Israel-Palestine have revolved around ethno-religious partitioning solutions, based on the creation of two separate nation-states. The founding of a Jewish homeland was accepted and promoted by Britain as part of the Balfour declaration. The establishment of a Palestinian homeland was a subsequent add-on following outrage by the Palestinian leadership and violent public protest. The partitioning favored a Jewish nation state, maximizing wide territory for the influx of further Jewish settlement. Coerced or, if necessary, forced exchange of population was recommended by the Peel Commission to deal with the demographic reality (Morris 2001).

From the first resolution regarding the conflict adopted by the UN General Assembly in 1947 – resolution 181 – the UN focus was also on partitioning along ethno-religious lines. Resolution 181 provided for the establishment of an Arab State and a Jewish State with a special international regime for the city of Jerusalem. Although Resolution 181 provided for religious, language and cultural rights for the minorities to be residing in the two future states, the partitioning was clearly along group lines. Section 1 of chapter 3 of the resolution outlined that persons over the age of 18 may opt for citizenship in the other state

> providing that no Arab residing in the area of the proposed Arab State shall have the right to opt for citizenship in the proposed Jewish State and no Jew residing in the proposed Jewish State shall opt for citizenship in the proposed Arab State.
>
> (UN Res181 1947)

In other words, Jews and Arabs would only be able to change residence into their "own" nation-state. Section 9 of Part 1B outlined that, during the transitional period, no Jew shall be permitted to establish residence in the proposed Arab state and no Arab shall be entitled to establish residence in the proposed Jewish state (UN Res181 1947). The resolution was never implemented, but it provided an international road map for solutions to come.

The demographic reality was only one of the several serious problems in implementation. In 1948, the day the British Mandate expired, the Jewish Peoples Council declared the establishment of the State of Israel, which was immediately recognized by the US. As noted in the introduction to this chapter, from the initial partitioning as designed by the United Nations, the new "Jewish" state had almost the same number of Arabs as Jews. For Israel, the "demographic majority problem" was partly resolved with the subsequent Arab–Israeli war when much of the Palestinian population either fled or was ethnically cleansed. Almost a million Palestinian refugees became scattered, most becoming permanent refugees within the surrounding Arab countries. Shortly after, almost a million Jewish refugees fled the Middle East countries, most of whom settled in Israel. Integration of Palestinians and other non-Jewish minority groups within Israel was very problematic. As noted by Joe Migdal, the state had constituted the Palestinian minority as "dangerous population," subject to state power but at the same time, excluded from the community of belonging (Migdal 2004).

Group strategies for the Palestinians are a complex combination of exclusion, cultural accommodation, and partitioning, with differing group strategies depending on the location. From the birth of Israel, policies of the new state towards the Palestinian minority were for the most part exclusive, since Israel was deemed a state for Jews, while Palestinians became either invisible or unwelcome guests. Judaism became not only a religious identity of Israel but the political, national and cultural identity of the state (Kook 2000). The policies of exclusion were built into the country's institutions and legal framework. As noted by Rebecca Kook, "ethnonational structures of inequality have been defined into the institution of citizenship, rendering it ineffective as a political and social equalizer" (Kook 2000, 264). The nature of the Jewish state led to institutionalized discrimination against its Arab minority. Until 1966, Palestinians living in Israel had been subject to military rule. As noted by Amal Jamal, ethno-religious affiliation, rather than civic membership, was established as the main principle of citizenship in Israel (Jamal 2009). This supported the policies of segregation, discrimination and intimidation, and served as justification for house demolitions and political arrests, measures which have continued until the present time. As discussed in Chapter 3, international norms regarding the status of minorities in states favor integration policies, which have been ignored by the Israeli government. Based on an exclusive cultural–religious framework, Israel is an ethnocracy. Until recently, the treatment of the Palestinian–Arab minority within Israel has been considered an internal Israeli matter and generally ignored by the international community.

Despite the dim reality of the "Israeli-Arabs", the quality of lives of Palestinians within Israel in some ways surpassed that of many Palestinians forced to become refugees in surrounding Arab countries. Although Israel discriminated against its Palestinian minority politically and restricted their integration and land rights, it set up a parallel educational system in Arabic and allowed, and at times fostered, economic advancement. This helped to create a well-educated middle class of Palestinian–Israelis, many of whom have become integrated economically in certain Israeli sectors such as health, business and the service industry. Many Palestinians who fled to surrounding countries faced much harsher circumstances, and were unable to integrate politically, socially or economically, thereby creating a generation of refugees dependent on foreign aid and vulnerable to regional conflicts. UNWRA (The United Nations Relief and Works Agency for Palestine Refugees in the Near East) currently provides assistance for over five million registered Palestinian refugees in Jordan, Lebanon, Syria and the Occupied Palestinian territory. Palestinians who have fled to neighboring countries such as Lebanon and Syria have remained refugees and have suffered an escalation of violence. In the past 60 years, spanning generations, their status has been maintained as refugees and their conditions have not improved significantly.

Palestinians facing the deepest hardship have been those living under Israeli Occupation. Since 1967, Palestinians living in the West Bank and Gaza have been partitioned from Israel, living under the harsh conditions of military occupation. In the West Bank and Gaza, the occupation has been perpetuated through strong-armed military rule and separation through the construction of a barrier. Illegal settlement policy, confiscation of land, house demolitions, arrests, and check points have been the daily policies in the West Bank, while Gaza has become a large, sophisticated open air prison. Israel's behavior in the West Bank and Gaza has been subject to much international focus and criticism, particularly by the EU and the UN.

Palestinian Prime Minister Salam Fayyad described Israel's current levels of micromanagement, where:

> Israel is involved in the minute details of the lives of Palestinians. It is important to remember that the entirety of the West Bank and Gaza Strip is ruled by military orders – not by politics, logic, or reason – but by military orders with (Israel's) "security" dictating the rules of the game.
>
> (Fayad 2007)

The barrier, at times a high wall and at times an impenetrable fence, has deepened separation between the groups, prevented movement of Palestinians between the Occupied Territories and Israel and limited movement within the Occupied Territories. The 815 km barrier was planned to annex 20 percent of the land from the West Bank; however, due to successful land suits, this was reduced to around 5 percent annexation (Arieli 2012).

The dire situation in the Occupied Territories, the separation barrier and the build up of the settlements, has only heightened Palestinian disillusionment with the peace talks and the potential of an international proposal of a two-state solution. Israel's occupation has come hand-in-hand with the buildup of settlements, which have carved up the territories. As noted by Aruri,

Slicing both the West Bank and Gaza into three separate zones was in fact Labor's solution to Likud's earlier dilemma: how to insure that its absorption of the Occupied Territories (which contrasted with Labor's formula of separation) did not lead to a bi-national state, in which Arabs and Jews would coexist in equality.

(Aruri 2003, 116)

The West Bank and East Jerusalem have become a collection of isolated areas and enclaves, separated from one another by roads that connect the settlements. The freezing of the build up of settlements has been one of the many hurdles to renewing peace talks. Despite Washington's continuing support of Israel, there has been some pressure on Israel to give in to international demands, including a settlement freeze. From Washington, the pressure has come with large carrots rather than sticks. In 2009, PM Benjamin Netanyahu announced a ten-month settlement freeze to return to the negotiation table. However, the settlement freeze did not include ongoing construction and settlement build up in Jerusalem and the surrounding area (Ravid 2009). In return for an additional 90-day settlement freeze, the US government offered Israel 20 F35 Fighter Jets worth three billion dollars. Despite its reliance on American support, cooperation from Israel has not been forthcoming. Former US Ambassador to Israel Martin Indyk said that, if Israel sees itself as a superpower that does not need any aid from the United States, then it can make its own decisions.

Given Israel's dependence on the United States to counter the threat from Iran and to prevent its own international isolation, an Israeli prime minister would surely want to bridge the growing divide. Yet the shift in American perceptions seems to have gone unnoticed in Jerusalem.

(Indyk 2010)

In response to the lack of progress towards a diplomatic solution based on a two-state solution, the build up of the settlements and the carving up of much of the West Bank, the Palestinian leadership has begun to move away from a two-state solution. Several key Palestinian leaders and think-tanks have started calling for a one-state solution. Former Palestinian Authority Prime Minister Ahmed Qurei, one of the architects of the Oslo Accords, called on Palestinians and Israelis to consider a one-state solution, noting that a two-state solution is no longer viable. Qurei "blamed Israel for 'burying' the two-state solution by building settlements and creating new facts on the ground in the West Bank and East Jerusalem" (Abu Toameh 2012). In 2008, the Palestinian Strategic Group, made up of prominent Palestinian intellectuals, outlined their "shift from a two-state outcome to a (bi-national or unitary democratic) single-state outcome as Palestinians preferred strategic goal" (Group 2008). Prominent Palestinian-American academic Rashid Khalidy noted that the one-state solution already exists, since "there is only one state between the Jordan River and the Mediterranean, in which there are two or three levels of citizenship or non-citizenship within the borders of that one state that exerts total control" (Shalev 2011). As noted by Khalidy, a two state solution "would not mean end-of-conflict and would still necessitate agreement on Palestinian refugees and on Israel's 'Palestinian minority' before a comprehensive settlement could be achieved" (Shalev 2011).

A bi-national state or a one state solution is currently unacceptable for most Israelis and is, at best, on the very margin of the international agenda. However, with the two-state solution being an ever-more-distant reality, the voices in favor of other solutions, including the one-state option, have grown louder. Paradoxically, it is Israeli politicians on the right that have pushed for an annexation of the West Bank and giving Palestinians full political rights. Former Israeli Minister of Defense and Likud member Moshe Arens noted in an opinion letter,

> What would happen if Israeli sovereignty were to be applied to Judea and Samaria, the Palestinian population there being offered Israeli citizenship? Those who, in Israel and abroad, consider the Israeli "occupation" of Judea and Samaria an unbearable evil should be greatly relieved by such a change that would free Israel of the burden of "occupation."
>
> (Arens 2010)

Although the international community continues to call for a two-state solution, the criticism of Israel for preventing a two-state solution, in particularly by the EU, have mounted. In its conclusions on the Middle East Peace Process, the Council of the European Union highlighted that the "viability of a two-state solution must be maintained" (Union 2012). The EU expressed "deep concern" about developments on the ground, which "threaten to make a two-state solution impossible." Among its concerns, it noted: the marked acceleration of settlement construction; the ongoing evictions and house demolitions in East Jerusalem and changes to the residency; the living conditions of the Palestinian population in Area C; and serious limitations in Area C for the PA to promote the economic development of Palestinian communities (Union 2012). EU statements, however, have had little impact in Israel.

The two-state solution, which is the current external prescription of group strategy in the conflict, ignores "Arab Israelis" or Palestinians living inside Israel. Although there have been some calls by extreme right-wing Israeli politicians for their forced removal, the official policy in Israel is one of integration within the state of Israel; however, in practice, the Palestinians living inside Israel have been subject to exclusion. As noted by Yiftachel, Israel has been established and continuous to function as an ethnocratic democracy (Yiftachel 2006). Ethnocratic rule builds on the concept of exclusion and is not conducive to positive transformation of the relations between groups. Although not surprising given the country's beginning and historical European persecution of Jews, the policies are unlikely to be sustainable. Ethnocratic rule has not only been subject to criticism from minorities within Israel, in recent years it has also been subject to deep external criticism.

Although not considered the core issue, the European Union has in particular become increasingly vocal in voicing its concerns. According to a classified paper drafted by diplomatic representatives working in Israel, "the European Union should consider Israel's treatment of its Arab population a core issue, not second tier to the Israeli–Palestinian conflict" (Ravid 2011). The document, which was sent to Brussels, noted; "The stalemate in the peace process, and the continuing occupation, inevitably has an impact on the identification of Israeli Arabs with Israel." The diplomatic representatives noted,

> It is in the interests of all Israelis to demonstrate that Israel is not only Jewish and democratic, but tolerant and inclusive, and that these are patriotic values. We believe in common with most Israelis that Israeli nationality is an inclusive concept which can accommodate equally those of other faiths and ethnic origins.
>
> (Fisher 2001)

Palestinians living inside Israel have pushed for equality, greater democratic inclusion and also to be allowed to form some links with Palestinians living in the West Bank and Gaza. In the 2006 *Future Vision Document*, written and officially submitted to the Israeli Knesset by the National Committee for the Heads of the Arab Local Authorities in Israel, Palestinian leadership living inside Israel noted that

> [t]o maintain the ethnocratic system, Israel has implemented several rules concerning the Palestinian Arabs in Israel: Cutting all identity relations between the Palestinian Arabs in Israel and the rest of the Palestinian people and the Arab and Islamic nation. Israel has tried to create a new group of "Israeli Arabs". Preventing Palestinian Arabs in Israel from keeping relations with their brothers in Jerusalem, the West Bank and the Gaza Strip, and, the Palestinians refugees.[3]

The document demanded equality for Palestinians living in Israel with the Jewish majority. The document noted that current Israeli policies, based on the "ethnocratic system," are "forcing the Palestinian Arabs in Israel to accept resource allocation on a basis of ethnicity rather than citizenship. This aims at maintaining the Jewish superiority and the Palestinian Arab inferiority in Israel."[4]

The inclusion of Palestinians living inside Israel may contribute to a peace process. Within internationally led discussions, the PLO has come to represent all Palestinians. Official talks not only excluded other groups and religious leaders in West Bank and Gaza but also moderate, educated Palestinian elites living within Israel. Through Oslo, Fatah effectively achieved monopoly of power over the majority of Palestinians but, with little achievement on the ground or in the peace talks and blatant corruption, the divisions have continued to widen (Ghanem 2010). The lack of benefits for average Palestinians not connected to the PLO and Arafat's political party Fatah, the largest and dominant faction of the PLO, formulated deep divides in the West Bank and Gaza beyond the conflict between Fatah and Hamas.

Solutions revolving around partitioning along exclusive ethno-religious lines have not been conducive strategies to resolving the conflict. The two-state solution is operating under an assumption that Israelis and Palestinians cannot live together. But it might be countered that Palestinians and Israelis already partially coexist, though not on equal terms. Although often referred to by Israelis as Israeli Arabs, Palestinians make up a fifth of the population of Israel. In many parts of Israel, on a daily basis Israelis are meeting Palestinians in streets, stores, busses and hospitals. Israelis even meet West Bank Palestinians in settlements. Many Palestinians, work, shop and some even live in settlements that are not closed to them. The recent escalation of violence has increased support for more divisions along ethno-religious lines. The question is whether strategies based on partitioning along ethnic lines offer transformative solutions to the conflict. Transformative solutions may come out of a one-, two-, or three-state solution, but they are unlikely to come out of exclusive identity strategies. As noted in Chapter 3 and witnessed in other conflicts, partitioning along ethnic lines is most likely to lead to ethnic cleansing and more violence. Land can remain important but "this land belongs to us" may need to be molded towards "we belong to the land" with the necessity of sharing and inclusion.

Conclusion

Despite the launching of the Quartet, the Arab Peace Initiative and a more cooperative US administration, external intervention in the Israeli–Palestinian conflict continues to be divided in practice, with the US supporting Israel and numerous other countries, particularly the EU, taking an increasingly stronger vocal opposition to Israeli practices as the occupier. The divided external intervention has been a hindrance to conflict transformation, hardening rather than softening the divisions between the Palestinians and Israelis. American partisan policy has a similar affect to that of an external guarantor, which provides moral, economic and military support to one of the groups in the conflict, preventing the necessity for the group's transformation. Similarly, some members of the Arab league have not taken any steps to prevent the support and arming of extremists, most specifically Hamas, empowering the group with not only technical and financial support but with moral ground, and this also prevents incentives for transformation. Thus, although there has been a small shift towards united–neutral intervention, it has been within the realm of principles while in practice the divided intervention continues to add fuel to the conflict.

International conflict resolution strategies in the Israeli–Palestinian conflict have also been far from ideal. From the beginning of the conflict, the one common element of external intervention has been attempts to divide territory between Palestinians and Israelis. International identity strategies have persisted along the lines of ethno-religious partitioning, giving little space for accommodation or inclusive integration. Although the birth of new inclusive democratic states can be a positive step, partitioning along ethnic or religious lines, which is the only current international solution, has only reaffirmed opposing identities. On the ground, the presumed connection between identity and territory has been translated into building settlements in occupied territories, evictions and separation walls.

As discussed in Chapter 2, a united intervention process, whether partisan or neutral, can have a constructive impact on the conflict. Lack of an international consensus has impacted on the potential of using more active or robust methods to resolve the conflict. Although boycott, divestment and sanctions (BDS) have gained some international popularity, particularly in Europe, the policy has had little support in the US. Indeed, some states have enacted legislation to divest from companies boycotting Israel, counterattacking the sanctions. Propped up by US support, the hardliners on the Israeli side have had little incentive to transform or end the Occupation. Thus far the United Nations and the European Union have voiced their concerns but lacked strength to have an impact. On the Palestinian side, the widening of the Israeli settlements in the West Bank and East Jerusalem and the chipping away at the possibility of a viable two-state solution have left the alternatives of a one state solution or another violent uprising. Lack of alternative solutions to the current partitioning strategies has also frozen the conflict in unsustainable conditions, which may get far worse before getting better.

Notes

1 Palestinian Center for Policy and Survey Research, Palestinian Public Opinion Poll, No. 34 December 10–12, 2009.
2 Joint Israeli–Palestinian Poll, Palestinian Center for Policy and Survey Research Unit and Harry S. Truman Institute for the Advancement of Peace. August, 2009.
3 *Future Vision of the Palestinian Arabs in Israel*, The National Committee for the Heads of the Arab Local Authorities in Israel, 2006, p. 10 www.adalah.org/newsletter/eng/dec06/tasawor-mostaqbali.pdf.
4 Ibid.

References

Abu Toameh, Khaled. 2012. "Qurei Calls for Reconsidering One-State Solution," *Jerusalem Post*, March 17.
Amnesty. 2009. *Operation Cast Lead: 22 Days of Death and Destruction*. Amnesty International. MDE 15/015/2009.
Andoni, Lamis. 1991. The PLO at the Crossroad. *Journal of Palestine Studies* 21 (1): 54–65.
Arens, Moshe. 2010. "Is There Another Option?" *Haaretz*. June 2.
Arieli, Shaul. 2010. *People and Borders: About the Israeli Palestinian Conflict*. Herzliya Pituach, Israel: Friedrich Ebert Stiftung.
Arieli, Shaul. 2012. "What we have Learned from the Barrier." *Haaretz*. July 10.
Aruri, Naseer Hasan. 2003. *Dishonest Broker: The US Role in Israel and Palestine*. Cambridge MA: South End Press.
Awan, Samir. 2007. The Arab Quartet and the Arab Peace Initiative. *Palestine–Israel Journal* 14 (4): 31–33.

Bar-Tal, Daniel and Dikla Antebi. 1992. Beliefs about Negative Intentions of the World: A Study of the Israeli Siege Mentality. *Political Psychology* 13 (4): 633–645.

Bennis, Phyllis. 1997. The United Nations and Palestine: Partition and Its Aftermath. *Arab Studies Quarterly* 19 (3): 47–76.

Bush, George W. 2009. "Ariel Sharon and George W. Bush's letters in full." In *Haaretz*. June 6.

Christison, Kathleen. 2004. All Those Old Issues: George W. Bush and the Palestinian–Israeli Conflict. *Journal of Palestine Studies* 33 (2): 36–50.

Congress, US. 2009. *H Resolution 867*.

Convention, Geneva. 1949. "Convention (IV) relative to the Protection of Civilian Persons in Time of War."

Council of Ministers, Council of the European Union. 2002. *Seville European Council 21 and 22 June 2002, Presidency Conclusions*.

Eisenberg, Zittrain Laura Neil Kaplan. 2003. The Israel–Jordan peace Treaty: Patterns of Negotiation, Problems of Implementation. *Israel Affairs* 9 (3): 87–110.

Eisenberg, Zittrain Laura Neil Kaplan 2010. *Negotiating Arab–Israeli Peace: Patterns, Problems, Possibilities*. Bloomington IN: Indiana University Press.

Fayad, Salam. 2007. *UN Sponsored Middle East Quartet Corners PLO, Hamas into Critical Options*. Presented at the Seventh Annual Herzliya Conference, Tel Aviv.

Fisher, J. Ronald 2001. "Methods of Third Party Intervention." In *Berghof Handbook for Conflict Transformation*. Berlin: Berhof foundation.

Foundation for Middle East Peace. 2011. *Settler Population Growth East and West of the Separation Barrier*. Washington DC: Foundation for Middle East Peace.

Ghanem, Asad. 2010. *Palestinian Politics after Arafat*. Bloomington IN: Indiana University Press.

Golan, Galia. 1986. The Soviet Union and the PLO since the War in Lebanon. *Middle East Journal* 40 (2): 285–305.

Goldstein, Joshua S. and Jon C. Pevehouse. 1997. Reciprocity, Bullying and International Cooperation: Time-series Analysis of the Bosnian Conflict. *The American Political Science Review* 91 (3): 515–559.

Group, Palestine Strategy Study. 2008. *Regaining the Initiative: Palestinian Strategic Options to End Israeli Occupation*. Ramallah: Palestine Strategy Group.

Gurion, Ben David. 1945. Ben Gurion's Survey. *The New Judaea* 21 (11).

Indyk, Martin. 2010. "If Israel Manages Alone, It Can Decide Alone." In *Haaretz*. April 21.

Jamal, Amal. 2009. Democratizing State-Religious Relations: A Comparative Study of Turkey, Egypt and Israel. *Democratization* 16 (6): 1143–1171.

Kelemen, Michele. 2006. "Key Roadmap Mideast Peace Envoy Resigns." In: NPR.

Khalidi, Rashid. 1997. *Palestinian National Identity: The Construction of Modern National Consciousness*. New York: Columbia University Press.

Kimmerling, Baruch and Joel S. Migdal. 1993. *Palestinians, The Making of a People*. New York: Free Press.

Kook, Rebecca. 2000. "Citizenship and Its Discontents: Palestinians in Israel." In *Citizenship and the State in the Middle East: Approaches and Applications*, eds. Nils August, Uri Davis Butenschon and Manuel Sarkis Hassassian. Syracuse, NY: Syracuse University Press.

Laqueur, Walter. 2003. *History of Zionism*. London: IB Tauris Academic.

Levy, Daniel and Michael Shtender-Auerbach. 2006. The Road Not Taken in the Middle East. *World Policy Institute* 23 (3): 15–22.

Makovsky, David. 1995. *Making Peace with the PLO, The Rabin Government's Road to the Oslo Accord.* Boulder CO: Westview Press.

Malley, Robert and Aqha, Hussein. 2001. Camp David: The Tragedy of Errors. *The New York Review of Books* 48 (13): 133–159.

Meloni, Chantal and Gianni Tognoni. 2012. *Is There a Court for Gaza? A Test Bench for International Justice.* The Hague: Asser Press.

Migdal, Joel S. 2004. State Building and the Non-Nation State. *Journal of International Affairs* 58 (1): 17–47.

Miller, Aaron David. 2013. "Oslo Stakeholders reflect on Peace Process after 20 Years," *Aljazeera America,* September 12. http://america.aljazeera.com/articles/2013/9/12/oslo-stakeholdersreflectonpeaceprocessafter20years.html.

Mission, UN Fact Finding. 2009. *Human Rights in Palestine and Other Occupied Arab Territories.* Geneva: Human Rights Council.

Morris, Benny 2001. *Righteous Victims: History of the Zionist–Arab Conflict 1881–2001.* New York: Random House.

Musu, Costanza 2006. The Madrid Quartet: An Effective Instrument of Multilateralism? In *The Monitor of the EU–Israel Action Plan,* eds R. Nathanson and S. Stetter. Berlin: Friedrich-Ebert Stiftung.

Nusseibeh, Sari 2007. *Once Opon A Country: A Palestinian Life.* New York: Farrar, Straus, and Giroux.

OCHA. 2015. *Fragmented Lives Humanitarian Overview.* Jerusalem: United Nations Office for the Coordination of Humanitarian Affairs.

Papers (4899), Palestine. 2009. *Meeting Minutes Dr. Saeb Erakat – Senator George Mitchell, October 21.*

Pardo, Sharon and Joel Peters. 2009. *Uneasy Neighbors: Israel and the European Union.* Lanham MD: Lexington Books.

Peres, Shimon. 1993. *The New Middle East.* New York: Henry Holt and Company.

Peters, Joel. 2010a. Europe and the Israel–Palestinian Peace Process: the Urgency of Now. *European Security* 19 (3): 511–529.

Peters, Joel. 2010b. Israel's Disengagement from Gaza: A Failure of Planning or a Flawed Plan? *Paper for American Political Science Association.*

Pinkas, Alon. 2013. "Oslo Stakeholders Reflect on Peace Process after 20 Years," *Aljazeera America* (September 12, 2013). http://america.aljazeera.com/articles/2013/9/12/oslo-stakeholdersreflectonpeaceprocessafter20years.html.

Pradhan, Bansidhar 2008. Palestinian Politics in the Post-Arafat Period. *International Studies Quarterly* 45 (4): 295–339.

Qurie, Ahmed. 2008. *Beyond Oslo, The Struggle for Palestine: Inside the Middle East Peace Process from Rabin's Death to Camp David.* London: IB Tauris.

Rabinovich, Itamar. 2004. *Waging Peace, Israel and the Arabs, 1948–2003.* Princeton NJ: Princeton University Press.

Ravid, Barak. 2009. "Netanyahu Declares 10-month Settlement Freeze to Restart Peace Talks." In *Haaretz.* November 25.

Ravid, Barak. 2011. "Secret EU Paper Aims to Tackle Israel's Treatment of Arab Minority." In *Haaretz.* December 16.

UN Res181. 1947. *UN Resolution 181.*

Ross, Dennis. 2004. *The Missing Peace: The Inside Story of the Fight for Middle East Peace.* New York: Farrar, Straus and Giroux.

Sanders, Jacinta. 1999. The Honest Brokers? American and Norwegian facilitation of Israeli–Palestinian negotiations (1991–93). *Arab Studies Quarterly* 21 (2): 47–70.

Saunders, Harold. 1967. *Memorandum by Harold Saunders of the National Security Council Staff to the President's Special Assistant.* Volume XIX, Document 457, Johnson Library, Washington DC.

Segev, Tom. 2000. *One Palestine Complete: Jews and Arabs under the British Mandate.* New York: Metropolitan Books.

Shahar, Smooha. 2007. "All the Dreams we Had are Now Gone." In *Haaretz.* July 19.

Shalev, Chemi 2011. "Leading Palestinian Intellectual: We already Have a One-State Solution." In *Harretz.* December 5.

Shulewitz, Malka Hillel, 2000. *Forgotten Millions: The Modern Jewish Exodus from Arab Lands.* New York: Continuum.

Swisher, Clayton E. 2004. *The Truth About Camp David: The Untold Story About the Collapse of the Peace Process.* New York: Nation Books.

Swisher, Clayton E. 2011. *The Palestine Papers.* London: Hesperus Press Limited.

Union, Council of European. 2012. *Council Conclusions on the Middle East Peace Process.* Brussels. 17438/12.

Waage, Hilde Henriksen. 2004. *Peacemaking is a Risky Business: Norway's Role in the Peace Process in the Middle East, 1993–96.* Oslo: International Peace Research Institute.

Waage, Hilde Henriksen. 2005. Norway's Role in the Middle East Peace Talks: Between a Strong State and a Weak Belligerent. *Journal of Palestine Studies* 34 (4): 6–24.

Waage, Hilde Henriksen. 2007. The "Minnow" and the "Whale": Norway and the United States in the Peace Process in the Middle East. *British Journal of Middle Eastern Studies* 34 (2): 157–176.

Yiftachel, Oren. 2006. *Ethnocracy: Land and Identity Politics in Israel/Palestine.* Philadelphia: University of Philadelphia Press.

7 Conclusion

Interpretations of group identities form the road map for the understanding of conflicts and guide international intervention process and strategies. An unconstructive international process may not only result in a lack of contribution to resolving the conflict, it can heighten divisions between groups. Interpretation of group identities as solid and unchanging contributes to intervention strategies that serve to build walls rather than bridges between groups. This book argued that two key aspects of international intervention impact on group identities: the intervention process and conflict resolution strategies. First, the type of intervention process, whether the intervention takes place in a united, divided, neutral or partisan manner, has significant impact on group identities in conflict. Second, the nature of group identity strategies – namely, the level of inclusion and exclusion within integration, accommodation or partitioning – also impacts group identities and their potential for transformation.

One of the strongest predicting contributing factors towards a successful intervention is the degree to which external intervention is united. As argued in this book, divided external intervention not only weakens the intention of the intervention, making it far less likely to succeed, it also hardens the identities of the conflicting groups. Receiving diplomatic, economic or military external support, conflicting parties dig in their heels and feel no need to transform their goals, positions or narratives. For an effective intervention, external actors need to shift from divided–partisan to either a united–neutral or to a united–partisan intervention. As noted in the research, a neutral intervention against an uncooperative or an aggressive group may have little impact on the behavior of the aggressive leadership. In the case of a powerful and aggressive group, a united–partisan intervention process may rapidly end a conflict, but not necessarily with just results. Reaching a consensus on a neutral versus partisan intervention is a fundamental element of a successful intervention.

As was seen in the case studies, a united intervention process took place in Northern Ireland and in BiH, but thus far has failed to materialize in the Israeli–Palestinian conflict. Although there was much division in the early years of the conflict, by the 1990s intervention in Northern Ireland became united. The divided intervention consisted of active support of Unionists on the part of Britain and passive and covert support of Nationalists by the Republic of Ireland.

Despite its official principled stance of neutrality, Britain in practice was act-ively supporting the Unionists. Unionist leadership depended on Britain for this support, and their perception of the loss of this backing had an impact on the group's goals and strategies. Likewise, Nationalists and Republicans expected the Republic of Ireland to retain a position in favor of their cause. The shifting of the position of the Republic of Ireland closer to that of Britain had a parallel impact on the strategies, goals and identities of the Nationalists and the Repub-licans. The united interventionist process was a result of a mutual shifting of the policies of Britain and the Republic of Ireland from partisan to a more neutral approach. It was also the result of a changing regional and international context, namely the growing predominance of the EU and the vital role played by the US in helping to push for a united process and overcome hurdles, bridging the gaps between London and Dublin. The unification of British, Irish, EU and American policies embodied a vital ingredient in the success of the GFA.

In the case of BiH, the unification of the European and American intervention process was an arduous battle over the interpretation of the causes of the conflict and consequently how to intervene. As discussed in Chapter 2, a divided inter-national intervention not only weakens the intention of the intervention, it also affirms or hardens the identities of the parties. This was certainly the case in BiH until the international community became united in its efforts. The interpretation of the conflict by external interveners as an ethnic war stemming from deep rooted ethno-religious hatreds became one of the catalysts and excuses for lack of early intervention in BiH. Linked to the interpretation of the conflict was the first type of external intervention, which was neutral and mostly humanitarian. Since this was largely a war of aggression between groups and states that were far from equal, and the strong side was determined to ethnically cleanse the Bosniak civilians, neutral intervention was ineffective.

In the BiH case, international interveners eventually reached a consensus to move towards a partisan intervention against the more powerful, uncooperative and increasingly aggressive leadership of the Bosnian Serbs. However, the shift towards a consensus took years and was subsequent to attempted genocide and massive ethnic cleansing. Although the united–partisan intervention forcibly ended the conflict, it had not decisively contributed towards a transformative impact on the groups in conflict. BiH has remained peaceful; however, thus far, the international community has had to remain present to ensure the viability of the peace.

The divided–partisan external intervention in the Israeli–Palestinian case has been a hindrance to conflict transformation, hardening rather than softening the divisions between the Palestinians and Israelis. External partisan support for Israe-lis and Palestinians has only added fuel to the fire. Key external interveners have failed to agree on the type of intervention process. For an international intervention to become effective in Israel-Palestine, interveners have to decide whether to move towards a united–neutral or a united–partisan intervention. As discussed in Chapter 2, a united–neutral intervention may contribute to a constructive process only in a case in which neither group is behaving in an aggressive or uncooperative manner.

This was the case in Northern Ireland, where a united–neutral intervention was sufficient to end the conflict since neither group was overwhelmingly more powerful or behaving aggressively. Reaching a consensus on whether Israel is behaving in a sufficiently aggressive manner to warrant a partisan intervention is a challenge. Although some measures in Israel-Palestine by the UN and EU have shifted towards the use of more partisan tools against Israel, thus far, this has taken place more in principle than in practice. The US has continued to block a united–partisan process by providing diplomatic, economic and military support to Israel. For an effective intervention, external players have to intervene in a united manner and without a consensus among key interveners on a partisan intervention; the default is a united–neutral intervention. The second element is that, although a united–partisan intervention may forcibly end the conflict, there is no evidence that it will necessarily have a transformative impact on the groups in conflict. Thus if the international community stepped in to forcibly end the conflict, as it did in BiH, they may have to remain present to ensure implementation of the peace.

The divergent international intervention processes in the three case studies to reach a final status agreement are also reflective of the different mediation processes. Although in all three conflicts it was American Democrats who took the leading role in attempts to mediate the end to the conflict, only in the Northern Ireland case was the mediation process transformative. The mediation process in Northern Ireland that culminated in the Good Friday Agreement was far more transformative than the coerced BiH agreement made at Dayton, or the unsuccessful and poorly managed US-led process at Camp David II. In addition, although in all three cases the regional actors were part of the problem, only in the Northern Ireland case have the regional players become a formidable part of the solution. The three mediation processes also differed in their inclusion and exclusion of moderates and extremists. In the BiH case, prominent moderates were sidelined in favor of violent extremists. Extremist leadership was involved in the mediation effort in Northern Ireland; however, international mediation focused on the creation of a coalition of moderates and the transformation or the ousting of the extremists.

The type of conflict resolution strategies also impacted on the groups in conflict and contributed to the hardening or transforming of hostile group identities. As noted in Chapter 3, although international norms for minorities recommend democratic and inclusive integration, the international solutions in violent conflicts focus on accommodation and/or partitioning. In two of the cases within this research, BiH and Northern Ireland, international interventions advised and implemented accommodative consociational institutional arrangements. The consociational identity strategies in BiH and Northern Ireland, however, widely differed. Intervention in BiH fluctuated between accommodation and partitioning and the eventual consociational arrangement formulated divisions between groups within a corporate accommodative framework. From the beginning of the violent conflict in BiH, intervention strategies promoted partitioning along ethnic group lines, which failed to stop, and even at times incited, ethnic cleansing. This is not to say that the IC promoted ethnic cleansing but rather that international identity strategies from the beginning of the conflict until after Dayton rested on a nexus between solid ethnic group identity and territory. Similar to the extreme nationals, the IC solutions revolved around exclusive prescriptions based on the assumptions that the communities could not coexist.

International strategies and inaction to stop the war crimes gave license to gangs to pursue their own lucrative agendas. The majority of the ethnic cleansing of the two million civilians had more to do with theft, looting and extortion by militant thugs than sectarian conflict between local civilian communities. The ethnic cleansing provided an opportunity for Serbian criminals released for the task from Serbian jails to exploit chaos, fear and desperations among fleeing civilians and pillage millions of dollars, devastating generations and pocketing their wealth. This began what was an odd common ground between the paramilitaries, the extreme nationalists and the international community, who tended to favor the ease of dealing with clearly defined ethnic territories.

The international institutions designed at Dayton solidified the divisions in a permanent peace agreement. International mediators shared the presumption of the inability of the groups to coexist. Moderate voices that promoted a multicultural Bosnia were ignored by the international mediators and muzzled by the local extremists. The end result was an ongoing cementation rather than transformation of group identities along ethnic lines. Despite good intentions to end a violent war, the framework designed and imposed at Dayton embodied a dysfunctional institutional system and exclusive territorial separation along ethnic lines. Thus, although the IC ended the war, thus far, external efforts in Bosnia have not managed to create a stable and a viable country. The Dayton Agreement drawn up during the conflict has been difficult to change and thus serves as a barrier to group transformation, resulting in the catch-22 situation, in which the desired outcome is impossible to attain because of the rules set up in the peace agreement. International strategies have had long-term consequences of reification rather than transformation of group identities.

The Northern Ireland case gives some evidence that external identity strategies that promote inclusive group identities contribute to the transformation of conflicting group identities. Despite the fact that this was also a consociational agreement, the GFA undertook a more creative, multi-layered and inclusive approach to group identity issues that did not close the door to the potential transformation of the groups in conflict. The GFA introduced institutions promoting the overlap of identities through accommodation and multiple layers of representations. The consociational framework drawn between the parties also benefited from the constructive intervention of Britain, the Republic of Ireland and the US. As noted in previous chapters, identity shifts make the difference between successful and failed settlement processes. Still, the GFA and the subsequent efforts have not gone far enough to promote inclusive integration advancing the potential of identity transformation. Accommodation or specifically consociational arrangements can, however, be created with some flexibility for the potential of transformation, as was the case in Northern Ireland, or with rigidity, as was the case in BiH, resulting in the freezing of relations between groups.

Partitioning along group lines has been the only international solution to the Israeli–Palestinian conflict and continues to dominate the official international discourse. The underlying assumption of the partitioning strategy is that the presumably solid opposing groups are unable to live together. As argued in Chapter 3, external identity strategies which promote exclusive group identities contribute towards solidification or hardening of identities of groups in conflict. In Israel-Palestine, partitioning options along ethno-exclusive lines have certainly not prevented, and arguably at times inspired, land grabs and settlements. The partitioning option in the Israeli–Palestinian case has also not provided any incentives towards a transformation of the conflict, and rather entrenched the divisions in unsustainable conditions. The hardships of the occupation and policies of exclusion and segregation have only served to further cement divisions between groups.

From the three case studies, only Northern Ireland can be argued to have had a positive international intervention process and, for the most part, constructive group identity strategies. As was discussed within the case study, the intervention in the Northern Ireland case contributed to the transformation of relations between groups in the conflict. Although in BiH the international community had in the end managed to carry out a united international process that ended the conflict, detrimental identity strategies have resulted in the freezing of the hostile relations between the groups. Finally, regardless of intention and the substantial amount of investment and intervention in the Israel-Palestine conflict, predominantly this case is an example of harmful external process and strategies. With divided external process and exclusive identity strategies, Israel-Palestine, I argue, is an example of detrimental external intervention, in which the IC contributed to hardening of the divisions between the groups in conflict. The end result is that in the divergent case studies external interveners in Northern Ireland, BiH and Israel-Palestine contributed to transforming, freezing, and heightening the respective conflicts.

Towards an effective and sustainable international intervention process

I suggest that an effective multilateral intervention process necessitates a consensus among mediators in three key spheres: *consensus on a neutral or partisan intervention, consensus on the tools used, and consensus on the red lines.* A multilateral intervention process necessitates a consensus on a united–neutral or a united–partisan intervention, ideally on the basis of a necessity to protect the lives of civilians. Second, a united multilateral intervention builds on a consensus among international interveners on the use of appropriate diplomatic, economic, military or other tools to augment a united–neutral or a united–partisan intervention process. Third, the decision to intervene multilaterally in a neutral or a partisan manner is ideally taken on the basis of the responsibility to protect lives and the human rights of civilians, and thus is related to the circumstances of the conflict and in accordance with international human rights standards and international law.

United intervention is also based on a consensus among the key mediators on the interpretation of the nature of the groups in conflict. It requires an agreement among mediators on defining the conflict and a common understanding of the perceived conduct of the groups in conflict. It necessitates a consensus among key interveners on whether the conflict is an act of aggression or the conflicting parties may be able to transform within a neutral intervention process. This is a challenge in many conflicts, since the decision to intervene neutrally or in a partisan manner is commonly based on external rather than internal factors related to the conflict. For an effective united intervention, the decision to intervene in a neutral versus partisan process should ideally be based on endogenous factors related to the behavior of the groups or state in conflict.

Given the complexity of considerations that go into interventions in any conflict, a united–neutral intervention is the ideal type of intervention in that at the very least it will not be responsible for escalating the conflict. In a multilateral intervention, a united–neutral intervention is the most likely to achieve international legitimacy and a consensus between interveners. It is the least likely to have unintended effects on vulnerable groups within society. A united–neutral intervention may contribute to transformation in a case in which neither group is behaving in an uncooperative or aggressive manner. A neutral intervention against an uncooperative and aggressive group may have little impact on the behavior of an aggressive leadership of the group. Thus, in cases where one or more of the actors or state is aggressive, uncooperative, and acting with impunity, a neutral intervention may be ineffective and a partisan intervention may be necessary to protect the lives of civilians. However, as discussed, a partisan intervention necessitates a consensus among international mediators on the use of diplomatic, economic, military or other tools to augment the intervention process on behalf of or against one of the conflicting groups.

In the case of an aggressive group, a united–partisan intervention process can have a transformative impact on the groups in conflict. However, partisan intervention against a group may also increase the salience of the said group, since the group may feel under threat. Thus, although a united–partisan intervention may end a conflict, it might not achieve the desired group identity transformation. A partisan intervention, in particular if it is military, may also have unintended effects on women in particular. Thus external process contributes towards group identity transformation under condition of a united–neutral intervention and may contribute towards transformation under conditions of a united–partisan intervention. A divided intervention process does not only have little constructive input in resolving a conflict, it is likely to widen the divides between the conflicting groups.

Opting for a partisan versus neutral intervention is fundamental, affecting the existing balance of power between conflicting groups. A shift from a divided intervention towards a neutral intervention or a partisan shift against one of the groups or the state in the conflict has an impact on the balance between the groups. As was analyzed in the case studies, a shift from a divided intervention to a united–neutral or to a united–partisan intervention tilts the balance between the parties affecting their behavior and the dynamics of the conflict. Consensus on a united–partisan intervention, however, needs to be linked to a parallel consensus on the use of appropriate diplomatic, economic, military or other tools.

In a multilateral international intervention, the mediators would benefit from reaching a consensus on the use of appropriate tools. The strength of diplomatic, economic and military tools is directly linked to a consensus among the key multilateral interveners. International mediation can be supplemented with diplomatic coercion, economic sanctions, and when necessary, military intervention. For an effective united–partisan intervention, external interveners have to agree on whether the reality on the ground allows for the use of particular coercive tools. Partisan intervention may include sanctions, boycotts, divestment and shaming against a conflicting group or a state. Recent research has pointed to the effectiveness of non-military coercive tools such as sanctions, the use of international judiciary bodies and "naming," "blaming" and "shaming" campaigns.

Reaching a consensus is directly related to the effectiveness of any tool. As one of the most divisive conflicts for the international community, the ongoing Israel–Palestinian conflict has failed to gain a consensus on either a neutral or a partisan intervention. Although the 2008 and 2014 Gaza wars resulted in many civilian deaths, threats of sanctions, and accusations of war crimes, lack of consensus among the key interveners meant that intervention had little impact. The UN inquiry into the 2008 Gaza war headed by Richard Goldstone accused Israeli Defense forces and Hamas of war crimes, crimes against humanity and serious violations of international law, recommending further investigation and bringing those responsible to justice (Mission 2009). The EU Parliament endorsed the report, while the US Congress voted the Goldstone report to be "irredeemably biased" against Israel and called on President Obama to maintain his opposition to the report. The recent Gaza crisis also resulted in accusations of war crimes. Despite the widely covered conflict and atrocities committed against civilians, lack of consensus among the IC has meant it has had little impact on the conflict.

Partisan diplomatic, economic, military or other tools are only as effective as they are united. Sanctions against South Africa only became effective after a consensus was reached among the IC on a partisan intervention against the apartheid state. In some cases, more forceful military tools can accompany a partisan intervention. As the first case study of BiH demonstrated, neutral intervention was insufficient to end atrocities against civilians. A neutral intervention by the United Nations not only placed international lightly armed troops at risk, it gave a false sense of security to refugees fleeing to UN "safe areas" which became the sites of the worst massacres. In the end, it was a more forceful military partisan intervention that successfully ended the conflict.

Consensus on the red line

A vital ingredient is reaching a consensus among the IC on the location of a red line where partisan intervention is required to protect lives of citizens. Global legal principles, enshrined in existing international laws within the UN Charter, the Geneva Convention and other conventions have not sufficiently contributed to the scholarly debate on neutral versus partisan intervention. In practice, international intervention norms have been influenced by the emergence of the Responsibility to Protect, which holds that the IC has the responsibility to protect civilians from war crimes. The International Commission on Intervention and State Sovereignty proposed that sovereignty "be made conditional on two basic responsibilities: respect for the sovereignty of other states and responsibility to provide basic security for one's own citizens – that is, to refrain from subjecting them to massacre, genocide, or ethnic cleansing" (Ignatieff 2012). As noted by Jon Western and Joshua Goldstein, the doctrine has become integrated into a practitioners' tool kit of conflict management strategies that "includes today's more robust peacekeeping operations and increasingly effective international criminal justice mechanisms" (Western 2011).

The behavior of groups or government in conflict should ideally be a primary reason why external actors intervene in a neutral or a partisan manner. Partisan intervention should only take place when the behavior of one group or a state warrants a strong intervention to protect the lives of civilians. The challenge is reaching a consensus among international mediators on a point at which the behavior of one of the conflicting parties is bad enough to warrant a partisan intervention.

Towards more effective and sustainable international intervention strategies

Scholarly debates and practitioners have focused on accommodation as the "tool of choice" to intractable violent conflicts within groups. Does accommodation represent the best strategy or does it foster the creation of an institutional framework that, while designed to mitigate conflict, sets up divisive institutions that hinder transformation and provide a path of separation or partitioning? The cases of Northern Ireland and BiH examined in this book offer different types of accommodation strategies that have received their share of praise and criticisms. While in both cases the accommodative peace agreements have been helpful in maintaining peace, around 20 years after the peace agreements one can analyze long-term achievements and failures.

Although accommodation may be demanded by representatives of some groups in conflict, corporate accommodation strategies, such as in BiH, make states less functional and thus can contribute to state failures. While international mediators may be attempting to resolve a conflict by negotiating between the conflicting groups, they may also be assisting in creating dysfunctional institutions marked by exclusion, future paralysis and intergroup division. Group accommodation can, however, be created with more flexibility for the potential of transformation, as was to some extent the case in Northern Ireland, or with rigidity as the case in BiH, resulting in the freezing of relations between groups. An accommodative framework may be designed as a temporary measure with the intent of contributing towards eventual inclusive integration of conflicting groups. Much of this depends on the level of inclusion and exclusion. There are also far worse strategies than accommodation, including occupation and exclusion.

Integration, accommodation and partitioning, depending on the level of inclusion and exclusion, each offers solutions to group identity that may either harden differences or soften divisions between conflicting groups. The main areas of concern in the type of strategy relate to the levels of inclusion and exclusion, the functioning of a state and the impact on the conflicting groups.

The ultimate purpose of accommodation is to prevent majoritarianism or the exclusion of minorities. Ironically, while the institutional framework is designed to mitigate exclusion, it may also institutionalize exclusion against other minorities. In BiH, accommodative group strategies institutionalized and solidified differences along ethnic lines. Indeed, clauses in the peace agreement created a basis for discrimination against the Bosnian Serbs in the Federation and Bosniaks and Bosnian Croats in the RS. The peace agreement did not allow for the basic individual right not to belong to a specific group or attain membership of multiple groups. The GFA is far better at protection of the rights of all groups, including mixed individuals as well as those who do not wish to belong to any specific group. The accommodative elements of the GFA ensure the end to discrimination and to the exclusion of the Catholic minority in Northern Ireland. At the same time, the GFA permanently privileges the Unionist and Nationalist identities above all other group identities.

It is clear that consociational arrangements such as group vetoes and rotating presidencies can hinder the functioning of a state. In both Northern Ireland and BiH, the consociational arrangements had, in some ways, stalled the functioning of their respective governments. The Dayton Agreement established a balance of power between ethnic groups based on the US belief that creating a balance between groups will result in peace. Thus, greater effort was placed by the international mediators on dividing territory between the conflicting groups and training and arming separate but equal armies than creating functioning institutions. The institutions created are not only cumbersome and dysfunctional, but also unsustainable without foreign assistance. Although the consociational design of the GFA contained more integrative components, it also included elements that have resulted in deadlocks and marginalization of smaller moderate parties. The deadlocks in the Northern Ireland Assembly were only overcome with constructive input from London and Dublin.

One of the many criticisms launched at accommodative frameworks is that they tend to strengthen nationalistic leadership. Currently, ethnic or nationalistic leaderships dominate the political spectrum in all of the cases, with little space for moderates. This is a reflection of elections where voters continue to select national representatives over those who stress civic values or cross cutting issues. On the other hand, at least in the case of BiH, this is also a consequence of a divisive electoral and institutional framework that is designed to function along ethnic lines. In the BiH case, citizens have no choice but to vote for a

President that represents their ethno-national group. In the Northern Ireland case, the electoral framework tends to favor the large parties over the smaller ones, marginalizing some of the centrist parties, and privileges National and Unionist identities above all other. Still, the more liberal accommodative framework in Northern Ireland left the electorate and the elected officials many more options and forced them to function at an executive level.

The final paradox in accommodation is that, while attempting to appease groups in the midst of a violent conflict, corporate accommodation cements divisions and hinders future group transformation. In BiH, conflicting group identities were deemed by the mediators as permanent, with no capacity to transform. This happened despite dozens of years of peace and coexistence. There was very little attempt at integration and most external solutions focused on the separation of the groups in conflict. Mediators in Northern Ireland played a far different role. The GFA did not link conflicting group to a specific territory and allowed the people of Northern Ireland to choose institutions that enabled them to form mixed identity linkages. George Mitchell did his utmost to construct a consensus among moderates. Although extremists were also welcomed around the table, provided they took a vow of non-violence, in the Northern Ireland peace talks moderate voices were heard. Elections were conducted with the aim of an inclusive representation of people in the talks, which included former combatants, moderates and women. In Northern Ireland, despite decades of conflict, there was a greater attempt at integration. The British, American and Irish strategies intended not only to produce an internal power-sharing arrangement but also to mediate a regional agreement with deep connections to neighboring states. External strategies in Northern Ireland included the promotion of multi-layered identities and flexible institutions were oriented towards a transformation of group identities.

Despite international norms that favor integration, the current prescriptive solutions to violent conflict are group accommodation or, in some cases, partitioning along group lines, both of which entrench the conflict and hinder group transformation. Thus, we have the catch-22 in which the institutions proposed and implemented during the height of the conflict make the desired outcome of transformation impossible. Currently, much of the international intervention that falls under the umbrella of accommodation and partitioning does not envisage the potential of group transformation. In the current global context, international mediators and scholars will profit from greater attention to flexible and inclusive accommodation and inclusive integration. Not only is integration supported in international norms, it also opens up the possibility of a long-term sustainable resolution. Divided societies do not necessarily need divided solutions.

Tony Blair noted wisely that "resolution to conflict is a journey not an event" and the above discussion is based on conflicts which still have a long road towards group transformation. The conflict in Israel-Palestine is the furthest from a resolution and indeed is currently not on the path in that direction. For the IC to become united over the type of intervention process in Israel-Palestine is fundamental and the most crucial step. Focusing on exclusive partitioning strategies as the only solution to the violent conflict is, however, not conducive to the path of group transformation. The divided intervention is not only preventing but at times fostering policies of exclusion and the justification of continual violence against civilians. Creating conditions for meeting the basic human needs of all groups is fundamental and, as noted in Chapter 1, is a key foundation of group transformation. In the case of Israel, the responsibility to protect norm under which states are obligated to protect civilians from war crimes and to "respond collectively in a timely and decisive manner when a state is manifestly failing to provide such protection" is ignored.

The three case studies illustrated the importance of selecting a process and strategies that do not hinder but rather promote group identity transformation. Further research is needed into inclusive integration as a potential solution for conflict strategies of groups in a violent conflict. Although there is evidence that partitioning along ethnic lines does not contribute to conflict transformation and accommodation can result in solidification of groups, there is little evidence, except in the case of the EU, that integration following a conflict may lead to conflict transformation. None of the cases studied here attempted inclusive integration, which in general is avoided by external mediators during a conflict. The lack of research into this area is partly due to the fact that, in violent conflict, integration is not looked on as having the potential for resolution, since it is presumed that conflicting groups cannot transform or coincide, and require accommodation and, in the most difficult cases, partitioning. Partitioning or separating of groups does not necessarily solve a conflict; indeed, it can heighten it.

As argued in this book, a priority for a successful intervention is to focus on a united process and inclusive group identity strategies that intentionally promote and do not hinder group transformation. Group identities, including their meanings and salience, can and do change. Group identities harden during a violent conflict and the international strategies selected should be those that promote identity transformation. Thus construction of power sharing institutions that are flexible and promote overlapping identities, as in Northern Ireland, are far better than the construction of institutional and territorial partitioning along ethnic lines as was imposed on BiH. Whether interveners adopt strategies of integration, accommodation or partitioning, the emphasis would benefit from the formulation of strategies that promote inclusion and transformation and the blocking of strategies that are exclusionary or harden differences between conflicting groups. Although the creation of two democratized inclusive states may become a part of a conflict transformation process, a partitioning along ethnic or religious lines is unlikely to resolve any conflicts and might only lead to ethnic cleansing and more violence. Land remains important but, in the modern age, "this land belongs to us" would benefit from being transformed towards "we belong to this land," with the necessity of sharing and inclusion. International interventions must not only be conscious of the process and strategies they are utilizing but also be engaged in building bridges rather than walls between the different groups in conflict.

References

Ignatieff, Michael. 2012. Reimagining a Global Ethic. *Ethics and International Affairs*. www.ethicsandinternationalaffairs.org/2012/reimagining-a-global-ethic-full-text/.

Mission, UN Fact Finding. 2009. Human Rights in Palestine and Other Occupied Arab Territories. Geneva: Human Rights Council.

Index

Page numbers in **bold** denote figures.

For Product Safety Concerns and Information please contact our EU
representative GPSR@taylorandfrancis.com
Taylor & Francis Verlag GmbH, Kaufingerstraße 24, 80331 München, Germany